MW00610499

Drawing by Louise Sagalyn.

A PROMISE FULFILLED

THE MEMOIR OF ARNOLD SAGALYN

To Edie and Jack

With appreciation for your

wonderful friendship

these many years.

Affectionately,

Arnold

Book and cover design by Yordan Silvera

ISBN 978-1-4507-0759-6

Printing supervised by
International Arts & Artists
Printed by House of Printing

This book is written for
Louise,
Laurie, Rita, Lisbeth,
Erik and Matt
Benjamin, Mitchell and Emma
to fulfill my promise to write down
the stories I told them over the years.

And in memoriam to Dana.

CONTENTS

PROLOGUE

President Franklin D. Roosevelt campaigning for reelection 1940.
Courtesy FDR Library.

This generation of Americans is living in a tremendous moment of
history. The surge of events abroad has made some few doubters among
us to ask: Is this the end of a story that has been told? My answer is
this: All we have known of the glories of democracy—its freedom...
its ability to meet the aspirations of the common man—all these are
merely an introduction to the greater story of a more glorious future.

> *Roosevelt's November 2, 1940*
> *campaign speech in Cleveland*

It was late in the afternoon on November 2, 1940 and Franklin Dela-
no Roosevelt had just finished the last major speech in his Presidential
campaign before an enthusiastic crowd of Democratic supporters in
Cleveland's Municipal Auditorium. I was seated in the press section
close to the President where, as an assistant to Cleveland's Public
Safety Director, Eliot Ness, I was assigned to oversee security arrangements for the press during the President's visit. I was thinking how
bowled over my parents were going to be when I told them that I had

been sitting very close to Roosevelt when he spoke to the nation on the radio from Cleveland that day.

Everyone was told to remain seated until the President left, and as the President now turned to leave—walking with the aid of a cane and holding the arm of his son, James, and surrounded by Secret Service agents—I rose to follow him to the elevator which would take him down to the underground garage. From there the presidential motorcade would leave for Cleveland's train station. There he would board his private train to return to his home in Hyde Park, New York to cast his vote for an unprecedented Presidential third term.

Although Roosevelt's legs had been crippled by polio as a young man and he needed help walking, I remember marveling at the impression of enormous vigor, vitality and strength he projected and the fact that his disability had absolutely no impact on his enormous presence. Through all of my most formative years, Roosevelt had been President and my parents had ardently supported him because of his outstanding leadership in creating jobs and combating the country's devastating economic depression. While I was then working for a mayor and immediate boss who were Republicans, I, too, became a dedicated Democrat in national politics. But I followed the family tradition of voting as an Independent in local and state elections.

I did not know it at the time, but I learned later that Colonel Edmund Starling, Chief of the Secret Service who was accompanying the President on this trip, had been worrying about recent threats against the President's life. And his concern had intensified when he learned that the Cleveland newspapers had published the estimated time and specific street route of the President's motorcade from the Cleveland auditorium to the train station, providing any potential assassin with a dangerously explicit roadmap.

On this November day, enormous crowds had been arriving from all over the city and outlying communities to position themselves along the publicized motorcade route. When I joined the Presidential party in the underground garage, I was told the sidewalks and adjacent areas of the streets leading from the exit of the auditorium garage were packed with festive spectators all the way to the train station.

Although most of Cleveland's police officers were deployed along the route to keep the streets clear and control the large assemblage of onlookers, and a covey of experienced, highly trained Secret Service agents would accompany the President on both sides of his open black presidential sedan, Starling knew how very difficult it was going to be to protect him against any determined assassin armed with a gun or bomb.

When I arrived near the exit where the motorcade was assembled, I saw Eliot conferring with the colonel[1]. I was startled and taken by complete surprise when Starling broke away from Ness and walked over to talk to me. "Would you like to ride with us to the train station?" he asked me. I sensed that he was accustomed to giving orders to young whippersnappers like me, and it never crossed my mind that there was something odd about the way he framed his question, almost as if it was a request. In my naiveté, the first thought that came to my mind was that he was just being kind to this very young plain clothes policeman who had been helpful with the security arrangements, and that I would get a thrill out of riding in the President's motorcade. I looked inquiringly at Eliot, who nodded his approval.

I followed Starling in a happy daze to the convoy of cars lined up in front of the exit ramp. Two Cleveland police cars filled with uniformed officers were parked in the lead position, while directly behind them were two large, open, black touring cars with sturdy-looking running boards, their canvas roofs battened down. A dark-suited swarm of Secret Service agents were stationed alongside them and from time to time, two or three of them would sequentially step up on the sedans' running boards to scan the surrounding area and then

---

1. *Eliot Ness, the son of a Norwegian baker, had won national acclaim as the youthful leader of an elite team of nine Federal prohibition agents, known as the "Untouchables," who had succeeded in crushing the notorious Chicago gangster, Al "Scarface" Capone's ruthless reign of criminal terror in the 20's.*
Ness had been hired away from the Federal government in 1935 by a new, reform Cleveland mayor to clean up the highly corrupt police department and widespread racketeering. He was overseeing and coordinating with Colonel Sterling the deployment of the city's police forces to assure the President's safety during his visit to Cleveland.

the vehicles parked behind them. Lined up behind the two lead open limos was a long cavalcade of closed sedans that would transport the various White House aides and campaign officials accompanying the President. Several police cars brought up the rear.

I was absolutely thunderstruck and more than a little confused when, instead of leading me back to one of the closed cars, Starling took me to the first convertible sedan, which was quickly surrounded by at least a dozen Secret Service agents. "Sit there," he said, pointing to the empty black leather rear seat. I looked at Starling quizzically. Sit in the rear seat of this car? Could this be right? Starling nodded affirmatively and then turned to walk back to an identical black open sedan behind me.

As I was getting into my car, my eyes followed Starling as he stopped at the sedan behind me, where Roosevelt was being helped into its empty rear seat. As the last remnants of the President's campaign entourage were being shepherded into the other cars behind it, I couldn't help looking back to the car where the President was now seated alone in the rear seat, chatting animatedly with his son, James, up front, who was sitting beside the Secret Service driver. I was all admiration for the great sense of style with which Roosevelt lifted up his chin and flourished the familiar, cigarette holder with a lighted cigarette trailing a thin ribbon of smoke

Then a voice called out and my driver, along with all the other drivers started their vehicles and, with the two Cleveland police cars escorting us, we began to move slowly up the exit ramp onto the street. I felt as if I was dreaming, as the Secret Service agents trotted along both sides of my car, and I could hear loud cheers from the awaiting crowd as they spotted the leading police cars with their flashing red and blue lights, and then the cheering increased and became almost delirious as my open sedan came into view.

"It's the President! There's the President!" the aroused crowd was shouting. Suddenly, it dawned on me that they thought I was FDR. And no wonder: There I was, a lone figure in the back seat of the lead open limousine with Secret Service agents alternatively walking or trotting to keep up with the pace of the Presidential motorcade, while the failing light made it virtually impossible for most of the spectators to see me clearly, much less distinguish my features or age. The cheering and wild clapping was infectious.

I was carried away with the spirit of the occasion, and began waving to the crowds who responded adoringly. It was an exhilarating feeling, to be mistaken for the President of the United States. I felt compelled to play my part. As I didn't want to disappoint the thousands who had come and waited so long to see their President, I waved vigorously to my right and my left and continued this intoxicating performance all the way to the station, until my driver turned off to a side street just beyond the track where the President's train was waiting.

At this point I was abruptly jolted back to reality. I was only Arnold Sagalyn from Springfield, Massachusetts, a very junior aide to Cleveland's Director of Public Safety. I was very young and was so used to taking in stride all my unusual and adventurous assignments without questioning them, that being used as a decoy to protect President Roosevelt against a would-be assassin had been just another, exciting experience in working for Eliot Ness.

Twenty-seven years later I would again be asked to assume the role of President of the United States (POTUS), this time in a war game at the National War College.

GROWING UP
1918-1939

Chapter 1

My father in front of 11 Florentine Gardens.

SPRINGFIELD

The childhood shows the man
As morning shows the day.
> John Milton

I grew up in Springfield, Massachusetts in a close-knit family of seven children, the third son and fifth child of Raphael and Dora Sagalyn. Springfield was tucked away in western Massachusetts on the peaceful Connecticut River. A quiet city of some 150,000, it had a small-town feeling and was a world away from the intellectual muscle and tumultuous politics of Boston. Its largely middle-class citizenry was proud of its selection by George Washington as a military arsenal during the American Revolution, as the Armory which made America's first military muskets and later the critical Springfield rifles in World Wars I and II. The city also prides itself on being the site of the invention of basketball and is now the home of basketball's Hall of Fame.

We lived at 1 Florentine Gardens in the Forest Park section of the city, in a large, white rambling clapboard house, with a covered, wraparound porch. Adjacent to our house was a wide expanse of lawn, where my brothers, Irwin and Bobby, and I played ball games and other sports with one another and our friends. Beyond it were rows of grapes that grew on wooden arbors next to the paved driveway that led from the side street to the three-car garage where our cars were parked: a large 7-passenger Cadillac convertible sedan, a smaller sports Reo, and my father's principal travel car, a black 7-passenger Packard with a sliding glass window between the driver and passengers, and two collapsible jump-seats behind the front seats. The Packard was my favorite because it had a radiotelephone on the window ledge behind the rear seat, with which I loved to play-talk.

Our front door opened into a large hallway that led to a spacious living room on the left, and on the right was a den, our family room, with a large RCA radio set and a tall Victrola. This phonograph was hand-cranked and on it we played our large collection of Caruso records and other operatic records as well as numerous albums of symphonies. After dinner the family usually gathered in the family room to listen to the evening radio network programs, such as Jack Benny, a leading low-key comedian, and Amos 'n' Andy, a popular family comedy program featuring impersonations of two, black, male characters.

Our living room extended almost the entire length of the house and contained a grand piano, on which my older sisters Lillian and Esther had their music lessons. My father was a firm believer that every child should be exposed to music and be offered the opportunity to develop any musical skills she or he might have. When I was eight, my older brother Irwin and I were required to take violin lessons, but after a few years of enduring regular, weekly instruction it became clear that neither of us had any talent for this lovely instrument. My father, after listening to us play, agreed it was futile to continue our lessons.

The dining room had built-in, glass-fronted cabinets where my mother's sizable, two sets of dinnerware were stored. In respect for her orthodox Jewish family tradition, my mother kept a kosher kitchen, which required one set of dishes to be used when meat was served, while the other set was used when dairy products were served.

1924: Bobby, Mother, Lillian, Irwin, Arnold, Esther, Julian, Father, Lenore.

On the second floor, there were five bedrooms and two full bathrooms. My father, who was very hip to new developments and always wanted the latest in everything (like the mobile telephone in his car) had specially installed in the largest bathroom what was reputed to be the first shower in Springfield. It consisted of a seven-foot square enclosure, with a floor and walls of white tile, in which circular rows of narrow, horizontal pipes ran from your ankles to your neck. Apart from its novelty, it was a wonderful, luxurious feeling to stand in the soothing jet streams of massaging, hot water shooting out of the holes in the encircling pipes. It became a family legend that whenever my father saw or heard of any advanced gadget or personal, technological development that was new and very special he would say, "I want it, I need it, get me two." To which my more parsimonious mother would always respond: "Don't get it, I've got it, what is it?"

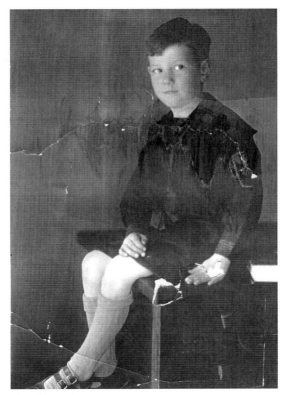

Arnold, age 6

The third floor opened on a very large, open space that ended in a suite of two bed-rooms and a full bathroom, where Mrs. Sullivan, our trea- sured, competent, no-nonsense, Irish housekeeper-cook lived. That big open room became my favorite indoor playground during the winter and in inclement weather; and every winter, my brothers Irwin and Bobby, and I spent many happy hours absorbed in setting up miniature train tracks that crisscrossed the room. We operated up to two or three electric, transformer-powered engines pulling long lines of various types of freight and passenger cars our parents had bought us for Hanukkah, which business friends of my father's would supplement with Christmas presents of railroad paraphernalia, such as repair shops, passenger sta- tions and bridges.

For a young boy who doted on mechanically-operated machines and toys, it was very exciting and thrilling to watch two or three engines, their whistles sounding and lights flashing, pulling long lines of alternating freight and passenger cars in and out of the dark tunnels. The excitement and tension built when my brothers and I, each of us controlling his own long train of cars on a separate track, approached an area where the tracks crossed, providing the risk of a collision. When that happened, as it frequently did, the resulting wreck would hurl engines, freight and passenger cars and their contents into a wild jumble of twisted tracks and overturned engines, cars, and freight, all sprawled over a wide area.

MY PARENTS

As a father's goodness is higher than the mountains,
So is a mother's deeper than the sea.
    Proverb

My father was born in Odessa, Russia, in 1879 and immigrated to the United States in his late teens. When we were growing up, we would ask him during dinner to tell us about his life in Russia and what led him to leave and come to America. We would listen spell-bound as he recalled the dramatic and fascinating accounts of his early life as an idealist and Socialist who tried to improve the terrible working conditions of the bristle workers (people who made brushes) in his community. It was those activities that attracted the attention of the Czar's police. He had to flee Russia to avoid arrest.

His earlier socialist activities notwithstanding, in America my father continued to try to help people in need, while also becoming an extremely successful businessman. He started out selling merchandise door to door, and within a few years had established himself as a wholesale, dry goods dealer: R. Sagalyn & Co., serving as a middleman between factories and consumers. This became the largest business of its kind in Western Massachusetts, with a New York office and connections to the largest textile mills in the country, including the Wamsutta Mills. One of his customers was the railroad industry's sleeping-car Pullman Company, for which he supplied sheets, pillow cases, towels, and blankets.

I have a photo of him in his dry goods sales office, a young man elegantly dressed, one hand debonairly in his pocket, his hip cocked, his lips slightly parted. He is gazing off into a world of his own, with what I recognize as the typically, absorbed, bemused expression he had when he was planning his next move or mulling over his affairs. In his face I see both his idealism and his pragmatism. He was one of those rare men who was a dreamer, yet had an acute understanding of the way the world worked.

By the time I was 10 and had entered Forest Park Junior High, my father had left the wholesale dry goods business to acquire a major interest in two Springfield department stores, Pooles and Stillmans, as well as an interest in a department store in Manchester, New Hampshire. He moved his personal office to Stillmans' top floor and while he had partners in the department stores, he wasn't at all interested in running them personally and he operated pretty much on his own in all his other ventures.

My father at Rapheal Sagalyn, Inc.

My father's personal blending of the visionary and the pragmatist was brilliantly on display in 1932. The '30s were the worst years of the Great Depression, which had brought the closing of Dwight Manufacturing Co. in neighboring Chicopee, one of New England's largest textile mills, along with the shuttering of scores of company-owned dwellings that had housed its workers. The company's departure for the lower labor and operating costs in Georgia had left its multitude of former employees jobless, and the city of Chicopee in dire financial straits with the loss of its principal tax base.

My father purchased Dwight Mills' extensive complex of five-story, red-brick mills, containing more than 1,000,000 square feet of space, and proceeded to create what is believed to have been the first industrial park in New England, if not the United States, the Industrial Buildings

Corp. For he foresaw an opportunity to restore the buildings to industrial use by finding new, small- and medium-size businesses and offering financial move-in assistance, including a year's free rent, to companies who agreed to move to Chicopee with its large supply of skilled workers. He was strongly motivated to create jobs for the thousands of former employees and restore Chicopee's devastated property-tax base.

Industrial Buildings Complex.

His friends, the area's business leaders, and the banks were unanimous in expressing their deep skepticism about his new venture in the midst of a terrible depression. They all warned him that he was courting financial disaster, and they were right. He was taking an extraordinary personal financial risk, committing all of his assets at a time when he was supporting a large family, with five children in or starting college, and three full-time, personal employees. As I now look back at those grim depression years I can only marvel at his incredible courage and self-confidence and the enormous, relentless pressures and mental strain he was under, day in and day out, as he struggled and contrived to make this pioneering venture a success.

New and unexpected problems and obstacles kept popping up all the time, such as his discovery shortly after his acquisition that the Dwight buildings were many thousands of dollars in arrears for property taxes to the city of Chicopee. When he tried to persuade the mayor that the city was going to benefit enormously from this venture and would help him succeed by not pressing him for payment of the taxes, the mayor refused. Whereupon, my father informed the mayor that he had no alternative but to start tearing down buildings to reduce their taxable value.

When the mayor remained obstinate, my father had a five-story building demolished; and when there was no response from Chicopee's mayor, he tore down a second mill building. But when there was still no response, my father informed the mayor he was going to begin demolishing a third brick building, and at that point the mayor finally called him, asking him to stop as he now was willing to cooperate and work out a plan on the taxes.

I remember vividly my conversation with my father not long after that when I was at his Chicopee office and he had just finished talking to a prospective tenant. "What will you do" I asked him "if despite all your efforts you don't succeed?" He just looked at me and, shaking his head and smiling sadly, he replied, "See all these buildings?" pointing to the surrounding five-story red brick buildings. "They have more than a mil-lion bricks in them and I will sell all their bricks for 10 cents apiece."

Looking back now, I realize that my visionary, determined father had not gone into this venture blindly. He had given it a great deal of careful thought and planning for contingencies, and was confident of his strategy and abilities to succeed. And he never wavered or gave up. He just proceeded to prove his critics wrong. He was an incredibly strong, gutsy guy. For the next several years, he scouted prospective businesses throughout the Northeast and surrounding areas, identified and persuaded a potential tenant here and another there that moving into Industrial Buildings would be in their best interest.

Over the next 10 years my father succeeded in renting all Industrial's 1,000,000 square feet of space. And in the process, he secured employment for the formerly unemployed Dwight Mills workers and created an even larger and more stable property revenue base for the city of Chicopee than Dwight had provided. The outbreak of World War II with its demands for industrial space for war production helped to facilitate his success.

One of the many ways in which being the fifth child in a large family was lucky was that by the time I was 14 and entering Springfield's Classical High, a respected public school with a high record of its graduates getting into all of the top Ivy League colleges, I was the only relatively mature male around the house, and my father started to ask me to play golf with him on weekends at the Oxford Country Club[1]. I learned to play golf, but more important, I was able to spend a lot of time alone with my father and got to know him better. The two of us would walk the course's nine holes, along the Chicopee River, accompanied by a caddy whose principal job it was, in addition to carrying my father's golf bag, to find the many golf balls I sliced into the dense foliage beyond the fairways. I could almost hear the caddy breathe a sigh of relief when my wild shots would land in the river instead of the woods.

Despite my poor golf performances, my father evidently enjoyed my company, as he also began to ask me to accompany him periodically in his chauffeured car on business trips to nearby towns. One of these trips was to the Hurlburt paper mill just outside downtown Stockbridge, where he would confer with the owner who was usually seeking his advice. Another day we took a trip to the Wales woolen mill, not too distant from Springfield, which was particularly memorable, because I learned my father had recently bought it. He later told me that he had to sell it after several months when he discovered that it was losing $10,000 a month. That was not the kind of financial success he usually enjoyed.

I loved going with him on these trips. It was fascinating to watch the different types of factories in operation; I enjoyed learning how things were made, how they worked. And it was thrilling to take part in his worldly and important life. On our outings we rarely talked very much,

---

1. This was Springfield's Jewish golf club, which he had helped found, and the only country club in the area where Jews were welcome.

however. He sat in front with the chauffeur, contemplative, reflective, and silent, preparing for his next meeting, while I sat in back, gazing out the window at the passing country scenery. He just wanted my company.

I realize now that my father's introspective musing was due to his total preoccupation with his business problems during those difficult economic depression years. He never wrote anything down, and his problems, options, and the need to solve them were all done in his head. He had a remarkable memory and a quick, retentive mind. And he could do long, complicated, mathematical calculations in his head.

He was constantly sought out for help as a business advisor and savior, not only by our relatives but by a continuous stream of business associates and even strangers. And he was always very generous in responding

Mother before her marriage.

to these requests for assistance. We children all heard accounts of his numerous kindnesses and good deeds everywhere we went. A family legend had it that he had left the ship on which he came to the United States in Philadelphia, which was not his original destination, in order to help a needy woman passenger with children. We could understand that, because we knew that he was especially prone to responding to a call for help from a damsel in distress.

On his regular business trips to New York, my father often picked up strangers whom he found interesting, telling them to look him up if they should ever need a job and came to Springfield. Before long, it became known that whenever a stranger arrived at the Springfield train station and seemed lost, the stationmaster or railroad policeman on duty would ask if he was looking for Raphael Sagalyn. And when the answer was yes, which happened often, he would give directions to my father's office.

One of my father's helpful impulses led to a very important corporate legal milestone, the historic landmark Massachusetts Supreme Court decision in Sagalyn vs Meekins, Packard & Wheat (MP&W), in which the Court established the rights of a minority stockholder in a corporation. This case had been initiated by my father when the distraught widow of a friend, who had been a senior official of MP&W, the city's largest department store, asked for my father's help. The company's directors had arbitrarily cut off the dividends on the shares of stock left to her by her husband and on which she had been completely dependent.

My father bought one share in the department store company and brought the successful lawsuit against them as a minority stockholder. Reflecting on my father's life after all these years, and the stories I heard later of the multitude of people whose lives were materially benefited by his acts, I have to conclude that he must have been born and grown up with an innate, moral obligation to help those less fortunate than himself. I believe his sense of moral duty also impelled him to stand up for people who had suffered a grave injustice. His life might be characterized best by what can be described as his continuous "acts of loving-kindness." This thought is deeply moving for me and has made me very proud to be his son.

Although my father was quite a religious man, I never knew him to go to the Beth El temple, the liberal synagogue where my brothers and I had gone to Hebrew school and were bar mitzvahed, or to the conservative synagogue my mother and her sister Ida attended. For he believed a person's relationship with God was a direct, personal one that did not require an intermediary like a rabbi, priest, or minister. At the same time, he believed it important for Jews to learn about their religious heritage and customs: He founded

Father in later years.

and funded the first Hebrew school in Springfield and was a major benefactor of Springfield's Jewish Community Center. At the domestic level, he also supported my mother's need to keep a kosher kitchen.

My mother, Dora "Dina" Katz, the youngest in a family of six brothers and a sister, had emigrated from Russia in 1890 when she was six and was living in Hartford, Connecticut when my father met her. She was a beautiful, petite young woman with a gentle nature who charmed and won the affection of everyone she met, particularly Raphael Sagalyn. A year later, they were married in Hartford on October 23, 1906 and moved to Springfield. It was a warm and loving marriage. My mother had an innate gentleness, and simple, plain goodness that was endearing, and she created an atmosphere of calm orderliness and quiet activity that permeated the house in which my six siblings and I grew up. This was a real achievement, considering the fact that she was raising seven very active, strongly opinionated, independent children while also running an efficient household with our competent, formidable — but sometimes difficult—cook-housekeeper, Mrs. Sullivan.

However, my siblings and I learned early on that our mother's quiet gentle nature and general deference to our father's opinions were misleading when there was a difference of opinion on issues concerning the activities and welfare of one of the children. On those few occasions when my father sought to overrule her, my mother was transformed into a woman of steel and dominating protection, like a lioness defending her cubs, and my father would always retreat and cede the argument and the decsion to her. For that reason growing up, whenever we needed parental approval for a social or school event, we would always bring it to my mother, because we knew she would be more understanding than our old-world father. Growing up, my mother made each of us feel special, and when my mother died, and my siblings and I were reminiscing about her at her funeral, each of us believed he/she had been our mother's favorite.

While his generosity to others tended to be very low-key and often anonymous, my father's displays of love for his adored wife were often extremely extravagant. He loved to surprise her with expensive jewelry, and on one occasion, which I'll describe later, he presented her with a sumptuous summer mansion and estate in Lenox, close to Tanglewood. But my mother, by contrast, was very thrifty. She dressed and preferred to live simply, and she always insisted on his returning these very expensive gifts, including the Lenox mansion.

He was, too, a loving, generous and caring father. He had a calm, firm but gentle mien, and I never saw him get angry or lose his temper, or shout at my mother or any of us. Nor did he ever hit or physically discipline any of his children. However, he was a stern, unrelenting autocrat when it came to approving the young men his daughters brought home, as none of them ever seemed good enough to meet his impossibly high standards. Thus when asked afterwards for his opinion of one their dates, he had a way of saying something very mildly dismissive but devastating, such as, "Oh, I thought he was a very nice young man. It's too bad he's not very intelligent."

One of my earliest memories of my family and home was sitting in a large white kitchen enjoying the wonderful, fragrant smell of fresh-baked bread my mother had just taken out of the oven. My mother made delicious bread and potted cheese, and a fantastic roast chicken, but otherwise left all the cooking to Mrs. Sullivan. Our kitchen had a large adjoining pantry, which opened into a walk-in cold room, and I have a very clear mental image of the 40-gallon can of fresh milk and the large crate of eggs that our farmer delivered each week. At the end of the cold room was a big built-in icebox, with a door to the outside of the house that was opened only by the iceman when he packed it with large blocks of ice as he made his weekly rounds.

My father was always home for dinner in the dining room at 6 p.m. and sat at the head of the large, highly polished, oak table. He never talked about his business affairs or dominated the conversation. Instead, we all talked about what we had been doing at school or other activities, and mostly the conversation involved my sisters and brothers talking back and forth across the table. My sisters were the most voluble. They were always more articulate than my brothers and myself, and I almost felt tongue-tied around them.

When disagreements or questions arose, my mother would usually moderate, but there was a certain finality when my father spoke. When we had guests for dinner, however, we all deferred to my father to set the topic of conversation and do most of the talking, for his views and opinions were what the guests were most interested in hearing.

BROTHERS AND SISTERS

I am he
As you are me
And we are all together
  John Lenon & Paul McCarney

My older brother, Irwin, and I shared a room with twin beds, just to the right of the stairway on the second floor, and we had a very close, warm, harmonious relationship for two very young, and highly active brothers only two years apart in age. Irwin was the quiet, even-tempered member of the family, and I can never recall having a physical fight or serious disagreement with him growing up. He was the older, kind and thoughtful brother who helped look after me and to whom I could turn for support whenever the need arose. Irwin was mechanically inclined and liked to spend his free time building things. So it was natural for him to want to attend Springfield's Technical High School and then obtain an engineering degree at the prestigious Massachusetts Institute of Technology (MIT). He later took over and ran the Holyoke Machine Company, which our father had acquired. Established in 1863, its specialty was producing custom-made machines and equipment for the manufacture of paper and textile products that were sold all over the world.

When our father bought and had installed a ping-pong table in our large third-floor playroom, I switched my interest in running trains to playing ping-pong with my brothers Irwin and Robert during inclement weather. Before long Bobby and I became almost addicted to playing it and, when we both got home from school, we would head for the ping-pong table. We quickly became very competitive opponents. Then, when good weather came, we played tennis at one of the many public clay courts at Forest Park, just a short walk from our house. Bobby proved to be a better coordinated, more graceful athlete than I and developed into a superior tennis player.

You couldn't help loving Bobby. He had a sparkling, whimsical sense of humor and was a natural comedian, who loved making all of us laugh with his hilarious impersonations, offbeat expressions and impromptu, innovative performances. He could just walk into a room, raise an eyebrow, or just stand there looking at you and everyone would crack

Thanksgiving reunion 1959. Rear: L to R, Bobby, Arnold, Irwin, Julian. Front: Lillian, Mother, Esther.

up. His birthday was June 8, and he found extraordinary, innovative and always amusing ways to let me know it, by leaving a hidden note in a pair of my socks, or in a jacket or pant's pocket that would read, "Remember June 8!"

Bobby loved classical music and, I believe he secretly wanted to become a conductor. I still remember walking into the family room from time to time to find him standing in front of the RCA phonograph with his hands and arms waving dramatically in complete concert with a Hayden symphony. But after graduating from Bard College, his deep love of the theater led him to study acting in New York's Neighborhood Playhouse, and to become a performer, stage manager, and producer of Broadway and Off-Broadway productions.

However, after he married Avital Schwarts, an attractive girl who had grown up in Belgium and whom he had met through our sister, Lenore, the reality of the theater's unreliable economic rewards and his need to support a wife and future family, resulted in his entering the family business, Industrial Buildings in Chicopee. Over the years, we had developed a very special relationship and maintained an active correspondence that continued until his sudden, untimely death following a massive heart attack.

During my early years, I rarely saw my brother, Julian, who, seven years older, had mostly lived away from home, first at a boarding school in Maine, and later at the University of Minnesota. Then, following a severe respiratory illness, he had moved to live with the family of a college classmate on a ranch in New Mexico where the dry climate was recommended for his recovery. While he was in New Mexico he became interested in biology and after his recovery he entered Clark University in Worcester, MA and earned a degree in science.

When he returned to Springfield to live and join my father at Industrial Buildings, I got to know him better and found that he shared many of my interests, including tennis. Like Irwin, Julian would become a considerate, introspective and very supportive brother. He married a charming, personable local girl, Peggy Hayes, joined our father at Industrial Buildings, and ultimately succeeded to the presidency after my father's death. And when the family decided to close down the dairy farm, sell the my father's herd of prized Guernsey cows and let the full-time farmer go, Julie took over most of the responsibility for looking after the farm.

My eldest sister, Lillian, had been a brilliant student and had won my parent's respect, graduating from Smith College when she was only 19, and then moving to New York to start a promising career at Macy's. But when she was attracted to and married Archie Burack, a recent immigrant from Scotland, she returned to Springfield, where both worked for my father's fledging Industrial Buildings Corporation. Her quick mind and mathematical skills proved very valuable to my father.

Lillian had a strong influence on me as I was growing up, and was a caring, thoughtful, and very generous sister throughout her lifetime. As the first-born child and the off-spring of immigrants from a country with different, stricter social traditions, she played an invaluable pioneering role in sensitizing my parents to her younger siblings' new and sometimes strange and worrisome ways and activities which were customary and appropriate for American children. My growing-up years, as well as those of my other sisters and brothers, were enormously smoothed and made easier by Lillian's experience and her ready, effective advocacy of our causes with our naturally concerned and protective parents.

Although my sister Esther was four years my senior, we developed a very close and affectionate sister-brother relationship after our successive graduations from college. The relationship included her husband, Malcolm Bick, whom she met when he was in medical school at Yale, and she was at the Yale Drama School, preparing for her future work as a playwright. (It was at Yale that she acquired her permanent nickname, Toby.) Their beach house on Casey Key, Florida, was a family rendezvous on many of my winter vacations, and Toby and I also shared our love and devotion for the house with Lenore, our youngest sister, and her children, Claudia and Peter.

THE FARM

My father's retreat and relaxation from the pressures and worries of his business ventures was a 200-acre dairy farm with a herd of pedigreed Guernsey cows in North Otis, Massachusetts, in the Berkshires. He believed his children would be healthier and learn important values if they got away from their life in the city and experienced the joys and values of living in the rustic, more primitive countryside. Here we could learn about and appreciate the beauty and rewards of living close to nature. Owning land where he could farm and grow things was especially important for my father, because a Jew in Russia was not allowed to own land. Our farm expressed my father's love of nature and man's connection to the land, and I was less than four months old when I spent my first summer there.

As I grew up, I continued to go there with my siblings every summer. It was an easy one hour drive from Springfield, and my father also liked to go there at other times of the year when the weather was favorable. We traveled together in either my father's commodious Packard or, in good seasonable weather, in the Cadillac convertible touring car. Both cars had two rear jump seats and could seat seven persons comfort-

Father at the farm.

ably. We drove from Florentine Gardens west on Route 20 past Westfield, and then on dirt roads over the mountains, past Blandford into Becket, and down until we hit and turned left on Route 8 to North Otis. There was a series of hills we had to go up and down just as we got to a high point in Becket, known as Jacob's Pillow. Irwin, Bobby, Lenore and I used to call them our roller-coaster hills. From time to time during the summer, we drove back to Springfield for dental or other necessary appointments, and my father's chauffeur would then drive us back. We loved these return trips, because when we reached Jacob's Pillow, the beginning of our roller-coaster hills, we would get the chauffeur to turn off the ignition, shift the gears into neutral, and see how far we could coast, keeping distance records to check against the next time.

The drive down from Becket intersected with Route 8, which ran west toward Otis. A few hundred feet past Pyenson's chicken farm in North Otis, we turned right and exited on a narrow dirt road known as Jones road, descending a few hundred yards past our sawmill on the right, adjacent to our 20-foot high, stone dam, which held back Hayden Pond, our lake. This lake formed the border of our dairy farm. Hayden Pond was fed by Greenwater Pond, on the western outskirts of Lee, as well as by a small mountain stream on our land and some cold underground springs. This was where we swam, canoed, fished, and, in very cold winters, cut the blocks of ice we stored in the small ice-house near our house that served as our summer-time refrigerator. The large blocks of ice were covered with sawdust from the sawmill to keep them from melting.

Just after crossing a small bridge and passing a weathered, gray barn which housed a wagon and machinery used for haying, we arrived at our family's summer home. This was an unassuming, rustic yellow clap-board farmhouse on the right side of Jones Road which sat back about 40 feet from the road. The house had a screened porch extending along its entire front and was shaded by a very large oak tree.

The front door opened into a large, comfortable living room that led to the kitchen on the right. The kitchen was dominated by an ancient but very efficient iron wood-burning stove that cooked our meals and warmed us on the habitually cold, summer mornings. A well-worn wood table surrounded by several plain, serviceable, chairs was where we ate breakfast, often lunch, and played card games at night. A narrow pantry extended from the rear of the kitchen. A staircase in the far left corner led to the bedrooms and a large, outdoor, screened porch, equipped with several single beds and cots where the girls slept. There was a full bathroom on each floor.

A door on the right side of the kitchen opened onto a large, screened porch for the boys, identical in size and shape to the 2nd floor screened porch above it. Our 1,200-foot elevation made for cold nights and we all slept under several blankets. I recall vividly waking up to temperatures in the low 30's, rushing into the adjoining kitchen to light the wood stove and huddle there to warm up before sitting down to breakfast. Our housekeeper-cook came with us to prepare meals and help my mother with the housework

A few hundred yards above our house, on a plateau on the left side of Jones road, was the commodious, weathered gray-shingled farmhouse where the farmer and his family lived. Close by stood the large main barn where the hay and a few of the wagons were stored. And adjoining the barn was a newly constructed wing that my father had built for his prized herd of 20 pedigreed Guernsey cows when he decided to make it into a dairy farm, equipping its lavish milking stalls with running water from the farm's mountain spring. It was a family joke that his cows had more comforts at the farm than his family.

To the west of the farmer's house and the barns was a large vegetable garden, where we grew all kinds of delicious vegetables during the summer. Above and beyond the barns were the fields where the cows grazed, while across Jones road on the east and to the north was our night-time pasture into which the cows were driven after they had been milked.

My mother loved the farm. One of her favorite pastimes was to go blueberry picking in the upper section of the cow pasture where abundant blueberry bushes grew. Despite all of our strongly voiced concerns about her safety, she always insisted on going alone. It was not until many years later when we had grown up and had families of our own that we realized that the blueberry picking sojourns were our mother's only free place and time at the farm when she could be by herself, without having her children, husband or anyone else to look after or worry about. "I need some blueberry time" became a respected and appreciated family homily among my sisters and brothers.

My father didn't do any physical work on the farm, but he often conferred with the farmer and was actively engaged in the management of the farm. Irwin, Bobby and I always looked forward to helping the farmer cut and dry the hay and pitch it up into the second floor of the barn for the cows to eat during the winter. I also remember, with some chagrin, my offering to take turns milking the cows, but my untrained hands and sore wrists would always end with my being forced to surrender this task to one of the farmer's several sons.

Just beyond our house we created and maintained a sand beach where we swam and kept a canoe and rowboat for fishing. During my early teens, my father arranged with a nearby riding camp to bring horses to the farm once a week to teach Irwin, Bobby and me how to ride, and we took long rides up the Jones's dirt road, and beyond.
We had no electricity during my early farm days, and depended on

kerosene lanterns to provide light for dining, reading, and playing cards and other games. When I was about eight, the first electric power lines reached our area. However, although my father had a disagreement with the electric utility company and refused to let them lay electric lines across our land, he was determined that we should have the advantage of electricity, especially during the evening hours of darkness. He was very enterprising and when he learned that the nearby town of Chester was upgrading its electric power system, he purchased the town's old electric generator, power panel, and related equipment and had them set it up in the large, barn-like building that had previously housed the saw-mill. As the power to operate the saw-mill had been provided by a water wheel drawing water from the lake where it was held back by the dam, my father arranged to utilize the power from the water wheel to help generate night-time electricity and hired an electrician to hook it all up.

We now had our own power plant. Each evening, as soon as it got dark, Irwin or Bobby and I went down to the mill, turned the water wheel to open the watergate, and threw the switches that started the generator, activating the electric current to our house. Then, guided by the bright glow from the lights shining out of the house, we walked back to read and play cards—pinochle and

Mother, circa 1940s.

bridge were favorites—as well as checkers and chess. We also did jigsaw puzzles. My mother wouldn't play these games, but would sit with us, making her prized, hooked rugs from our old bathrobes and other wool clothing which she found discarded or deemed should be.

At bedtime, two of the male Sagalyn children walked back to the mill with flashlights and reversed the process: throwing the electric panel switches to the "off" position and then closing the water wheel gate to the lake. It was a ritual. It was empowering: 'Here I am bringing light; and now I am taking it away.'

The telephone, which had arrived earlier at our farm, consisted of a "party line" that we shared with our neighbors who were hooked up to the same line. There was no dialing system; rather, each telephone had a box with a bell and an attached crank that made a distinctive ring when it was turned. The sound traveled along the telephone line and rang a bell attached to every telephone hooked to that particular party line. A short crank or half turn would transmit a short ring, while a full turn would result in a louder, sustained ring. Each party was assigned a number and sequence of long and short rings, indicating which calls were intended for them. These shared, party-line telephone calls naturally became a source of local gossip, as everyone would listen in to the conversation whenever the telephone's bell rang, whether it was for them or somebody else. If you wanted to telephone someone outside of your neighboring party-line subscribers, you had to call the operator who put the call through for you. Operators were very special and important people in the community, because of their role and first-hand knowledge of what was going on.

One summer Saturday afternoon when I was about fourteen, my father drove up to our farm house, followed by a farm truck hauling a large, handsome, black covered carriage with coach lamps above the doors. We all came running out to inspect the carriage and my father proudly announced that he had just purchased it at an auction along with the Hanna farm in Lenox, a large estate with sweeping, landscaped lawns that extended from the enormous main house down the sloping, manicured lawns to Route 183 which led past the front entrance to Tanglewood just a few miles away. The carriage had been in a barn that housed the stables for a large number of horses, and had been part of the estate. My mother, who had followed us out, stared disapprovingly at her husband and stated in a unequivocal tone: "Raphael, you can take this carriage and that fancy farm you just bought back to where you got them. I am not going to move there. I am staying right here." I remember how unhappy I was at my mother's reaction and how I and my brothers Irwin and Bobby had pleaded in vain with her to change her mind.

However, later we all understood and appreciated the reasons behind my mother's refusal to move. Our simple, unpretentious, farm house and her blueberry bushes provided her an escape and refuge where she could have time alone, and she was not going to allow anyone or any situation to ruin our summer tranquility on our modest family farm, which we used to proudly boast had more rocks per acre than any other farm in the Berkshires. If we were to move to the large Lenox "cottage" with its many rooms and landscaped acres, she would have the unwelcome burden and demands on her time of managing and taking care of this enormous house and estate.

Arnold, high school graduation, 1935.

COLLEGE YEARS

Adventures must start with running away from home.
William Bolitho

As my senior year at Classical High was drawing to a close, I was looking forward to entering one of the several New England colleges to which I had confidently applied. So I was very disappointed when my first reply was a letter of rejection and, as the other colleges responded, I opened each successive letter with an increasingly stunned disbelief. When I read the last turndown, I was overwhelmed with a feeling of shock, despair, and a depressing sense of emotional devastation. How could this have happened to me?

Springfield's public schools then were widely known and acclaimed for the high quality of their teachers and their students' education, and I entered first grade at the nearby elementary school. I continued at the neighborhood's Forest Park Junior High, to which I also walked, first with my older brother, Irwin, and later with my younger brother, Robert. Close by were the Forest Park tennis courts, a large block of public, well-maintained, clay courts, where I would learn to play and frequent often after school, while just beyond the courts was the city's zoo, which also was an attractive place to go.

In elementary and junior high schools, I had been a creditable but rather average C+ student, cruising along with occasional A's and B's. I was also active in various student activities, including drama, tennis and ice hockey. Being number five in a large family of seven, with two older brothers and sisters, and a younger brother and sister, meant that there was very little attention or pressure on me to excel, or do better in school. My older siblings had taken the brunt of my parents' natural concerns for their children to do well in schools. So when I came along, I was able to coast contentedly on my average-but-okay grades through all of my early school years.

The reality, I had to recognize, was that I had not been a very diligent student, especially during the past three years, but had spent a disproportionate amount of time on extracurricular social and sports activities instead of studying, still content with comfortable C's, occasional B's, and very few A's. Also, all of the colleges I had applied to were highly selective and always had far more applicants than available space, making my high-school grades and poor performance on the national scholastic aptitude exams (SAT's) an easy basis for rejection.

I felt humiliated that I had disgraced myself and had let down and disappointed my parents, as well as my four older sisters and brothers who had all been good students and had gone on to good colleges. However, when I went to tell them my bad news, my mother and father were sympathetically calm and uncritical. Instead of berating me, my father led me into the study and said: "Well, we have a problem. Let's sit down and discuss it. First, what do you want to do now? Is there some way I can help?" I told him I thought the rejection from Wesleyan had not been as final as the others, and I would like to call the Wesleyan admissions director to find out what I could do to convince them that I was capable of doing college-level work. With my father's approval, I called and was able to talk to the admissions director. He said they had their own exam to test my aptitude for college-level courses and, if I passed it satisfactorily, I would be accepted.

After reporting this to my father, I told him that I was confident that I could pass Wesleyan's test if I was tutored during the summer. I added that I had talked to Edwin Smith, one of my favorite high-school teachers who told me he would be willing to drive out to our farm, where I would be spending the summer, to tutor me, provided that my father approved and paid for the lessons. Happily, my father agreed and for the first time I really applied myself to my studies, working hard that summer with Ed Smith as he tutored me twice a week. With his help and my determination, I succeeded in passing Wesleyan's tests with respectable B's and was admitted as a freshman to Wesleyan's class of 1939.

Despite my passing Wesleyan's special entrance exam, my disastrous performance on my College Boards had left me a little apprehensive about whether I could keep up with my classmates, many of whom had gone to top prep and boarding schools like Andover, Exeter, and Choate. So I was feeling a bit anxious when I left home to enter Wesleyan in the Fall. I was also determined to buckle down, hit the books, and work hard to get good grades. I had learned the humiliating and scary consequences of goofing off, and now I was going to be a very serious student and make my parents and brothers and sisters proud of me.

WESLEYAN

The schools ain't what they used to be and never was.
    Will Rogers

Only my parents, my eldest sister, Lillian, who was married and living across the street from 1 Florentine Gardens, and my younger siblings, Bobby and Lenore, were there to see me off for college. My brother Irwin had already departed for MIT to begin his junior year and my sister Esther had graduated from Wellesley and was enrolled in graduate studies at the Yale Drama School. Julian, my oldest brother, was living in New Mexico recovering from a respiratory illness. I can still sense the feeling of relief from my father, mother, and Lillian that the earlier weeks of suspense and concern about my future were temporarily over. I was going to be at Wesleyan and living relatively nearby in Middletown, Connecticut. Travel arrangements to college were easily made when I discovered that two of my high-school classmates, Robert Kirkland and Malcolm Hobbs, were also going to Wesleyan, and Kirkland's father was driving them there. There was room enough for me to join them. My father told me that his secretary, Ms. Reardon, would take care of paying for my college tuition and books, and she would send me a monthly allowance to cover food, clothes, and other personal expenses. Ms. Reardon was the secretary-genie-fairy godmother in my father's office, a warm, attractive, diplomatic, incredibly competent, Irish woman and a family legend. She had gone to work for my father as his secretary as a young girl, never married and stayed with him until his death in 1949. For more than 30 years, she devoted herself to serving as my father's alter ego, managing his office and his life, as well as being a warm, caring, confidant and best friend to me and every one of my brothers and sisters.

A major away-from-home college problem—my laundry—was resolved by the purchase of a sturdy plastic rectangular carton in which I could send home my dirty shirts, socks and underwear, to be returned clean via the U.S. mail, just as my older siblings had done before, and as countless college students all over the country were doing.

Wesleyan, Amherst, and Williams were traditional rivals, known as the Little Three, who competed in sports and, like most small New England colleges, did not admit women. Their campus social activities were dominated by private Greek-letter fraternities where a great majority of the students lived and ate. Freshman students, however, were usually required to live in campus dorms.

I was assigned a single room in the North building, a small, clean, sparse room barely big enough for a narrow single bed, a clothes bureau, and a simple pine desk squeezed under a lone window. This was to be my new home. Following the promise I had made to myself to be a diligent, serious student, I applied myself during freshman year to my courses in English, French, History, Latin, and Biology. I found my classes and professors far more interesting and stimulating than those in high school and my commitment to my studies was rewarded.

With the exception of Biology, which I barely struggled through, I received an A- in History and B's in my other courses. My satisfactory academic performance in my freshman year encouraged me to engage in a more active social life as a sophomore. I went out for the soccer team and played, although usually briefly, in several games with rival colleges. I joined a community theatre group, played a major role in Chekov's Cherry Orchard, and was a dancer in a college performance of Gilbert & Sullivan's Pirates of Penzance. While I thoroughly enjoyed each of these extra-curricular activities, as well as the break from my studies, I must confess I was not a soccer star, and while an enthusiastic dancer, I clearly posed no threat to Fred Astaire. I did feel that my acting, however, was quite respectable for a novice thespian and took pride in the compliments I received.

On Saturdays, I joined the long ranks of Wesleyan students who left for weekend dates and partying at women's colleges. Planning and logistics for these weekend jaunts would usually start in the middle of the week, when I would meet with two or three of my socially close classmates to discuss the most critical problem, transportation—who had a car and could drive us. Once this was solved, we focused on the destination and our dates, who tended to be available and were often roommates of the date of one of our group. We took off Saturday morning in suits or jackets and ties. Those of us lined up with blind dates would try to pump as much information as was available to assure us that the girl we were to escort would not prove to be a total disaster. And, inevitably, the law of averages would result in some blind dates who were dreadful bummers and occasionally one who was a real dish.

When I look back, I have to acknowledge that the inherent nature of these weekends and blind dates put a premium on keeping our conversations and behavior on the light side, avoiding anything that threatened to be of substance or depth—except to try to impress a date. But, win or lose, I always found the weekends an enjoyable diversion and remarkably educational with respect to my fellow college men and women at that time and place.

While I liked my courses and professors and, with the exception of a science course in astronomy, my grades remained at the B level, I found that having fun and partying had a higher priority than academics among most Wesleyan students. Their prevailing attitude—that college time was better spent having a good time than studying—was exemplified and promoted by the college's fraternities, where the amount of beer you could drink at a sitting carried more prestige than your grades.

I found myself somewhat ill-suited for this type of social activity, as I did not enjoy drinking or smoking. I diligently tried both, but found that I just did not like the taste of hard liquor or the smoke of cigarettes and pipes. And since one glass of beer was pretty much my limit, this made me a poor companion for most of my fellow students.

My unsuitability also included my religion. None of Wesleyan's fraternities admitted anyone Jewish, and as most students after freshman year lived and socialized in the fraternities, their houses automatically created a physical barrier, as well as a presence and a daily reminder of my difference and separation. I cannot remember anyone else in my class who was Jewish. The few other Jewish students at Wesleyan were in classes ahead of me, so I never became friends with any of them. During my freshman year, I was invited to dine at a fraternity from time to time by a classmate pledged to the fraternity, and I would join him and other friends I had made on weekend dates. Beginning with my sophomore year, however, when the lives of virtually all my classmates and friends revolved around their fraternity brothers, non-fraternity outsiders like my-self inevitably tended to be shut out of the college social life. I had developed a close relationship with one of my professors and my class advisor, Ralph Bischoff, a very pleasant man with a warm personality. He was an inspirational teacher who made his course on government come alive, and he was a major influence on my developing an interest in government. One afternoon at the end of my sophomore first semester, I was meeting with Professor Bischoff discussing my work in his class and my other courses. He suddenly put up his hand to signal me to stop talking. Then, leaning forward, he looked at me intently and in a measured, thoughtful manner said, "I think you are wasting your time here at Wesleyan. Have you given any thought to transferring to another college?"

Taken completely by surprise, I searched his face and eyes trying to decipher from his expression whether he was joking. But it was clear that he was serious. His unexpected comment and the look of concern that accompanied his question acted like a powerful beam of light cutting though a thick fog, as the significance of what he was proposing jolted me. I suddenly realized that I was not really happy or satisfied with either my work or my life at Wesleyan, beginning with the general attitude that college was for partying and studying and was not to be taken too seriously. Added to that was the reality that if you weren't part of a fraternity, you were shut out of a large part of Wesleyan's life.

I replied that no, I hadn't really given much thought to whether I was wasting my time at Wesleyan. But now, thinking about it, I realized he could be right and I found his idea of transferring to another college very intriguing. "Do you have a particular college in mind?" I asked. He did and proceeded to tell me about Oberlin, a small liberal arts college in northeastern Ohio, not far from Cleveland, which he had attended. Bischoff observed that I didn't seem to have the same interest in my class and work as I had my freshman year, and he thought that Wesleyan's fraternity system had to be a major factor. Oberlin, on the other hand, had no fraternities and was also coeducational and, he believed, I would find these two factors advantageous and its strong academic environment much more satisfactory and rewarding.

The more I thought about transferring to a school like that the more I liked the idea, and with his assistance and guidance, I wrote to Oberlin, enclosing my grades, and applied for admission as a junior. It wasn't until after I had received a favorable response that I talked to my father and mother when I went home during a school break. My father said he understood my reasons for transferring, that they made sense, and that he approved. My mother's reaction was hesitant and she seemed disturbed. She asked me where Oberlin was and, when I told her it was in Ohio, her unease and troubled look deepened strongly. "Why do you want to go out so far west," she inquired, very concerned. "Aren't there wild Indians out there?" I finally succeeded in persuading her that there was no longer any danger from wild Indians in Ohio and that I would be safe at Oberlin.

OBERLIN

The ultimate goal of the education system is to shift to the individual the burden of pursuing his own education.
  John Gardner

After Wesleyan, Oberlin was a whole new world, academically, intellectually, and socially. This was particularly true with respect to the students, whom I found more open and interesting than Wesleyan's—as well as more representative of America's social and economic strata. Unlike most of my Wesleyan classmates, who all seemed to have been molded by the same socioeconomic background and reflected a preppy look and outlook on social values and life, I had the sense I had just discovered a new land, the Midwest and heart of America, where most people came from public schools, not prep schools, and whose backgrounds, customs, and social and political views were far more diverse and open to new ideas.

The change was as if I had just taken a cold, refreshing shower. In retrospect, I see this new academic environment as a heritage of Oberlin's history as a pioneering educational institution in Ohio, then America's western frontier, when it was started in 1833. Its covenant pledged its students to "the plainest living and highest thinking." Unlike most Eastern colleges of the time (and for many years to come) Oberlin never had fraternities and had always admitted both blacks and women.

It was not surprising, then, that I found this small-town Ohio college welcoming. For example, Oberlin believed all students should participate in athletic activities, and it emphasized and sponsored intramural competition rather than intercollegiate sports like football and baseball. I was soon playing on junior tennis and soccer teams. I found the presence of women in my classes and on campus especially fortuitous and an enormous improvement over Wesleyan's all-male student body. There was no need to take off every weekend to have dates and party at other colleges. I quickly found myself in the swing of things, meeting and frequently dating an attractive coed for a movie or college event. One of my discoveries at Oberlin was that I could enjoy the company of girls in all kinds of social activities without any sexual connotations or the necessity of making a commitment to a particular individual, as was sometimes a problem at Wesleyan. It was possible and o.k. just to enjoy being with and enjoying a girl's company and friendship.

As I had found my Government course at Wesleyan more interesting than all my other courses, it had aroused my interest in the field of government. I picked Political Science as my major at Oberlin. In the process, my attention was piqued by an outstanding Czech refugee and political science professor, Oskar Jaszi, whom Oberlin had attracted. I promptly enrolled in his courses. Professor Jaszi's courses turned out to be extremely absorbing and stimulating and would have a major influence on my career path[2]. Prof. Jaszi was an arresting, erect, impressive looking man with a dominating, authoritative, yet appealing, personality. His knowledge of events in Europe enriched his lectures with vivid images of Nazi Germany's developing threats of an expanding war— images so compelling that I always looked forward to his classes.

As was the case in my first year at Wesleyan, I worked hard enough to get a respectable B average, but by the time my junior year ended, I had also made time for a few selected, nonacademic activities such as tennis and soccer, a few theatrical performances and writing a column, "So 'tis Said," in the student newspaper, the Oberlin Review. In my senior year I made the Dean's list.

I kept my parents and siblings informed of my activities by way of several carbon copies of my letters, and my family responded in turn, so that all of us were kept in touch of what was going on in our respective lives. When my sister, Esther, enrolled in the Yale Drama School after her graduation in 1935 from Wellesley, she changed not only her name Esther to Toby, but also her family name Sagalyn to Bick after meeting her future husband, Malcolm Bick, a Yale senior. The summer before I entered Oberlin, I had a job as a tennis instructor and counselor to a group of eight 12-year-old boys at Camp Equinox in the Pennsylvania

---

2. *Professor Jaszi's course required a term paper on an important aspect of local or federal government. And as I had been fascinated in reading newspaper stories describing the successful exploits of nearby Cleveland's Public Safety director, Eliot Ness, in cleaning up the city's flagrant crime and corruption, I interviewed Ness and wrote my report on how he had achieved his success. I then visited Ness, gave him a copy of my term paper and told him I would like a job working for him when I graduated.*

Pocono Mountains. It was my first real job, and I loved the work and experience, although I knew I had only been hired because Malcolm's father was a co-owner of the camp. I returned to Equinox as a counselor the following summer and then joined my entire family at the farm on a warm, cloudless September day for the happy celebration of Toby's marriage to Malcolm in an outdoor ceremony.

In my senior year, however, my column in the *Oberlin Review* got me into "hot water" at the college. It all started when, after rummaging around for an interesting and challenging subject to write about for my forthcoming column, I decided to write about Oberlin-in-Shansi, an educational institution established by Oberlin missionaries in Shansi, China, many years earlier. This institution was one of the beneficiaries of the college's compulsory student activity fee, which funded the college's extracurricular, cultural, and intramural events. While I believed Oberlin-in-Shansi was a worthy non-profit institution deserving of support, my column questioned whether it qualified for inclusion in the mandatory student activity levy since very few, if any, of the college's students participated in the China institution's activities. Instead, I proposed that support of Oberlin students for Oberlin-in-Shansi should be voluntary, not mandatory—and certainly not part of the Student Activity Fee.

I had thought that my column might generate a useful, stimulating discussion of the propriety of including the China school in the Student Activity Fee. But I was flabbergasted and completely unprepared for the swift enraged reaction to my suggestion and the flood of vitriolic and abusive phone calls and letters that came flooding into the *Review*'s office, denouncing me and the newspaper for publishing it. I was particularly shocked and disappointed that some of the angriest and most derogatory criticism came from members of the faculty. I couldn't believe that what I had thought was an off-hand and rather mild recommendation had stirred up this incredible hornet's nest.

As I started to think about the critical faculty members, the very people I would expect to stand up and support the discussion of this college issue, I became very angry. My mother always said I was a "nudge," and sometimes I did have a stubborn, relentless streak in pursuing ideas and projects that intrigued me. But in this case, I felt that I was only expressing my constitutional First Amendment right of free speech and freedom of the press, and I was determined to fight back. Fortunately, the editor of the Review, Tom Boardman, a classmate and good friend, wasn't intimidated by the backlash, and he staunchly backed me up when I told him that I wanted to write a follow-up column on the same subject in the next issue of the school paper, demanding a referendum on the Oberlin-in-Shansi and Student Activity Fee issue by the entire student body. The referendum was held, but I was denied my request to talk to the students in any college room and denounced again by some of the professors. Moreover, the students voted overwhelming in favor of keeping Oberlin-in-Shansi on the Student Activity Fee.[3]

HOW I MET FRITCHEY & NESS

When I returned to Oberlin in September 1938, Professor Jaszi reminded all of us majoring in Political Science that we were required to turn in a term paper on a government subject. I remembered the paper I had to write for Professor Bischoff's political science course at Wesleyan. It had described the ineffectiveness of the local police and the success of the FBI in curbing the notorious bank robbers who were terrorizing many Midwest cities, and I recalled how much this law enforcement role and function of government had interested me.

Coincidentally, Tom Boardman had been serving as a stringer (part-time reporter) for the Cleveland Press, the state's largest afternoon circulation newspaper and I had been reading in the copies of the Press

---

3. *However, this incident was to have future adverse, personal consequences as I discovered years later when I had to undergo Federal background and character investigations for security clearances at the Pentagon and the Treasury. "Anonymous" Oberlin faculty members had seized on the Shansi incident to defame me by telling FBI investigators that I had been a "troublemaker" at Oberlin. I was so outraged by this charge that I terminated all contributions to my class and Oberlin. I wrote a note in response to a college solicitation shortly after this, saying that I would make no future donations and would explain why if I were contacted, but no one ever called or wrote me. Interestingly enough, after graduation from Oberlin in 1939, I rented an apartment in Cleveland and was a roommate with Tom Boardman, who would go to work for the Cleveland Press and become its chief editor, and also later serve as Oberlin's board chairman.*

he was receiving a series of intriguing articles about the extraordinary achievements of Cleveland's new public safety director, Eliot Ness. Previously, Ness had directed an elite team of Federal agents whose activities had led to the imprisonment of Al Capone, Chicago's top, notorious gangster, and the end of his gang's criminal reign. Ness had been challenged by the offer of a new Cleveland reform mayor to clean up that city's infamously corrupt police department. The stories in the Press had vividly described how Ness, against all odds, was systematically ferreting out the long elusive, critical evidence and sending to jail Cleveland's key, high-ranking, crooked police officers, as well as the city's imbedded racketeers they had been protecting.

I was completely fascinated by Ness's activities and excited that I had finally found the needed subject for my term paper: Eliot Ness in Cleveland. As I had to start work on my project immediately to meet my deadline, I decided that direct action was the best, that I should take a bus into Cleveland to talk to the Press reporter whose by-line was on the Ness stories, Clayton Fritchey, and get him to introduce me to Ness. The next day I found my way to the Cleveland Press office, where I was directed to Fritchey's desk. After introducing myself as an Oberlin student who wanted to write a term paper about Ness that was required for my political science class, I told him I had been inspired by his captivating articles and asked if he would introduce me to Ness so I could meet and interview him for my college project? I naively added that I would share with him the results of my paper.

Fritchey was clearly taken aback by my request and stared at me in surprise and disbelief at the presumptuousness of this college kid. Then, shaking his head at what he was about to do, he said he was just leaving to meet with Eliot Ness and I could accompany him. My good luck held, for I not only met Eliot, but he was also amused at my brashness, and like Clayton, approved of my aggressiveness and follow-up relentlessness. He talked to me for nearly an hour and agreed to additional interviews with him and other key police and city officials. He also arranged for me to obtain important public safety reports and data I needed to support my findings and conclusions.

I had discussed with my parents, when I was home on Christmas vacation, my earlier expressed interest in a job and possible career in government after my graduation. My father had always been very protective and resourceful in helping all my brothers and my eldest sister, Lillian, with jobs and settling down in Springfield. He told me he had already talked to several people in the state government in Boston, and there were two or three possibilities I could check out when I returned home from Oberlin. But I found myself feeling uncomfortable and restless in following the same path as my siblings, and felt strongly about being more independent,

Clayton Fritchey.

even adventurous, as to where I wanted to live and to find my own job. Meeting Ness and writing my term paper had stirred up my interest in the possibility of working for Eliot and living in Cleveland the summer after graduation.

As a result, after I returned to Oberlin and finished my term paper in early March, I made an appointment to see Eliot. I also made a copy of my completed term paper report, which I took with me to give to him. When I met with him and handed him the copy of my paper, I told him how much I had enjoyed writing the report about him and that I would love to get an intern-type summer job with him in June. Eliot riffled quickly through my report and the numerous pages of background data, tables and charts in the index. Then, he turned and, after looking at me thoughtfully for a long moment, said, "Why don't you just come and work for me full-time?"

Aside from the temporary furor over my column, my life at Oberlin had been thoroughly enjoyable, academically and socially rewarding, and unmarked by any other unpleasant or discordant event. I continued the practice of sending carbon copies of my letters to everyone in my family over the years that followed; my recipients continued to respond in turn. These letters from home and from my siblings have always been important events for me. I stopped everything I was doing to immerse myself in reading about what was going on with the writer and catch up on the latest doings and gossips about close friends and relatives. These letters were lifelines that buoyed my spirits and brought a warm, loving sense of the importance and empowering comfort of my family ties.

The day after my graduation June 13, 1939, with an Oberlin A.B., and saying thank you and goodbye to my parents who had come to see me graduate, I traveled to Cleveland to begin my law enforcement career with Eliot Ness.

CLEVELAND
1939-1942

Chapter 2

ELIOT NESS

The day shall not be up as soon as I
To try the fair adventure of tomorrow
 Shakespeare, King John

I was up early that special June morning in 1939. I shaved, showered, put on my conservative gray flannel suit with a blue-and-white-striped tie, ate a bowl of corn flakes with a sliced banana and two slices of whole wheat toast, drank a cup of Nescafe, and caught a streetcar to Cleveland's City Hall and my first day of work for Eliot Ness, the city's dynamic Director of Public Safety. I was going to be working closely with a man whose exploits I had been avidly following in the pages of the Cleveland Press during my two years at Oberlin, and I felt hyped up, both excited and nervous.

Lieutenant Walter Walker, an experienced and trusted police officer who was on full-time assignment to Ness, led me to a small metal desk with a worn wooden swivel armchair near a side entrance to Ness's office. "The Director wants you to sit here," he instructed me, and then, pointing to a metal inbox filled with correspondence addressed to Ness, he added, "He wants you to look through these speaking invitations, which he is accepting, and prepare responses for his signature."

I quickly discovered that Eliot's very small staff did not include a personal secretary, but that he would call on the City Hall's secretarial pool when necessary. So I was, in effect, to become his personal aide and secretary. Part of my job entailed handling many of his calls and correspondence relating to the media and requests to speak, for which I drafted responses for his signature. In addition, Eliot would appoint me secretary of his Police and Fire Committees, on which he relied to assess and acquire essential police and fire equipment and discuss major innovations. And because I was immediately available, he would assign me to handle special investigative and other unexpected but urgent projects that developed periodically.

Virtually all of Eliot's small, crack team of civilian criminal investigators—on whom he depended to ferret out the critical evidence required to clean up police corruption, racketeering and other illegal activity—worked outside of Eliot's office. Beside myself, only Lt. Walker and a few other itinerant plain-clothes police officers on special assignment had desks in Ness's large, open, outer office. Eliot's Deputy Director, Robert Chamberlin, had a private office just beyond Ness's, as did Tom Clothey, who coordinated special investigative and intelligence assignments. (Both Bob Chamberlin and one of Eliot's chief investigative aides, Keith Wilson, later played a very important role in my army career.)

Like most large cities, following the passage in 1919 of the widely unpopular 18th Amendment (and the Volstead Act, which prohibited the sale of alcoholic beverages), Cleveland had been devastated and corrupted by the arrival of brutal criminal enterprises and ruthless gangs that sprang up to meet the great public demand for outlawed liquor, wine and beer. Perhaps the most notorious criminal gangs were those in Chicago, none more infamous and symbolic of its lawless reign than that of Al Capone, whose downfall and imprisonment was largely achieved by a special Federal investigative team led by the young Federal agent, Eliot Ness.

When Prohibition was repealed in 1933, after President Roosevelt's election, the entrenched criminal organizations shifted their focus to other highly profitable and illegal activities, such as gambling, racketeering (extorting money by threats of violence), prostitution, and drugs. They were able to operate successfully in most large cities, including Cleveland, Ohio, by bribing the police, judges and other city officials, creating an atmosphere of public distrust of police and public officials. Therefore, in December, 1935, Cleveland's newly elected reform mayor, Harold Burton, asked Ness to be the city's Public Safety Director, with jurisdiction over the police, fire, and buildings departments and with a mandate to clean up Cleveland. Eliot's knowledgeable friends and colleagues warned him that he would be accepting an impossible mission. The police department was notoriously and hopelessly corrupt, and widespread racketeering and lawlessness were both prevalent and protected by bribed law enforcement and judicial officials. But Ness, who was then stationed in Cleveland as the agent in charge of the new post-Prohibition successor, the Treasury Department Alcohol Tax unit, was intrigued by the challenge and accepted the job.

When I joined Ness's personal staff four years later, his list of major accomplishments—uprooting and sending to prison crooked high ranking police officers and corrupt labor officials and restoring public confidence in Cleveland's city officials—had been publicly acclaimed as heroic and historic. Eliot had largely completed the reorganization and modernization of the city's police and fire departments, replacing incompetent officers and commanders, establishing one of the nation's first two-way radio-equipped police forces, and also its first police academy. He had succeeded in transforming the former dysfunctional police department into an effective, accountable and respected public safety agency.

Ness had also reformed the fire department. He instituted innovative fire-hazard-inspection and training regulations that required fire officials and firemen to conduct daily inspections of all commercial and industrial buildings in each battalion's area, instead of just hanging around in their fire stations waiting to respond to fire alarms. In their daily inspections, battalion chiefs were asked to record on waterproof maps the location and nature of all potentially combustible hazards in individual buildings, and to note lack of exits that could pose threats to men fighting a fire. Their two-way radio communications equipment would enable them to respond rapidly to any fire alarm within their battalion area just as quickly as if they were sitting idly back in their fire stations.

There was still much work to be done to complete public safety reforms designated to clean up the city's remaining gambling, racketeering, and related criminal enterprises. To educate and prepare me for my role as his personal aide, Ness arranged for a training program. I spent one to three weeks in each branch of the police department, including the detective bureau, patrol, traffic, radio communications and crime prevention, crime lab, and vice squad (primarily prostitution and gambling). Over the next several months, working under the wing of a senior officer, I was completely immersed in learning about each of these police functions. This on-the-job training was invaluable in my basic education and understanding of the fundamentals of protecting the lives and property of citizens and the maintenance of law and order in an urban community, 24 hours a day, seven days a week.

In the course of accompanying, observing, and talking with these police officers and their commanders and, in the months that followed, working directly with Ness, I learned firsthand of the enormous pressures and temptations inherent in policing, as well as the critical importance of instituting an effective system of oversight controls and accountability to prevent the corruption and abuse of a police officer's power in enforcing the laws. These temptations can affect police conduct dealing with everything from minor traffic and regulatory violations to serious criminal felonies. The police officer is entrusted with broad discretionary authority to stop and to arrest civilians. The officer has the power of life and death over those he has sworn to protect and defend, and he is provided with a gun to do so. I also learned of the huge psychologicagap and barrier between the average policeman and the average civilian. The police officer's "us" versus "them" mentality grows out of daily contact with hostile civilian reactions evoked in the process of maintaining law and order.

I found the operations of the vice squad especially interesting. Its commander and my instructor, Captain Mike Blackwell, was a big, brawny, hard-driving, flamboyant Irishman—a self-promoter who loved getting his name in the papers. Each night for three weeks we went on forays with a squad of officers and raided brothels or arrested prostitutes who were soliciting "johns" on the street. The first time we made a raid and were leading several prostitutes into the "paddy wagon" to take them down to the police station to be booked, I became very embarrassed when one of the veteran prostitutes suddenly stopped, looked over at me in great surprise, then turned to Blackwell and said, "Hey, Captain, who's the kid here? He's pretty cute." After awhile I was able to assume a very blasé attitude on these raids.

Many of the raids I went on with the vice squad targeted large gambling dens, where the squad would systematically destroy furniture, telephone and racing wire equipment, and other items of economic value in order to inflict severe financial loss and make it more costly for the owners to resume their illicit operations. While the normally aggressive Captain Blackwell tended to handle the prostitution raids in an uncharacteristic lethargic manner, on gambling raids he became a completely changed, highly energized and enthusiastic lawman. After breaking down the door, he would charge ahead of his equally motivated squad, smashing up the furniture, and ripping out the telephone and wire service lines that transmitted results from the nation's various race tracks. The excitement generated in these raids was contagious, and I quickly found myself wading in alongside my fellow raiders, breaking a sturdy leg off of a heavy oak table or swinging a metal chair to demolish vulnerable gambling room equipment. The enormous exertion expended would leave me sweating and exhausted, but also exhilarated. I had struck a blow at the gambling gang owners whose activities and bribes were corrupting the police and other city officials[4]. The day after each raid I would write a letter for Eliot's signature addressed to the President of the Ohio Bell Telephone Company, stating that the telephones at the address of the raided gambling establishment were being used for gambling purposes and should be terminated. The loss of their telephone service essentially put these gambling joints out of business.

My special police authorization.

The officers who oversaw gambling, however, were vulnerable to being bribed because a policeman made only $35 a week. He could receive double that amount for merely ignoring the designated address of a gambling operator who would then deposit the money in a bank account for him. Ness explained how such offers would be accompanied by highly persuasive arguments: it was legal to place bets at the race track or in a poker game at a friend's home, so placing a bet with a bookie or in a gambling establishment wasn't really that different, just a technical violation. The breaking point for accepting a bribe would usually come when an officer was confronted with an unexpected expense, and he rationalized that he wasn't being asked to do anything illegal by simply ignoring or staying away from a certain location.

Concerned about the large amounts of gambling money available that were being used to buy protection from susceptible police and other government officials, Ness set up a special gambling surveillance squad to detect when bribes occurred. Whenever a report came in that Sgt. Smith or Lt. Jones of the intelligence unit was "on the take," Ness's policy was to recognize the temptation inherent in these gambling intelligence assignments and routinely reassign the officer to a different

---

4. *The racing wire services were vital in providing track results to bookmakers, men whose business was to illegally collect bets. These services were owned and controlled by Moses Annenberg, who later went to prison for tax fraud. It's interesting that his fortune, based on these illegal activities, was the origin of the reputable philanthropic activities of his descendants, including his son, Walter Annenberg, President Reagan's U.S. Ambassador to Great Britain.*

type of duty that lacked such risk. Ness also staffed the gambling intelligence beat with young graduates from the police academy, replacing them annually, thus limiting the time period of their vulnerability to bribes.

One evening after I had concluded my indoctrination training on gambling, I asked Eliot his views on gambling and police enforcement. "How do you justify raiding and shutting down race track and other sports gambling in some places and ignoring other types of gambling in the city, such as poker games, that go on in private clubs? What is the public enforcement policy difference?" Ness leaned back in his chair, nodding approvingly at the question. "My concern is where the money is going and how much money is involved," he replied. "If people want to gamble with friends in their homes or clubs, that's their business. But when you have large scale organized gambling where enormous amounts of money go to criminal enterprises and individuals who use it to bribe public officials, I believe this is a threat to the public, and it's my business to try to stop it." As an example, Ness told me about his experience in Chicago where the large amounts of money generated by Capone's illegal operations enabled him to buy protection from Chicago's police, judges and other public officials.

When I had finished my intensive training in policing, Eliot commissioned me "Special Policeman in the Department of Public Safety." After I completed a full course in the handling and shooting of a police revolver at the police firing range, Eliot issued me an identification card signed by him and the chief of the Cleveland Police Department, authorizing me to carry a gun and to make arrests. Ness's very limited office staff and operations budget were set by a frugal city council, and he was forced to find creative sources of revenue to pay for the small criminal investigative team on which he was dependent to carry out his mandate to clean up the city. It was not a big surprise, therefore, when I learned that I was listed as an employee in the police garage at a salary of $31.50 a week, an amount that was more than ample for me to live on in those days.

My first assignment was to spend two days as a temporary replacement for a regular member of the detective bureau, who was on surveillance of a major suspect in one of America's most horrible, serial murder cases, that of the Torso Murderer, who has not been identified to this day! Starting in the fall of 1935, this serial murderer made it his practice to cut off the heads and limbs of his victims and left them in empty railroad boxcars. The press tagged him the "Mad Butcher of Kingsbury Run." (Kingsbury Run was a vast area of huge iron and steel mills, oil refineries and long rows of warehouses that operated day and night producing chemicals, paints, electrical equipment and tools. It was a grimy, smoke-filled area that was home to thousands of victims of the Great Depression. This was where the serial killer found and butchered his victims.)

Ness had the detective in charge of the investigation, Lt. Peter Merylo, brief me on the man I was to follow. The suspect was a middle-aged man from a respectable family who had served as a doctor during World War I and had been given a medical discharge after being badly gassed. A medical report that included a psychiatric examination stated that he had a "frustrated desire to operate," and this mental condition, combined with his surgical experience and evidence that he had been in the vicinity at the time when each murder occurred, made him a suspect who needed to be kept under surveillance.

Lt. Merylo, instructed me to go to the southeast corner of Euclid Avenue and 3rd Street, close to the Public Square, where I was to look out for the detective I would relieve, a balding, hefty man in a light gray suit wearing a blue polka dot tie and a gray fedora. When I reached the described area, I spotted the detective standing in the doorway of a tobacco shop next to a small restaurant. I walked over and joined him. He acknowledged my arrival with a quick nod and informed me that our quarry was in the restaurant having lunch. He would be coming out soon and was likely to take a trolley up Euclid. "This guy can be tricky," he warned me, and left. Merylo had given me a description of the "Doctor" and how he was dressed that day. I easily identified the rather ordinary-looking person who ambled out of the restaurant, wearing a green plaid cap and a light tan topcoat. He paused briefly to scan the faces of those nearby, and proceeded up Euclid Avenue at a leisurely pace. I waited in the smoke shop's recessed doorway until he had progressed a few hundred feet with several pedestrians between us before stepping out to follow him.

My suspect passed two trolley stops, pausing at a third, standing back from the curb, close to an office building. I ducked into the doorway of a shoe store, out of sight, watching. He leaned against a red brick wall while several trolleys passed by. Suddenly, just as the last in a string of trolleys was departing, he ran to the streetcar and jumped on. Although surprised, I managed to grab a steel stanchion at the trolley's rear door and boarded. I now knew what Lt. Merylo meant when he warned me that my assignee was "tricky." His maneuver had exposed me which was an embarrassing beginning to my career as a detective. He now knew who was following him, and my job was to make sure that I didn't lose him. He sat in the front of the trolley and I took a seat in the back and tried nonchalantly to ignore him by looking out toward the passing stores and office buildings. Suddenly, without any indication of his intentions, he got up, jumped off the trolley at the first cross street, and ran to catch a crosstown trolley.

When I realized what was happening, I ran after him, but was unable to reach the cross-town trolley in time. On inquiry, I was upset to learn that the next tram wasn't due for 30 minutes. I had no other means of pursuit. I had lost my assigned quarry on my very first surveillance. My humiliation was complete when I got back to police headquarters to report to Lt. Merylo and found that he had received a telephone message from my Torso Murders suspect. I could sense the disappointment in Merylo's voice when he relayed the message. "That young kid you had following me wasn't very good. If he wants to try again tomorrow, tell him I'll be in the men's department at Higbee's Department Store at 2 p.m."

The elusive Torso Murders suspect knew that Cleveland police detectives were following him. He thought it was a game and thoroughly enjoyed outfoxing the series of police detectives who were assigned to track him. I learned 40 years later, when my U.S. Treasury Department responsibilities included the training of 4,000 criminal investigators, that successful surveillance of someone in a large city requires an experienced team of investigators, equipped with sophisticated communications, transportation, and tracking capabilities, especially when the individual may suspect he or she is being followed.

Merylo conceded it would be futile to send me out alone again on a surveillance mission. The Doctor continued playing "hide-and-seek" games with the Detective Bureau. He even sent Ness a postcard, with a photo of a lone tree in the middle of field with an X underneath and a note: "DIG HERE." Despite his known tendency for pranks, such actions had to be followed up. The tree in the photo was found and dug up, to no avail.

Merylo continued his relentless though unsuccessful efforts to find the "Mad Butcher," and a few weeks after my cover was blown he called me up with a "brilliant" plan for catching him. "Since we know where the murderer picks up his victims and where he takes them to cut them up," he said, "I think we can capture him with your assistance." I was surprised but unsure how I could help, considering how badly I had muffed my earlier sleuthing assignment and the very limited detective bureau support I could expect. "What do you want me to do?" I asked. Merylo's plan involved my impersonating a hobo, dressed up in ragged, smelly clothes and camped out in the nefarious Kingsbury Run area. "Get acquainted with the area and the people and try to get picked up by the guy we're looking for," he said.

"You want me to be a decoy!" I replied incredulously. "And what happens if he does grab me?" Merylo was reassuring: "I'll have several of my best men planted there under cover who will be keeping a close watch. If our killer makes his play for you, we'll move in and grab him." I didn't think this was such a great idea at all. "It's dark there during the day as well as at night," I reminded Merylo. "And it's hard to follow anyone in that rough terrain. What happens if your men lose us or get to me too late? I don't mind being the bait, but not if I end up dead bait." He tried to persuade me, but I stuck to my guns and ended up rejecting his great plan for my help in capturing the Mad Butcher of Kingsbury Run.

Eliot called me into his office one November morning and informed me that he was going to put me in jail. His face broke into an amused smile when he saw my startled, bewildered reaction, and he quickly explained in a reassuring voice, that it was just for a day or two to get vital vote fraud information from a suspect in the recent City Council election. I was to go back to my apartment and change into a casual wool shirt, slacks and warm leather jacket. Lt. Walker would pick me up and drive to a remote precinct station (where no one was likely to know me) where the election fraud suspect was being held in a lone holding cell. I would be charged with armed robbery, and put in the cell with the suspect. My job was to get the suspect to talk about the fixed election: who had put him up to it, who were his associates and how they had illegally rigged the votes.

I stopped at a liquor store near my apartment and bought a pint of Jack Daniels and then changed from my suit to the casual clothes, putting the bottle in my jacket pocket. When Walker called to say he was outside, I went down and got into his car and as we were driving to the out-of-the way police station, I told him about my bottle of bourbon, and my plan to share it with the suspect. Walker nodded approvingly, and said he would see that I wasn't searched. When we reached the police station, he handcuffed me before we got out of the car, and informed me he would check in with me first thing the next morning to see how things had gone. Then, he walked me through the front door up to the sergeant's desk and booked me on a charge of armed robbery. When an officer arrived to lead me to the cell, Walker assured him I had already been searched, and departed.

My burly jailer grabbed my left arm and propelled me roughly down a long, dimly lit, gray corridor to an isolated cell at the end, containing two narrow iron cots on opposite sides of the small barred room. A forlorn looking, young man in his thirties wearing a disheveled, open white shirt and leather jacket lay slumped dejectedly on the cot nearest the door. After opening the cell door, my brusque uniformed escort removed my painfully tight, chafing handcuffs and shoved me unceremoniously into my new temporary Cleveland lodging. Now it was time for me to begin the job for which I was sent here, to get this guy to talk to me. I looked over at my cell mate, hoping he might be curious about me and start the conversation.

When the other occupant remained quiet, I could sense he was feeling lonely and abandoned and might welcome someone to talk to. To get a conversation started, I asked him, "What are you in here for?" He quickly responded, telling me the police thought he had something to do with some disputed votes in last week's city council election.

I laughed hilariously, shaking my head and staring at him in disbelief. "They have you here in jail just over some votes in a little, not very important election? That's pretty ridiculous." At this point I pulled out my bottle of Jack Daniels, held it up in a salute to him and pretended to take a big swig. From his expression, it was clear that he was upset and believing I was making fun of his alleged crime, for he quickly asked me what kind of offense I had been arrested for . "I'm in for armed robbery! " I replied with a tone of pride in my voice. And I took another long drink of Jack Daniels without swallowing it. I held the bottle out to him, saying he should have a drink, too. It was clear he was impressed with my armed robbery offense, and after a moment of hesitation, he took the bottle and drank a liberal amount of the bourbon.

Before long and with a few more slugs of Jack Daniels under his belt, he started to talk and tried to impress me with his achievements. And with my asking casual questions from time to time, the information Eliot needed came dribbling and then pouring out-- providing the names of the key people involved, and what and how they had managed to rig the votes for their client.

Lt. Walker arrived early the next morning and had me released. I had spent a very uncomfortable night on a cot with broken springs that jabbed viciously into my defenseless body, and in a cell with a malodorous odor that a skunk would admire, and a cellmate who had finished my Jack Daniels and fallen sound asleep and was still snoring. If I had to spend another day and night here, I told Walker, I would have been motivated to bring charges of cruel and unusual punishment against the city. But the information I had obtained provided the evidence needed to reverse the previous election results!.

Not all my time with Ness was spent tracking murderers and raiding dens of iniquity. I did have a social life although it, too, revolved around Ness and his circle of friends and acquaintances. Eliot's first wife, Edna, had become increasingly unhappy with the social demands that came with Ness's position as Cleveland's Director of Public Safety and her unhappiness resulted in their divorce. Eliot was a very social person who enjoyed partying with friends after work and also liked being married. In 1939, a few months before I began work, he had remarried. His new wife was a very attractive commercial graphic artist, Evaline McAndrews.

I developed a warm personal relationship with both Eliot and Evaline. Frequently after work Ness invited me to his attractive Lakewood house outside Cleveland. I was a steady visitor at their evening gatherings, where I made myself useful making and serving drinks and hors d'oeuvres. Often, we went out to the Hollenden Hotel where there was dinner and dancing and, while I was no Gene Kelly, I was able to acquit myself well enough on the dance floor, doing the waltz or the then popular Foxtrot—described as a "smooth progressive dance characterized by long flowing movements. My partners were often friends of Eliot , his wife, Evaline, and Clayton Fritchey. An extra single man was always welcome, especially on the dance floor. But I formed no deep attachments to the girls I met. I didn't want any commitments then. My job was so absorbing and unpredictable that it left no room for a serious relationship.

During most of my stay in Cleveland, Clayton was essentially a bachelor. His wife, Naomi, was a beautiful and talented artist who tragically contracted tuberculosis, became a patient at a sanitarium and later died.

L to R: Mayor Frank Lausche, Dean Landis, U.S Office of Civilian Defense, Keith Wilson and Eliot Ness. Lausche became Ohio Governor and then U.S. Senator.

Clayton grew up in Baltimore and dropped out of school at an early age to support his mother and two siblings after the death of his father. He began as a reporter and rose to be managing editor of the Baltimore American in his early 20s. He moved to the Cleveland Press as its star feature writer, garnishing his resume with a Pulitzer Prize for the dramatic series of articles about Eliot Ness cleaning up Cleveland. His intensive self-education efforts led to his continuous success, he became editor of the New Orleans Item, then in 1950 he went to Washington to serve Secretary of Defense George Marshall as Director of Information at the Pentagon where I met up with him again. Two years later he was working at the White House as special assistant to President Truman.

Among those I met in Cleveland through Fritchey was an uncommonly attractive and talented writer, Kay Halle, member of a prominent local family that owned Halle Brothers, the city's leading department store. Kay's father was Jewish while her mother was Irish, and it was common gossip that some years earlier Winston Churchill's oldest son, Randolph, had fallen in love with Kay.

Later, when I went to Washington with Eliot to help him start a wartime Federal venereal disease control project, my friendship with Kay deepened and I became her frequent escort to social events. Kay was well known for the popular salon she held regularly in her Georgetown house, a gathering that attracted Washington's top government, political and foreign diplomatic leaders. All the while, she clandestinely worked for OSS, the newly established U.S. foreign intelligence agency, which evolved into the CIA after World War II. She retained her close ties to the Churchill family, wrote several books about Winston Churchill, and became responsible for getting Congressional legislation making Winston Churchill an honorary citizen of the United States. Years later, when my wife and I visited Churchill's former country house, Chartwell, now a museum, the official U.S. State Department certification of Churchill's honorary U.S. citizenship was on display there. And I felt an additional personal attachment to it when I saw the certifying name and signature was that of my former partner at the *Northern Virginia Sun*, George W. Ball, who had served as an Under Secretary of State under Kennedy and Johnson and was then serving as Acting Secretary of State.

From time to time, Eliot dealt with sensitive new public safety issues that were far afield from his normal area of focus, and I quickly grew to appreciate his talent for innovative, yet practical, solutions. One of these odd cases that I remember in particular had to do with his contretemps with Cleveland's Catholic Archbishop, Joseph Schrembs, over the church's definition of obscene literature and the city's responsibility for censoring or even banning it from sale. I first became aware of this highly controversial problem in January 1940 when Eliot, after concluding a meeting with Schrembs, told me that he had agreed to establish a Committee on Obscene Literature and I was now its secretary. My first assignment was to arrange for all of Cleveland's wholesale distributors of popular weekly and monthly magazines to deliver to me ten copies of each issue for distribution to the new committee members Eliot would be appointing. The members were to examine these publications, looking for obscenity. Eliot explained to me that although he was personally opposed to such a committee, he was under political pressure to cooperate with the Archbishop.

The committee he appointed represented a broad range of professions and views, including the director of the local civil liberties organization. Following Eliot's instructions, I kept the members flooded with reading material so that it would be a long time before they would be able finish their examination and draw conclusions. Eliot, in the meantime, saw no need for the committee to meet. I was receiving regular reports from the Archbishop, who took offense at the caption of a cartoon in the respectable family magazine, the Saturday Evening Post, a double entendre with a sexual innuendo. After several months of waiting for the committee to meet and report, the Archbishop called Eliot requesting a personal meeting to express his concerns about the lack of progress.

I remember that occasion vividly as I was in attendance and listened to their conversation and its dramatic ending. The somber, impressive looking prelate in his rich black clerical suit with a white Roman collar and a simple cross held by a chain across his chest—who was accompanied by a stern-looking aide dressed in stark black—expressed his disappointment at the slow pace and inaction of the obscenity committee. Eliot listened quietly and nodded thoughtfully as the Archbishop expounded on the importance of speeding up the committee's progress in identifying the obscene materials and the moral urgency of rooting them out to safeguard the public from their depraving influence. When Schrembs had finished, Eliot leaned back in his chair as if he needed to think about what he had just heard. After a few seconds he sat up straight, leaned forward, and looked Schrembs directly in the eyes as he spoke in his distinctive soft voice: "I fully understand your position and can appreciate your concern over the slow progress being made," said Ness. "But I would like you to understand my position, particularly the opposition that I have been getting from religious and civic organizations who don't agree with your definition of obscenity and oppose the drastic measures you want me to take."

He then proceeded to describe his dilemma in responding to a moral issue that had been raised by these same civic and religious organizations that had been strong supporters of his ongoing campaign against organized crime, particularly against the gambling activities that had historically been used to bribe and corrupt city officials. A number of these groups believed that gambling was inherently evil. They couldn't grasp why police officers, who were working tirelessly to wipe out the gambling operations of Cleveland's nefarious gangs, were ignoring gambling organized by the Catholic Church: the regular bingo games conducted in its buildings throughout the city. "If you help me solve this problem by closing down your bingo gambling," said Ness "I, in return, will strengthen and accelerate my efforts to curb the distribution of obscene literature in Cleveland."

A long silence followed as the Archbishop stared at Eliot intently and reflected on the meaning of what he had just heard. Then, very slowly, he rose to his feet, nodded a goodbye to Eliot and walked out of the office, followed by his aide. There were no further calls from the Archbishop's office on this matter. I wrote a letter to the committee members for Eliot's signature, thanking them for their service and dissolving the committee, and telephoned the wholesale distributors asking them to discontinue sending us their magazines.

Eliot was an extremely newsworthy public figure in Cleveland, and virtually anything he said or did was of interest and written about in the daily papers. I was always conscious of the sensitive and highly confidential nature of my work. As a result, the close personal relationship

I had with Eliot and the trust he placed in me, mandated discretion. I never talked about him, or in any other way revealed anything I heard or saw that might adversely affect or embarrass him. I also made it a policy not to write anything about him or to describe in detail any of my own activities with anyone including my family and friends.

Cleveland's previous high crime rates and serious traffic accidents had been dramatically reduced by Eliot and the city was now enjoying its new reputation as one of the nation's safest. I was suddenly startled, therefore, on a Tuesday morning in March, 1941, to read in the regular crime analysis report about a sharp rise in robberies, primarily against visiting businessmen. When I called the head of the detective bureau's robbery squad for more details, I learned that while the robbery designation resulted from the victims' claims to the police, the follow-up investigation disclosed that each of the "robbed" businessmen had been visiting a local nightclub or "clip joint" (in police parlance). There he was persuaded to drink heavily, taken to a nearby hotel for sex and, after he had fallen asleep, his female companion would "roll him," strip him of his money, and depart. Concerned that these reported robberies would hurt Cleveland's reputation as a safe place to visit and would discourage future conventions and business visitors, I reported my findings to Eliot. With his approval, I set out to try to curtail these false robbery reports. After getting a list of all the "clip joints" involved in the robbery reports, I called the heads of the inspection and safety bureaus of the fire and buildings departments, asked them to conduct thorough inspections for any violations of building, fire or safety regulations, and to follow up by fining each property owner for every such violation.

I knew there would be quick results and quick reactions, for the reality in every large city is that a careful inspection of virtually every medium-to-large commercial building will reveal violations of the city's building code, as well as fire and safety regulations. Cleveland was no exception. Violations were found, some that would require very costly repairs to remedy. I was confident that the harsh economics involved would motivate the owners of the clip joints to clean up their act and lean on their hostesses to stop rolling visiting businessmen.

But I was naïve about city politics and soon to be educated in the political reality of city government. Within a week after my building and fire inspectors had issued their citations, Eliot called me in to order me to end my campaign against the clip joints. He told me he had just had a visit from the irate councilman who chaired the city council committee with jurisdiction over the police and fire department budgets, and whom Eliot was depending on to approve his request for the purchase of a new fleet of police cars and much needed fire trucks. The councilman, responding to angry complaints from the owners of my targeted clip joints, important supporters and financial contributors to the councilman's election campaign, had checked into who was behind the inspections. Now his clear message and warning to Eliot was "if you want to see those new police cars and fire trucks, tell that young kid in your office to lay off." Eliot was very sympathetic to what I was trying to do, but right now getting his police and fire equipment had a higher priority, and I had to close down my clip joint project.

Soon after that, I was given an assignment that made up for my recent disappointment and, as I later learned, would have far more important local and even national consequences. Eliot told me to investigate the presence in Cleveland of a nationally prominent woman member of the German American Bund, an organization with reportedly close ties to Nazi Germany, who had recently arrived with a German national male. The manager of the Hollenden Hotel had just called Eliot to report this couple had just checked into a room there. As a concerned American with the war in Europe heating up and likely to involve the United States, he thought this situation might warrant looking into.

"I want you to go over to the Hollenden and talk to the manager to find out what's going on," Eliot told me. As it was late in the afternoon, he said I should run back to my apartment, which was only 30 minutes away, pack a small overnight bag and plan on spending the night at the hotel. Ninety minutes later, I was at the Hollenden Hotel, introducing myself to the manager who told me his suspicious couple had just left the hotel, but that they left a message that they would return within the hour. In accord with Eliot's prior arrangements, he gave me the key to a room that adjoined theirs. It was on the fourth floor, rather small, with a single bed made up with a light blue bedspread and two uncomfortably hard white pillows. There was a small, narrow bed table with a black telephone and a lamp with an opaque frilly shade and a 40-watt bulb. Inside the table drawer was the usual Gideon bible. After putting my ear to the wall that divided my room from the German couple's room and hearing no sound of occupancy, I stretched out on the bed with a paperback mystery I had brought, munched slowly on the ham and cheese on rye with mustard I had picked up on route to the Hollenden, drank a bottle of Coke, and waited for my next door neighbors to return.

It was just after 9 p.m. when the sound of a door being shut and the faint sound of voices made me sit upright. I swung my legs off the bed, brushed away a few bread crumbs that had fallen on the bedspread, and walked over to the wall, carrying a cylindrical metal device that helped magnify sound. Now I was able to hear more clearly the guttural voices speaking German, though what was being said was unintelligible as I had no knowledge of the language. After awhile, I heard clearly recognizable sounds: two heavy bodies bouncing on bedsprings accompanied by passionate moans and the cries of a couple experiencing intercourse. There was no need for the hearing aid as the Germanic voices and the thumping of the mattress and metallic squeak of the springs grew louder and increased in intensity. It was a formidable performance that was to be repeated several times throughout the long night, but after awhile the monotony put me to sleep.

When I woke up and checked my watch, it was almost 8 a.m. and very quiet. I quickly ran over to the dividing wall and put my hearing device to my ear. I could faintly hear a male voice on the telephone asking about breakfast, and shortly afterwards the sharp thud of their outer door closing. Hurrying to my door, I very slowly opened it just a crack, wide enough to peek down the corridor to see a very large, blonde woman in a light blue dress and a more sparsely built, trim, light-haired man in a dark gray suit walking down the corridor toward the elevator. This was my opportunity, I decided. They were going to breakfast and chances were they wouldn't be back for almost an hour.

I felt my heart thumping and clammy sweat on my forehead as I walked to their door, fumbling nervously with the key given to me by the manager. I finally managed open the door, and entered their room warily. After scanning the room quickly without spotting anything of interest,

I opened the closet door and saw on the shelf what I was looking for: a black leather briefcase. A quick search revealed a file folder with copies of correspondence in English, written on the letterhead of a major German industrial firm. The letters were addressed to the CEOs of several major Cleveland and Detroit machine-tool companies and appeared to be offering very large, lucrative, long-term contracts for the manufacture of various intricate German materiel. I hurriedly scribbled down in my notebook the names and addresses of the American companies and key paragraphs of the letters. It was clear that the room's male occupant was the representative of the German firm and had been sent to the U.S. to complete negotiations.

Press credentials

It took me longer than I had expected to finish taking notes of the correspondence. My heart was now racing and my fingers trembling at the thought that the room's legitimate occupants would return and catch me. Putting the letters carefully back in the folder in the order I remembered, replacing the folder in the briefcase, and returning the briefcase to the same position on the shelf in which I had found it, I scurried out of the room and, closing the door softly, dashed to my own room where I had left the door unlocked for a quick reentry. As I was closing my door, I heard the sound of the elevator door opening and the heavy footsteps of a man approaching down the corridor. I let out the frightened breath I had been holding and dropped, exhausted, on my bed. I had made it just in time.

Thirty minutes later I was back in my office briefing Eliot and writing up my notes, which he then passed on to the FBI agent in charge of the Cleveland field office. I learned later that the FBI assessed this matter as a very clever attempt by the Nazi government to tie up the country's major machine-tool manufacturers, whose output was crucial to future U.S. production of critical military weaponry. The complex and profitable terms being offered to the vital U.S. machine-tool companies were designed to prevent the production of essential weaponry needed—initially by Great Britain and, after Pearl Harbor, by the U.S. I was told that the heads of the machine-tool companies were informed of the Nazi plot and persuaded to terminate the contract negotiations.

One of Eliot's tactics, and a major factor in his winning vital public support, was wooing the press to build up public understanding and support for the policing reforms and changes he was making. One of my functions was to maintain a close relationship with the news media and insure a response to any of their questions. Hardly a day passed when I was not talking to a reporter about Ness's activities. I developed a deep appreciation for the news media's important role in a democracy, informing the public and influencing political decision-making.

In February 1941, after two years of working for Ness, I became imbued with the idea of a career in journalism. Eliot had been an incredibly kind and inspiring mentor, and I had loved the work and found my job continually exciting and stimulating. While my original purpose and goal after graduating from college had been to get my first real job on my own and sever my dependence on my father, I had been working with Eliot as an interim measure to acquire experience and perspective on what I wanted to do with my life in the long term.

Now, I felt, it was time to cut my dependence on Eliot and to move on. Writing my column for the Oberlin college newspaper and then working closely with Cleveland's local press and other media had provided experience and motivation. I decided to discuss these thoughts and feelings with Eliot one Friday evening, after I had driven out to his lakefront house to join him and Evaline. Before talking to Eliot about my journalistic ambitions, I freshened up his regular scotch, then sat down to join him. Evaline was working late and their guests that evening would not be arriving for another two hours. I told Eliot how much I had loved working for him and expressed my appreciation for the invaluable knowledge I had acquired under his tutelage. But Eliot's public safety problems were relatively quiet and under control, and I believed it was now time for me to utilize the skills and experience I had gained working for him to begin a new career that offered different but equally challenging opportunities. My first choice of where to start was the afternoon newspaper, the Cleveland Press, the city's largest, most influential newspaper. I had established good relationships with its editor, Louie Seltzer, and our mutual friend, Clayton Fritchey, worked there, as did my current apartment roommate and former Oberlin College classmate, Tom Boardman.

Eliot's response was warm and understanding. He told me how helpful and valuable my work had been and how much he had enjoyed having me as his personal assistant. I did not know then that Eliot was under tremendous pressure from the city's Civil Service Commission to discharge all of his criminal investigators hired under the guise of clerical and manual labor workers but not providing the service specified for those positions by Civil Service. And two months later, in April, Eliot would be forced to comply. But all the members of his small team of undercover investigators soon found employment in the various intelligence services of America's armed forces, where they were desperate for people with such skills

CLEVELAND PRESS

I keep six honest serving-men
They taught me all I know;
Their names are What and Why and When
And How and Where and Who.
       Rudyard Kipling

Louis Seltzer, the editor of the Cleveland Press, had an open-door policy. Two weeks later on a cold wintry morning in February 1941, I walked into his office without an appointment, wearing my best gray flannel suit with a dark blue-and-red-striped tie. He was an amiable, shrewd, short, balding and highly energized "little dude" who wore flashy ties. Louie's focus on local news and his aggressive watchdog coverage of public officials had made the afternoon Press the largest and most influential newspaper in Cleveland, and my press liaison work for Ness had made us well acquainted.

When he looked up and saw me, his face broke into a welcoming smile. "What brings you here today?" he inquired. "I just want you to be the first to know that I'm leaving Eliot and that I would like to come to work for the Press," I informed him in my best conversational voice. He looked very surprised. Then in a more businesslike tone, he said that was not his department, and I would have to talk to Norman Shaw, the City Editor.

As I headed for Norman's desk, which was in the middle of the Press's large, open newsroom, I was feeling less optimistic, and even a little apprehensive, as I remembered the Press's standard practice of assigning all new reportorial hires to work as copy boys, where they would spend their first year running copy from the news to the press room before they were eligible to become reporters or to write copy. Competition for even the job of copy boy was very fierce, as had been demonstrated by the experience of two recent Harvard graduates, one of whom was one of my current roommates, Bob Dimke. My concern increased as I remembered my various meetings with Norman during the past two years. He was always cooler and much more serious than Seltzer, and likely to be more demanding with respect to my qualifications to start as a reporter. So I was very nervous when I arrived at his desk and said, "Louie told me to see you." "What about?" Norman asked. "I'm leaving Ness and would like to work as a reporter for the Press," I responded simply. Norman looked at me thoughtfully for an intense moment that seemed to stretch to eternity. "When can you start work?" he asked.

Two weeks later I reported for work and was assigned to the midnight–eight a.m. shift of the "Police Beat," the basic starting job for a reporter. I spent the next five months covering the serious crimes, accidents and other human tragedies that occurred regularly during the late-night hours, but lessened appreciably as the later, early-morning hours reflected the somnolent state of the city's humanity. My job was to monitor the continuous radio reports coming from the various two-way radio-equipped police patrols. These reports were beamed into the pressroom and I checked out the ones that merited my driving out to the scene. When they did, I went out and interviewed the police officers at the scene, and any survivors and witnesses that might add value to the story. When I finished, I called the Press and dictated my story to the rewrite desk. Where there was a fatality, I drove to the residence of the parents, spouse or next of kin to get biographical information and, very important, to obtain a photo of the victim.

My other strong memory is of the inevitable blanket of deep weariness that enveloped me around three a.m. and my unsuccessful struggle to keep my eyes open as a vise-like pressure kept dragging my eyelids down to close over them. And, as it was highly unlikely there would be any newsworthy events for me to cover for the next three hours, I dragged my weary, protesting body and heavy-lidded eyes to the large, heavily scarred oak table that stood in the middle of the Police Department press room. There I promptly fell asleep until awakened by the sharp, amplified voice of the police dispatcher booming out of the police radio sound box receiver attached to the adjacent wall.

After a while, the initial reaction and sense of shock—and often-physical revulsion at the violent nature of some of these fatal accidents and human deaths—would start to wear off, as these experiences became more routine. Interviewing the mother or father of a child in the midst of their grief was usually a very emotionally charged task, especially if the request for a photograph was unsuccessful. I was expected to "borrow" (in police-beat jargon, that often meant "steal") one. But one day I was both young and naïve—and uncomfortable enough—to question Norman, my city editor, about the ethics and propriety of a reporter invading the privacy of a family and exploiting the tragic death of a child or family member when the family was deeply upset and suffering. "What right do we have to do this?" I asked. His response was brief and simple: Anyone who is involved in a public event automatically becomes a public figure and thus subject to coverage by a free press. I must confess that from a moral point of view, I still find that his unblemished "right" of the press troubles me.

However, my term as a police reporter ended soon, as the war in Europe and the increasing likelihood that the U.S. was going to become more directly involved led the Press to establish a Civil Defense beat. Happily, I was taken off the police beat and assigned to cover the new civil defense plans and related activities. One of the first benefits of my new beat was being sent to Washington for a couple of days to cover New York Mayor Fiorello LaGuardia and write a story about his plans as President Roosevelt's part-time appointee to head a national Civil Defense program for U.S. cities.

My first impression of Washington back then was that I was in a rather placid small town, with few good restaurants and little nightlife. While Mayor LaGuardia was a colorful and dynamic personality and his civil defense plans made a good story, the highlight and most exciting part of my trip came later when I attended a small press briefing in President Roosevelt's office. I and about a dozen other reporters stood around his desk in the Oval Office in a half circle and had an informal question and answer exchange that seemed like having a friendly chat. Roosevelt was an attractive, impressive figure even when just sitting at his desk. This impression was heightened by his full-of-life, jovial mood when he talked and as he listened to the courteous questions of each reporter. His responses were larded with good humor and an occasional hearty laugh when he thought a question did not warrant a serious answer There was no sign of his infirmity; rather the impression was one of forceful strength and an energetic personality.

But my life, and that of everyone I cared about was to change radically on Sunday, the 7th of December. I was driving to Canton, Ohio, accompanied by my Press associate and good friend, Bill Miller, to cover a story for the Press when a news bulletin broke into the radio program we had turned on; The Japanese had attacked Pearl Harbor. We stopped the car, listened to more details, and both agreed we should return immediately to Cleveland. The most immediate, significant and far reaching consequence of that attack and the declaration of war against Japan and Germany that followed, for me and for my roommates and fellow Press associates, Tom Boardman and Bob Dimke, was our common determination to get personally, actively, involved in the war. It was clearly a strongly emotional, patriotic response and is natural and expected when you're young, idealistic, and believe your country has been severely and unjustly attacked.

The Pearl Harbor attack had also outraged and mobilized public opinion, which had previously been deeply divided over U.S. involvement in the war in Europe, particularly against Germany, in the large midwestern sections where the Chicago Tribune and America First organization symbolized the strong pro-German and anti-British sentiments that existed at that time. The abrupt change and unification of national support of U.S. intervention fanned a reactive, overwhelming patriotic sentiment and strong public support for everyone volunteering for military service, which made you feel you were doing the right and necessary thing, defending your country and your family. While Tom and Bob were quickly accepted by their choice of armed service, the Navy and Army Air Force respectively, I was chagrined and deeply disappointed to be turned down by each of these in turn because of my poor eyesight. And when I settled for military service in the Army, I was disappointed as well as surprised to learn that I had a hernia, which disqualified me. But, determined that nothing would stop me from joining my friends and serving in a military service, I arranged for an extended leave from the Press and went home to Springfield where I had the hernia problem corrected by surgery.

When I returned to Cleveland to restart my prospective entry into a new military life, I was relieved to find awaiting me a notice from my Draft Board informing me I had been classified 1A, fit for service, and to report for an examination and induction. Delighted at the news and my pending success in joining one of the armed services, I hastened to comply. After completing the prerequisite physical and confident that my former hernia would no longer block my path to military service, I waited for the standard announcement informing me where to report for military service. In the meantime, I informed the city editor, and the business office of my resignation. The long anticipated letter from the Draft Board arrived shortly and I eagerly tore open the official government envelope and pulled out the letter, tearing it in my haste to find out where and when to report for active duty.

My eyes blurred and my throat tightened as I read the unbelievable news: Rejection due to eyesight. Reclassified as unfit for military service. I couldn't believe it. How could this happen to me after all the effort and trouble I had gone through. And after saying goodbye to my friends and associates and receiving one of Louie Seltzer's traditional mushy, very sentimental letters which he sent to everyone who had left the paper for military service, praising me for my patriotism in serving our country and expressing his best wishes for my future life—only to be rejected again. I felt miserable and frustrated, and rather humiliated. But good fortune had not yet abandoned me. I was rescued and sailed on to new adventures when Eliot called to tell me he had just taken a new job with the Federal government in Washington, that he needed me and wanted me to join him there.

THE WAR YEARS
1942-1946

Chapter 3

...we shall fight on the beaches, we shall fight on the landing grounds, we shall fight in the fields and in the streets, we shall fight in the hills; we shall never surrender.
    Winston Churchill

JOIN NESS IN WASHINGTON

Although I had been unsuccessful in my attempts to join the armed forces, Eliot's call to help him organize a new Federal law enforcement program was a timely rescue and would, finally, result in my getting into uniform! The Office of Defense, Health and Welfare Services (ODHWS) had the mandate of providing health, recreational and welfare assistance to the millions of young, recently drafted soldiers, sailors and airmen who were training in military and naval bases across the United States.

Throughout history in times of war, prostitutes have always arrived to provide companionship and sexual services for young, lonely servicemen, but now our Army and Navy were experiencing the loss and hospitalization of thousands of their newly drafted servicemen by a dangerous domestic enemy, venereal disease (VD). The U.S. Public Health Service had identified professional prostitutes, who engage in frequent and indiscriminate sexual relations with servicemen, as the primary source of this near-epidemic disease. The ODHWS ' Social Protection branch, which Eliot was directing, had been established and charged with the special mission of suppressing prostitution to the point where VD was no longer a serious military health problem in the U.S. As ODHWS information and reports specialist, I would again be devoting virtually all of my time working with Ness.

Congress had responded to the military VD crisis by passing the May
Act, making it a federal offense to solicit for and engage in prostitution
near a military installation, which, in effect would cover most major
urban areas as well. While the FBI was assigned to enforce this law, the
Office of Social Protection (OSP) was responsible for developing the
strategy and programs to reduce the high VD rate among servicemen
to a minimal, acceptable level. The May Act and the FBI law-enforcement powers provided Eliot's office with a powerful, effective weapon.
It forced recalcitrant urban police chiefs and rural sheriffs who had frequently tolerated and protected professional prostitutes in their jurisdictions, to close down those operations rather than suffer the embarrassment and adverse consequences of publicized FBI raids and arrests.

Eliot's approach was to get at the core of the problem by preventing
a prostitute from having any physical contact with a serviceman. And,
as ODHWS' information and reports specialist, I would be focusing
nearly all of my time working with and helping Eliot stamp out professional prostitution, and its health threat to U.S. servicemen.

I was fascinated and intrigued as I witnessed Eliot's planning and
implementation of a successful strategy to solve the military's critical VD problem in the U.S. Essentially, it addressed the basic issues of
how prostitutes and soldiers/sailors met, found the time and place for
the physical intercourse that resulted in VD, and the development of
appropriate countermeasures. He designed a systematic, comprehensive program that made it virtually impossible for a prostitute to meet
and pick up a serviceman; and if she did succeed, impossible to find
and transport him to a hotel or a motel that would give them a room.
Concurrently, he had the Army and Navy require every VD-infected
serviceman fill out a standard form reporting where he had picked up
the prostitute (usually a bar or nightclub), who had provided the transport, and the name of the hotel or motel where intercourse took place.

By appealing to their war-time patriotism, Eliot obtained the agreement
of the country's major beer and alcohol distributors to stop selling
their alcoholic beverages to any bar, nightclub or restaurant that a VD-
infected soldier, sailor or airman reported to be the place where he met
the prostitute. This in turn resulted in these establishments barring any
prostitute. He also made agreements with the governing agencies for

taxi owners cited in reports to lose their right to buy rationed gas and tires, while the abetting hotels and motels would be closed as dangers to the public health. But he didn't need to do much arm-twisting. The prostitutes had now become an economic liability to such inns, and they wanted to demonstrate their cooperation with the government in a time of war.

As he had done in Cleveland, Eliot created a corps of undercover investigators who would identify the active prostitution operations near Army, Navy and Air Force bases and urban installations, to provide the OSP with the names of the principals and individual prostitutes involved. This intelligence enabled Eliot to assess the progress and success of his plan and to verify that the police chiefs and sheriffs concerned did in fact close down prostitution operations. In those initial cases where prostitutes continued to operate, a call to the FBI and an FBI agent's visit to the police chief or sheriff were sufficient to prompt the local law enforcement agency to do its job.

It says a great deal about Eliot that he also considered the plight and welfare of the prostitutes affected and that he took measures to help them. He told me that research had revealed that the average prostitute was very young, lacked an education, and was often unable to read or write, leaving her virtually incapable of earning a legitimate living as a waitress, clerk, or secretary. Almost none of them preferred prostitution as a profession, but most of them came from impoverished families who looked to them for critical financial assistance. They were under great pressure to earn the money needed, and prostitution offered one of the very few, if not only, ways they could provide this help. Eliot's solution was to get the prostitutes into government training programs where they would be taught the skills needed for jobs that were opening up in factories producing war equipment and materials.

His strategy of making it extremely difficult for a serviceman to meet or have physical contact with a prostitute, and at the same time closing down the prostitution houses and their operating facilities worked brilliantly. And his follow-up program of providing training and income-earning jobs dried up the previously available pool of prostitution recruits. In a remarkably short time, he eliminated the professional prostitute as a serious source of venereal disease among military servicemen within the United States. For the rest of World War II, the VD rate among members of the military services in the U.S. was the lowest in history.

I remember very clearly my last meeting with the Public Health officers working with us when their senior officer rose to make his report, stating, "For all practical purposes, the professional prostitute no longer exists in the United States. Instead of having 20 to 40 contacts a day, she now has only one or two because of the difficulty she faces in plying her trade. What we have left is what we now call 'women with a low threshold of sexual approachability.'" He explained that these were women who, out of a sense of patriotism or their appreciation for having been taken out to dinner, would take a serviceman home to their beds.

Being involved in a war-related program that affected the health and readiness of thousands of members of the armed services was fulfilling. It gave me the sense that I had helped solve an important military problem, and I was actively engaged in the War. My position also called on me from time to time to work on special projects for the overall Office of Defense Health and Welfare, which was established to improve the health, welfare, and social aspects of American servicemen drafted in World War II.

One day I was asked to attend a conference to discuss a very odd and surprising request that had come from a high-ranking Army official. When I arrived, I was handed a copy of a letter which deplored the nature of the songs currently being played and heard by the American public: maudlin, sentimental songs like "Somebody's Rocking My Dreamboat" and "I Don't Want to Set the World On Fire" and derisive songs that were trivializing the enemy. That could make us weak and lose the war![5] We were told we could help by starting a project that

---

5. *I was to learn some years later that this attempt to censor the playing of songs that were either too effusively sentimental or that ridiculed the German and Japanesemilitary leaders was torpedoed when the ODHWS music censors reportedly tried to suppress Donald Duck singing a hilarious song, "In Der Fuehrer's Face," in an animated Disney film about Hitler that won a 1943 Academy Award. Their attempt was leaked to a popular nationally syndicated columnist whose report on the incident blew them out of existence.*

would discourage the composition and playing of such songs and, instead, encourage the writing and playing of more patriotic and positive lyrics. Although everyone at the meeting was bemused by this bizarre request, it was agreed our agency should try to respond to the Army's request, turning it over for implementation to the ODHWS section that was responsible for sending records and musical entertainment to U.S. servicemen.

But I hadn't given up hope of active military service overseas, and working at ODHWS had brought me into direct contact with a number of well-placed military personnel. It was during a conversation with an army major in the Adjutant General's office when I learned that, due to some unknown recruitment quirk, the regular Army, which had closed its recruiting activities when the draft began, was still manning an unmarked, unknown recruiting station in a small, hard-to-spot building just off K Street.

At lunchtime, I slipped out of the office and, armed with the address, hurried down to what for me was a hidden treasure. This time I was prepared for the eye exam. I had just acquired a new set of prescription sunglasses, which were very uncommon then. As it was a bright sunny day, I was not out of place among the other ordinary sun glasses-equipped pedestrians on the street. At the recruiting center, the lone government-issued gray steel desk was manned by a heavily beribboned staff sergeant who looked up in great surprise to see a stranger in civilian clothes, apparently a rarity there. When I told him I wanted to enlist, he handed me a thick Army personnel questionnaire to fill out.

I kept my sunglasses on as I filled out the form, and when I had finished, the sergeant led me to the far corner of the office where I had noticed an eye chart. As I approached it, I quickly read and memorized the third line down, figuring that line would indicate satisfactory vision. When he asked me to remove my sunglasses, I folded and thrust them nonchalantly into my topcoat pocket. "Read the first line you can see clearly, " he instructed me. I stood there for a moment squinting my eyes intently as I pretended to scan the chart. "The third line is clearest," I said and then proceeded to "read" the sequence of numbers and letters that I had memorized.

My performance seemed to have satisfied the sergeant, for he said, "Okay. Come back tomorrow at 0900 for your physical."

I had shared my discovery of the recruiting station with Ness, who was very understanding and supportive. Our VD control program was well under way and fully staffed with trained, competent personnel, and I knew I would not be missed. One week after passing my eye and physical tests, a very contented Private Arnold J. Sagalyn, serial number 13145294, began basic training in the rugged red clay hills of Ft. Mc-Clellan, Alabama.

JOINING THE ARMED SERVICES

As it did for many others in my generation, World War II had an incredibly powerful influence in defining me. The war was an extraordinary emotional experience that bordered on the spiritual for millions of impressionable young men. Prior to entering the Army, I had lived a protected, comfortable life, always looking to others for guidance and support. But my Army experiences as a wartime officer forced me to tackle and solve tough new life-and-death problems that made me wiser, more self-confident, and willing to take on new challenges. However, that's not the way my Army career started out.

As a raw recruit, the Army's first mission was to make me physically fit and skilled in the use of weapons. I spent my first three bone-wearying months as a private at Fort McClellan, Alabama in basic training. Each day (and frequently each night) involved arduous physical conditioning, including long hikes over rough terrain, carrying weapons and a heavy backpack under a merciless sun. Hardly a day passed without instruction in the use of the deadly M1 rifle and bayonet. "These weapons are your best friends, so take good care of them," I was constantly reminded. Like most of my fellow trainees, I found our hand-to-hand combat-training exercises emotionally difficult, even loathsome. The worst of these exercises was the close-up bayonet practice, where I was trained to kill another person only a few feet away. My training sergeant would point to the straw-filled "enemy" mannequin 15–20 feet distant and shout "charge!" and I had to rush at my "enemy," yelling at the top of my lungs, with my rifle and its attached bayonet raised to my shoulder. And when I reached "him," I had to thrust my bayonet into "his" midriff with a hard, vigorous thrust of the sharply honed blade. My sergeant kept urging me to keep twisting the long, sharp steel blade deeper and deeper into "his" body, all the while screaming, "Die, you bastard" and other profane phrases.

The first time I practiced this exercise, the sergeant, noticed my lack of enthusiasm for the simulated bayoneting, walked over to me and in his harshest tone—which he used on every green, squeamish trainee— barked: "Get smart, soldier! You're in the infantry, where it's kill or be killed. If you don't kill him, he's going to kill you! Which one do you want it to be?" The battle-tested sergeant's words sank in. I realized that this war and my training were not a game; they were for real and very deadly, especially for people like me in the infantry, who were considered expendable. I knew that if I wanted to stay alive I had better take my training seriously, so I concentrated on becoming proficient in stripping, cleaning, and reassembling my M1 rifle, keeping my bayonet sharpened to a fine point, and worked hard to improve my physical fitness and combat skills.

After Fort McClellan, I found myself on desert maneuvers near Yuma, Arizona, member of a two-man heavy weapons (machine-gun) squad of the 8th Division. I was pleased with my new infantry combat capabilities and high state of physical conditioning. But this sense of military accomplishment quickly dissipated in the days and weeks that followed as my new training consisted of enduring the relentless rays and furnace-like heat of the sun. I lugged the searing steel barrel of the weighty 50-caliber machine gun next to my sunburned neck on my aching shoulder. It was more than 102 degrees in the shade, except there was no shade available.

I trudged slowly through endless blazing-hot dunes, lifting up my Army boots, which kept sinking deep into the sand. When our company captain finally called a halt, we would be ordered to set up a defensive position and my partner and I dug deep foxholes with our small personal shovels, jumped down into the sandpit, set up our gun barrel on the heavy steel tripod which he had been carrying, and carefully positioned it so that it covered a full field of effective fire. But no sooner had we dug in and set up than we would get new orders to break down our gun and tripod, fill up the foxhole, and slog on to the next halting point, where we repeated our previous tasks. On and on this went, in the brutal sun. When our training exercise finally ended late in the day, I was disconsolate at the utterly boring nature of our simulated desert combat exercise and its lack of any mental challenge. Exhausted, I would crawl into my one-man pup tent to await the promise of cooling desert air.

Arnold as a Private on maneuvers in Arizona. 1943

Soon enough evening brought welcome relief from the daytime sun, but also heightened my disenchantment with my marginal responsibilities and the plodding routine. At night I was faced with the regular arrival of scorpions and black widow spiders who shared my desert shelter, and whom I had to carefully remove from my sleeping bag and boots before retiring. In stark contrast with the hot days, the nights were so bitter cold I had trouble sleeping.

While I was determined to become a creditable soldier, I thought there had to be a more useful, productive, and interesting way to serve in what I believed was a vitally important, fully justified defensive war. The best way to do this, I decided, was to become an officer and I set out to find out how this could be accomplished. The investigative skills I learned working for Ness and as a reporter, together with knowledge

acquired as a government information officer in Washington, helped
me learn how I could parlay my rank from an army private to become
a commissioned officer. I learned I could become a Second Lieutenant,
the starting officer rank, if I successfully completed a rigorous three-
month course at an Officer Candidate School (OCS) recently established by the various armed services to meet the demands for trained junior officers. But I first had to obtain an "okay" from my commanding
officer, then pass an I.Q. test with a minimum score of 110 and, finally,
appear personally before a board of skeptical senior infantry officers
to convince them that I merited their approval for admission into the
Army's Infantry OCS. I concentrated all my energy on achieving this
goal and in short order I obtained my commanding officer's approval,
passed the intelligence tests and persuaded the board of senior officers I
had what it would take to be a good junior infantry officer.

A few months later I underwent a very rigorous, intensive academic and
physical three-month training course at the Fort Benning, Georgia, Infantry School's OCS program, Class of 287A . Our training focused on
instilling an understanding of the importance of providing leadership.
The infantry officer's motto was "Follow me!" And we were trained
to always take the initiative. My primary responsibility was to lead my
men into battle and make sure they followed me and did their job. In a
letter written to my mother dated June 29th, 1943, that she had saved,
I described a typical day:

"We're back after a three day bivouac. In that time we crawled over half
of Georgia on our bellies and then on our knees, simulating scouting
and patrolling. We took turns in leading a platoon and squads in
attacks on enemy machine guns, skirmish lines and finally a German
village. We used live ammunition and hand grenades, which added to
the realism.

"It was a pretty grueling affair, on the go all the time from 6 a.m. until
11 every night with time off only for meals. Not even that hard ground
could keep me from sleeping soundly came bedtime. About everyone was
bitten by "chiggers," little red bugs of pinpoint size that bore into you.
Evidently I tasted pretty bad to them for I wasn't bothered at all.

"Today was spent on combat intelligence—mostly demonstrations. We had a two-star and one-star general and a flock of colonels, majors, etc. sitting in. Wednesday the 6th week begins. We're losing about 41 men as a result of the 5th Week Board. The empty beds in the barracks stand out as grim reminders of 'it can happen to you!' Otherwise all's well from here. All my love, Arny"

As graduates of the program, we were tagged as the "90-day wonders." At my OCS graduation on August 23, 1943, our commanding officer congratulated the 212 graduates on our newly commissioned rank as "2nd lieutenants and gentlemen" and then jolted us with this stark fact: "A year from now, 50% of you will be dead!" Pausing briefly, in the hushed silence that followed this chilling statement, he added in a matter-of–fact tone, "Gentlemen, you can't expect to be 2nd lieutenants of the infantry and live long." The same grim statistics awaited all of us, for each member of our class had received orders, assigning us to report to an Infantry Replacement Training Center (IRTC) where we were all destined to replace the large number of junior infantry officers expected to die or be seriously wounded in the anticipated, fiercely resisted Normandy invasion landings in June of 1944. At the end of the War, I could only find three other members of our class who had survived.

Arnold, newly commissioned as a 2nd Lieutenant.

Despite our commanding officer's grim pronouncement, my graduation as a second lieutenant of the infantry was, perhaps, the most
gratifying day of my life. I glowed with pride that I had confronted and
successfully overcome what had seemed an impossible barrier, and had
proved my physical and mental capabilities, first to endure and perform creditably the demanding duties of a private in the infantry in the
rugged hills of Ft. McClellan, and then hauling a heavy machine gun
through the devil's own burning desert sands in Arizona, and now the
tough regime of the Infantry School—all this after my Draft Board had
called me "unfit" to serve. I realized that I had reached a new level of
maturity and that now, at the age of 25, I was fully capable of taking
care of myself. I could make my own decisions. It was a bit scary to be
a grown-up, but a wonderful thing to discover.

Before I had to report to the IRTC to which I had been assigned, I
used my two weeks' leave to head for the farm in the Berkshires, where
I knew my family would be assembled, except for my sister, Toby, who
had accompanied my brother-in-law, Malcolm, to his new Air Force
medical post at Wright Field in Dayton, Ohio, and my younger brother
Bobby, who was undergoing training at an Army camp. I had been
a conscientious correspondent and had kept my parents, sisters, and
brothers posted on my whereabouts and activities, so they knew of my
successful completion of the Infantry OCS. When I arrived at the farm,
I proudly showed off my new Army uniform, with the glistening gold
bars of a second lieutenant on its shoulders and the shiny new crossed
rifles insignia of the Infantry on my upper lapels. I must confess I was
on a high and very much pleased with myself.

Although both of my older brothers had been found to be ineligible
for military service—Irwin because he was discovered to have diabetes
and Julian because of his asthma—they performed their patriotic duty
by working at war production jobs: Julian at the Springfield Armory
and Irwin at the Holyoke Machine Company. It was wonderful to be
home and able to luxuriate in the warmth and mutual affection of my
family, away from the relentless tasks of the Army. I was content just
to be home at the farm, catching up with everyone, helping the farmer
with my father's herd of Guernsey milk cows, and generally enjoying a
complete change of pace to civilian daily life.

My two-week leave raced by and I left the farm for a new post, Ft. Blanding, Florida, an Infantry Replacement Training Center. But I wasn't there long: earlier orders from Washington caught up with me and I was transferred to the Army's Civil Affairs Division (CAD) with orders to report to Northwestern University in Chicago for courses in the language, government, and economy of Germany. This was followed by a special one-week course at the Military Police School, Ft. Custer, Michigan, and my shipment overseas to England in March 1944.

There's an old proverb that states: If you are ever given a choice between choosing talent and luck, choose luck every time. Reflecting on my personal odyssey and its various critical tipping points, I have come to believe that I am the beneficiary of "luck," although I have also always believed that a "lucky" person usually has to help make good luck happen. You have to take some positive measure or otherwise prepare yourself to take advantage of the good fortune when it comes. The opportunity to become an officer was the first part of this luck. The second part was my transfer to the CAD. Instead of being an expendable replacement for one of the many junior officer casualties, I was given the opportunity to serve in a far more personally challenging capacity, which contributed to the creation of a reformed, democratic Germany. My selection for Civil Affairs occurred only because two of my former Cleveland colleagues, Bob Chamberlin, Eliot Ness's deputy director, and Keith Wilson, who had headed Ness's undercover investigators, both happened to be on the staff of General Eisenhower's Allied Expeditionary Headquarters Civil Affairs (G-5) staff in London and were looking to recruit Civil Affairs personnel with government public safety backgrounds.

CAD had been created following Pearl Harbor. After America's temporary military occupation of Germany at the end of World War I, the U.S. Army was called upon to help restore a multitude of civilian problems arising from damage to the infrastructure and essential services that had afflicted many German cities and towns. The Army's inexperience and lack of skills in solving these civilian problems seriously jeopardized both U.S. military readiness and the foreign policy objectives of the Occupation. The lessons learned in that period led to the decision to establish the CAD, to provide vital civilian population support and control services in future U.S. military occupations.

The Nazi occupation of France, Belgium, Netherlands, and other allied countries presented very special, highly sensitive civilian problems for our troops when they had to attack and fight their way through German armed resistance. Civil Affairs teams were assigned to accompany the infantry battalions and regiments when they liberated former Nazi-occupied French, Belgian, Dutch, and other allied cities and towns, freeing the combat troops to focus on fighting, leaving civilian problems

The Averys, Arnold's English host family.

and threats to Civil Affairs detachments. Since these units served as the Army's liaison in providing support and assistance to the representatives designated by the government-in-exile of the allied country concerned, France, Belgium, the Netherlands, et al., they were known as Civil Affairs Army personnel. A large number of other officers and enlisted personnel had been selected and received special training to serve in Germany as representatives of the Military Government. Unlike their Civil Affairs counterparts assigned to work in liberated allied countries, this group (which included me) would not become operational until U.S. combat troops crossed the German border, after which they became active as Military Government personnel. (My unit and most other Military Government units prior to the 1944 invasion had been destined for duty in specific cities at the war's end. Our detachment's final destination would turn out to be Hof, a large city in the northeast corner of Bavaria, next to the designated Russian Occupation Zone.)

On my arrival in England in early March 1944, nobody was there to meet our ship. There was dead silence on the deserted Liverpool docks since the whole city had shut down for a Bank Holiday. A lone guard on the dock informed us that nobody would be working for several days. "Don't they know there's a war,?" someone called out. "It's the Bank Holiday," the British guard said, as if that explained everything. One of the critical elements of leadership that had been drilled into me at Infantry School was, "First, take care of your men!" There were nearly 1,000 soldiers aboard our troopship who needed to be unloaded and billeted. So I got some of the other officers to join me and hunt down a British officer to arrange for our ship to be unloaded and for the men to reach our designated billets. Finally, after a number of futile telephone calls, we reached a senior officer who, slightly miffed at having his Bank Holiday disturbed, helped our troops to be transported to where we were scheduled to be housed. American officers were housed with cooperative British families, and I was given a comfortable room with a hospitable, middle-aged couple in a small residential community outside Manchester. There most of the Civil Affairs personnel were stationed and received special training courses and instruction related to their forthcoming military assignments.

Spring, with its gentler air and colorful, fragrant flora had always been my favorite season, but that English spring brought me little joy or pleasure. Instead the surrounding bountiful country gardens targeted me with a devastating allergy that assaulted my eyes and nose and left me weeping, my nose streaming and altogether completely miserable. When I sought help at CAD's nearby infirmary, I was told I needed to have some allergy tests to determine a more specific cause of this English airborne attack, but they were not equipped to do these tests. Instead, I was directed to their daily shuttle van to the U.S. Army's 10th Station Hospital to be tested. I followed their instructions, boarded the shuttle, and checked in at the 10th Station Hospital Admission Office.

After an hour's wait, an Army nurse walked into the Admission office and called out my name. I got up, acknowledged I was Lt. Sagalyn, and was led to a bed in a hospital ward, where she handed me a hospital robe and told me to undress and get into the bed. Dumfounded by her request, I said there must be some mistake, that I was only at the hospital for some allergy tests. The nurse became very huffy and in a sharp authoritative voice, told me not to argue with her. Her orders were to get me into the bed. I was getting increasingly confused and alarmed.

They had to have me mixed up with another junior officer, and I now informed the nurse this was all a terrible mistake, that I wanted to see the medical officer in charge to clear up this misunderstanding. Very shortly, a visibly annoyed Army medical captain strode into the ward and in an impatient tone asked me why I was causing so much trouble. Pointing out that I was now under the hospital's authority and full control, he said I had to get into the bed because I was scheduled for an operation early the next morning. I was now in a state of near shock, thinking I had gotten myself into some kind of insane asylum. "What are you operating on me for? There's nothing wrong with me except an allergy, and that's why I came here, for some tests."

The medical captain then explained. I had an acute case of tonsillitis and it was urgent that my tonsils be removed immediately I quickly told him this operation wasn't necessary, because I, together with my two brothers, all had our tonsils removed when I was seven years old. To humor me, the doctor examined my throat, and he was clearly surprised to find what I told him was true. But my elation was short-lived when the Army Captain said that this discovery didn't change anything, insofar as the hospital was concerned. "We know there's something seriously wrong with you. We are going to take some tests now and hope to have an answer tomorrow."

I didn't sleep very well that night, as I no longer trusted the medical captain and what he might find. And my fears proved justified when he returned the next day to announce triumphantly that I had typhoid. He then went on to explain that they would have to send their test results to another medical facility to be absolutely sure of their typhoid diagnosis, and it would be a week before they could receive its results. However, in the meantime, they would begin treating me for typhoid. While I wasn't certain that the 10th Station Hospital was run for demented army personnel, I was sure I had a doctor who was one.

I firmly believed my life was at risk in the hands of this mad medical captain, and I had to get help to get out of there before it was too late. I remembered my brother-in-law, Archie Burack, had a brother who was a colonel in the Army medical corps and stationed in England. After a series of phone calls to army hospitals, I located him and explained my desperate plight and asked him what could be done to get me out of the hospital and the clutch of this mad Army doctor. To my great despair, I was told my hospital and its doctor had complete authority over me and there was nothing he, or anyone else, could do.

The week that followed seemed surreal. Every day I had to swallow numerous, very large pills accompanied by huge amounts of water. And as I was the only officer patient in the ward, the rest of my time was committed to reading and censoring the mail of my ward mates, who were military casualties of our ongoing North African campaign. One day I was offered a Purple Heart, a medal given to all wounded soldiers in combat that were being distributed to all other, wounded patients. At the end of the week, my medical captain showed up to report on the results of my tests for typhoid. "The tests were negative. There's nothing wrong with you," he added cheerfully. "But that's okay, we weren't very busy."

I dressed quickly and hurried out of the 10th Station Hospital to catch the shuttle that took me back to my sane CAD associates. I never did take their allergy tests, nor would I seek them at any other military hospital. I felt much safer that spring enduring the discomforts of my allergy.

Cal Stillman, Peter Strassberger and Arnold on leave in England. 1944

My Military Government Detachment, #I4B3, was one of a number of small Military Government (MG) teams whose mission was to accompany the forward infantry battalions and regiments who would be the first American soldiers to enter newly captured German towns and cities. It consisted of ten men—three officers and seven enlisted men—and commanded by an extremely competent, savvy, and wonderfully considerate leader, Captain Beverly P. White, a former lawyer from Lexington, Kentucky. Captain William Cochran, a former police officer, served as the Public Safety Officer, while I completed the commissioned staff. The enlisted personnel included three men proficient in German who served as interpreters.

The following months, I joined other officers assigned to military government units in special training courses, designed to provide me with a practical knowledge of the Nazi Party's and Germany's governing structure and my duties and responsibilities as a military government officer. But not until I heard and read Eisenhower's surprising, thrilling announcement on June 6th of the D-Day landings in Normandy did everything I was learning and training for suddenly became very important and worthwhile.

Two months later, D-Day would become very real for me when I stepped off of a small naval vessel onto one of the Normandy beaches, and saw a beach that was strewn with the stark remnants of sunken landing craft and wrecked vehicles. And as we drove north up Normandy's narrow winding country roads, I witnessed grim scenes of the luckless American tanks that had been stranded and abandoned after they had tried vainly to maneuver through the impenetrable, thick Normandy hedgerows that bordered the roads and farmers' fields. Everywhere we traveled I saw the appalling evidence of the war's horrific bombing and destruction in the shattered buildings and landscape.

We followed the U.S. armed forces as they advanced slowly toward Paris and camped out in individual Army pup tents in a wooded area near Rennes. As a designated Military Government detachment, I4B3, that would not become operational until we crossed the German border, we were in an inactive, holding position. On August 25th I had just finished breakfast and was sitting outside my tent, cleaning my mess kit, when my good friend Cal Stillman, a fellow Civil Affairs officer, came running over to me. "Did you hear the news? Our troops have reached Paris! Peter's family has a house there and he wants to go to Paris to see what shape it's in. Why don't we join him?" Peter Strassburger was another colleague and the three of us had established close ties in the course of our idle days.

I knew we weren't supposed to leave our camp without orders, but just sitting around all this time had become very boring and frustrating. Who would know or care if we took off for a couple of days? Of course we could get into real trouble if anyone wanted to make a case of it. "Great, let's go!" I exclaimed getting to my feet and tossing my mess kit into the tent. The once-in-a-lifetime opportunity of being in Paris during its long-awaited liberation overcame my normal prudence. We hitched a ride with an Army ordnance truck convoy carrying supplies and joined the thousands of other American uniformed forces liberating the city which was a teeming mass of wildly cheering, enthusiastic and friendly Parisians, who wanted to hug and kiss us and invite us to share their joy.

When I returned to Paris only three weeks later, this time properly authorized, I discovered a complete change of attitude toward Americans. The Parisians were cool and aloof and filled with disdain; it was as if the Liberation's fabulous welcome had been an aberration. Still, in the many times that I've returned to Paris since the War, I always recall the unforgettable welcome I received in the electrifying celebration of the city's Liberation in August, 1944.

Lt. Cisner and Arnold in France. 1944.

That winter my unit was holed up in an unheated cattle shed in a small town in Belgium,, the only shelter we could find. We shivered in the biting cold, still waiting for our troops to break through what continued to be strong German resistance. As soon as the breakthrough occurred, we could cross into Germany and our Military Government Detachment could finally go into action. The cold was so intense I could feel it in my bones, along with a persistent numbness, especially in my toes. I had no means of keeping warm and one especially frigid night my toes became frostbitten. I am still bothered by the numbing, aching effects of that frostbite. I remember playing a quiz with myself, nudging my memory to conjure up my feelings of being intensely hot, and wilting as I recalled how I had sweated and burned all day under that broiling Arizona desert sun, two years earlier when I was a private in training. I decided that being cold was worse than too hot, because in the desert there was always a chance for relief from the sun in the shade, if any could be found.

My time in Belgium that winter of '44 was one of the most dreadful experiences of my life. The bitter cold degenerated into even worse weather, with dense blowing snow and heavily overcast skies, making visibility so poor that all Allied air missions had to be suspended. This lulled our ground forces and commanders into a feeling of safety. They hunkered down and worried only about keeping warm while waiting for the weather to improve before continuing their advance into Germany.

Our troops were completely surprised on December 16, 1944, by the sudden appearance of German armored units, followed by hordes of German soldiers, many of them virtually invisible in white camouflaged attire, while other notorious SS units wore deceptive American uniforms. The Germans burst through the unsuspecting, snowbound American lines and overwhelmed the totally unprepared GI's. It was a brilliantly planned and implemented lightning-like assault, and it created pandemonium among the American forces. Frantic commanders sent urgent demands for immediate reinforcements to the Allied Supreme Commander, General Eisenhower, while they tried to regroup and turn back the German assault in what became known as the Battle of the Bulge.

My detachment was in the center of the German breakthrough, temporarily attached for administrative purposes to the 106th Division, which
had just moved into our area and was awaiting winter uniforms, arma-
ment, and ammunition for its troops before being activated. These unarmed, poorly-clad soldiers were among the first prisoners to be taken
by German SS troops, who marched them nonstop back to Germany to
a concentration-type facility under terrifying conditions, which included selecting for torture those soldiers they suspected of being Jewish.[6]
Luckily for me and the other members of Detachment I4B3, our small,
relatively isolated living quarters were outside the 106th's main camp,
so we were not immediately aware of the German invasion nor were
the invading SS aware of us.

But when we did find out what had occurred, our lives as members of
a tiny unknown military unit detached from any other recognizable
military organization became an unanticipated, terrifying ordeal. We
continuously had to persuade the deeply shaken, highly suspicious soldiers of the various American regiments and divisions we encountered
that we were not some of the invading German enemies dressed in
American uniforms, thus susceptible to being shot on the spot.

My own life was particularly in jeopardy when the U.S. military units
in our infiltrated area established a baseball sports test for screening
bona-fide soldiers in American uniforms from the German pretenders at
numerous military roadblocks and checkpoints. Each passerby was interrogated with a sports quiz, such as: "Who was pitching for the Car-
dinals at their last game? Who is playing second base for the Red Sox?"
and "Who is leading the American League in runs?" As I was probably
the only GI in the U.S. Army who didn't read the sports pages or follow baseball, I was in real daily danger of getting shot as a German in
an American uniform. Afterwards, whenever I had to go somewhere,
I latched on to a colleague who was a knowledgeable sports fan to

---

6. *Charlie Guggenheim, who later became a documentary film producer, was
serving in the 106th Division at that time, although by fortunate happenstance
he was absent from the Division that day and missed being part of the large
group that was captured. He produced a moving documentary film depicting what
had happened to the men of the 106th, especially those men the SS units had
believed to be Jews.*

accompany me and let him answer the guard's questions. It was a few weeks before the arrival of reinforcements and a break in the weather, which enabled our Air Force planes to attack, ending the German offensive. This Battle of the Bulge had come very close to disrupting the Allied advance, setting back Germany's surrender for many months.

The independence with which I and the other members of I4B3 operated cut me off from what was happening outside my small sphere of military activity. While I enjoyed an extraordinary degree of authority to make decisions and act on daily problems and crises once we entered a German city or town, I never knew what was happening outside my little realm, such as what battles were being fought elsewhere and won or lost. And equally important, except for sporadic letters from my family, I didn't know what was happening back in the United States or in the Pacific in the war against Japan, where my brother Bob was stationed. There remains to this day a big blank in knowledge about those war years.

The break our Detachment had been waiting for came when General Patton's 3rd Army crossed the Rhine on March 23 and we received our long-awaited orders to follow these troops into Germany, where we finally become operational. I had earlier "liberated" a Mercedes convertible sedan that had reportedly belonged to the Oberbürgermeister of Dresden. When my low-slung Mercedes got hung-up on a span of the pontoon bridge Patton's Army had erected across the Rhine at Remagen, an angry Major General strode up to see what was holding up his Armored Division. "Get that damned car off this bridge, Lieutenant, or I'll have my men throw it into the river!" he shouted at me. But I wasn't about to lose my Mercedes and called over to several of his men, "Hey, give me a hand, will you?" and they responded by quickly lifting my car and setting it free, enabling me to drive it rapidly across the bridge. I had become very fond of that car. It was so much more comfortable than my Jeep, and I kept it until the end of the war, despite the occasional hazard of getting fired at by American GI's who thought it was a German officer's staff car. (I turned the Mercedes over to one of my fellow officers when I left Hof to report to my next assignment in Berlin.)

As I was writing this, I had only limited success in my search through Army records to pin down all the places and dates our Detachment had accompanied battalions or regiments when they captured German towns and cities and where we established the first Military Government proclamations and laws, appointed new mayors, etc. Too often the records I did find were very poor copies and hard to decipher, instead I've relied on letters I had sent home which my mother and sister Lillian had saved, along with the few notes and records I had kept. I clearly remember March 27, an extraordinary day for me when Capt. White, my commanding officer, ordered me to take an interpreter and one of the Detachment's corporals and capture the Fortress of Ehrenbreitstein, ahead of the 69th Division battalion, which was already en route there. I was to post the Fortress off-limits to the 69th and leave the corporal there to enforce the posting, pending the arrival of a representative from SHAEF (General Eisenhower's headquarters.) I learned that the Nazi government had stored valuable works of art in the Fortress, priceless records of a number of cities, and the archives of the Grand Duchy of Luxembourg. The Luxembourg government-in-exile had been pressing Eisenhower to make sure these records were protected from any damage or loss. So when Eisenhower learned that the 69th Division, a National Guard division with a poor reputation for discipline among its soldiers, was due to capture the Fortress, he wanted to make sure the stored archives and art treasures were safe from 69th Division "liberators."

In retrospect, I am astonished that together with only an interpreter and a corporal, I was ordered to capture a mountain fortress guarded by an armed German garrison. The commanding general of the 69th Division had assigned a fully armed and supported infantry battalion of some 800 men to do the job. Even knowing this, I was undaunted. I picked up the interpreter and corporal in my jeep (it would have been too dangerous to drive my Mercedes under those conditions), raced madly toward the Fortress, and succeeded in catching up with the slower moving 69th Division's battalion. Ignoring the shouted warnings of the GI's that the enemy was just ahead, I passed the entire procession, driving up a steep, winding mountain road that ended at the entrance to the massive 12th century fortress. Then, pounding on the heavy gate with the butt of my Army revolver, I shouted for the garrison commander to surrender. Fortunately, the garrison commander, knowing that thousands of approaching American troops had already crossed the Rhine with no German forces to stop them, opened his gate and formally surrendered to me.

I posted a Military Government Off-Limits notice and left the corporal to explain the posting to the soon-to-arrive 69th Division. Sixty years later I received a letter from the Office of the Chief of Military History in response to my inquiry about the capture of the Fortress, stating: "it had been captured on 27 March 1945 by the lst Battalion of the 273rd Infantry Regiment, 69th Infantry Division. The capture of Fortress Ehrenbreitstein was an historic occasion because it was here that the last American flag was lowered following the occupation of Germany after World War I...Plans were made to have the same flag raised at the fortress on Army Day, 6 April 1945, as a symbol of the victorious return of American troops to Germany for the second time in a generation. General Bradley, 12th Army Group Commander, and Major General Reinhardt, 69th Division Commander, presided over the ceremonies."[7]

The quickening pace and progress of our advance into Germany was reflected by the frequency with which our Detachment was moving into and out of newly captured German towns and small cities, remaining only a day or two to post our Military Government proclamations, hours of curfew and new laws and to appoint a new mayor. The small size of our Military Government detachment and the large number of civilian communities our fast-moving troops were entering daily made it necessary for me, assisted only by my interpreter, to execute the first

---

7. *After the war, foolishly thinking the Army historical section might appreciate getting the actual facts of an Army "historical" event, I visited an Army Historical center in Washington, and asked to see its director. After showing him the Army's official version, I told him what really happened—that I had captured the Fortress and put it off-limits to the 69th. The director looked at me in astonishment, shaking his head slowly from side to side, as if I were a certified idiot. "What makes you think the Army would want to have your version of the Fortress's capture in its official records?" he asked me dismissively. However, my search in the Army archives in Maryland turned up a copy of an I4B3 March 27 report signed by Captain White describing his later visit to the fortress that day, accompanied by the V Corps' G-5, Fine Arts and Monument Officer, to document the archives, art and other treasures stored there and arrange for the assignment of a special, large security force to guard them.*

Arnold enroute to Belgium. 1944.

Military Government duties and responsibilities in a number of German towns. These ranged from posting Proclamation No. 1 from the U.S. and Allied Forces Supreme Commander, General Eisenhower, establishing his and the Military Government's supreme legislative, judicial, and executive authority. We also posted notices requiring the surrender of arms, curfew and travel restrictions, appointing a new mayor (Bürgermeister) or, if the incumbent was politically acceptable, issuing him orders to assure maintaining civil peace and the health, safety, and housing of U.S. troops in the area. I kept our Detachment commander, Captain White, informed of our activities and findings for inclusion in his daily report to SHAEF on each city or town's health, public safety, status of water and electric utilities, food, status of any Displaced Persons in the area, security conditions, and other important conditions and needs.

Frequently I would have to take care of urgent situations, such as the one I described in a letter I wrote home on March 25, 1945:

> *"I had quite a time in this place today. My interpreter and I were the only Military Government people in the area, the rest being a few infantry advance quartering units. After getting one area of the town evacuated by all Germans for use by the troops due in later, trouble started. In the next town are about 300 Russians who had worked in a large factory there as slave labor. They got wind that the German homes were empty and our troops had not yet arrived. Next thing I knew the Bürgermeister came running in to see me. The Russians were entering all the vacant houses and looting them. In addition, they had gotten into some wine cellars. There were fights breaking out between them and the Germans who tried to stop them.*

> *"I got things more or less quieted and ordered the Russians back to their camp in the adjacent town with the appropriate harangue and threats. Then I shot over to see their leader who turned out to be a seemingly intelligent and capable fellow. 'I thought the Russians were the friends of the Americans,' I told him 'but your people are doing things which force me to regard you as enemies. They are going into homes and stealing and looting. That is against our laws and the Russian laws as well. These are the acts of criminals. If they continue I shall have no choice but to regard these people as criminals... Our troops cannot devote all their energy to killing Germans when they have to keep order among you....*

> *"Then I saw the Burgermeister and told him that while this outbreak was regrettable and we were taking action to stop it, he must realize that the Germans themselves were to blame. They had brought these Russians here and had treated them badly, and it was not to be unexpected that they would turn against their oppressors. That really stopped him and he became apologetic and confessed the Germans had sometimes mistreated them. But these DP's sure cause a hell of a lot of headaches for us now. Not that I blame them for what they do——only we have to handle it. And you can't let a private little war start between them and the Russians.*

"Then I drove out to a nearby town (we have a number of them to look after) and found myself running smack into another mob scene. This time it was a large mass of Germans who were looting a factory coal stockpile. There was a German wearing a Military Government "polizei" armband trying ineffectually to stop them. Women, children, and men were grabbing coal briquettes and hastily filling up large grain sacks, then throwing them to their aides who waited below with carts and wagons. (The pile was on a small hill.) I stopped and called the policeman over and asked him what the score was. He explained somewhat hysterically that these people had descended upon the coal like locusts and were making off with it, that it was supposed to be distributed by their Bürgermeister.

"I climbed up to a vantage point with my handy interpreter and had him shout a little louder than the rest for quiet. The sight of our uniforms (and my stern commanding attitude, naturally) halted them. I then ordered them all to gather around immediately. When they were assembled in silence I read them the riot act (figure of speech). What was the meaning of this? This property has been taken in custody by the American military authority. You are guilty of a serious violation in stealing this coal. Unless you want to be regarded as criminals, you will put all this coal back at once and return to your homes. If there is any reoccurrence, the criminals will be shot as looters. Furthermore, this policeman is our representative here and you will obey him.

"Yes, this work is really o.k. now that we are out in the field and operating. It's also surprising to find the prestige that Military Government has among the troops. They think we are something hot and special."

From time to time I participated in an adventurous, non-military government assignment, one of which I recounted in this letter I wrote home:

"Until yesterday I was operating with an infantry battalion and living with one of the companies and I swung back into a routine I had left more than a year ago. I was detached from the rest of my (MG) detachment, together with my interpreter, on a special assignment. I

> even went on a night patrol with a squad hunting Germans, though
> we returned empty-handed. It's nice being attached to the infantry
> and not yet being assigned."

April 9, 1945, we established the first Military Government in the university city of Göttingen, where we had to deal with the many urgent
multifaceted, problems. (Although Göttingen was officially within
the British zone of occupation, our V Corps' 2nd Division[8] had been
moving faster through the German defenses and Göttingen was in their
path when they crossed the Weser River on April 8.) The city's population had jumped from 50,000 to more than 70,000, including some
10,000 hospitalized German military patients, plus an additional nearly
10,000 foreign forced laborers who had been looting, rampaging and
otherwise terrorizing the frightened civilian population with the weapons they had taken from local railroad cars which had been carrying
rifles and ammunition.

I left our unit to manage major problems while I sped out with an
interpreter to investigate a report from an excited 2nd Division Sgt.
that some German civilians were burning files in some kind of technical
laboratory just outside of the city. When I got there, I discovered the
place was a research testing facility for aircraft. I found the director and
ordered him to stop the destruction of the files, evacuate the building,
lock it up, give me the keys, and report to me at the Military Government office first thing in the morning for instructions. On my return, I
reported to Capt. White the results of my investigation.

The next morning, a very hush-hush delegation of American civilians
dressed in American uniforms and carrying high-ranking credentials
was brought in to see me. In confidential tones, they informed me they
were on a secret mission to find and take charge of a high-tech German

---

8. A Corps is a military organization consisting of two or more divisions and
other troops, and V Corps (the Fifth) was primarily the administrative subdivision
of General Eisenhower's Supreme Headquarters, Allied Expeditionary Force
(SHAEF) from whom our MG detachment received its assignments and through
whom Captain White made a brief, biweekly Field report on overall conditions,
and a more comprehensive monthly report (in triplicate to V Corps' MG officer,
G-5, to SHAEF on overall conditions.)

laboratory developing supersonic aircraft. I told them this was their lucky day, handed them the keys I had taken from the lab director, and led them to the room where the German Supersonic Lab director was waiting.[9]

I learned later that this American delegation was part of a carefully planned project to find and bring back to the U.S. Germany's scientific discoveries and advanced technological developments, as well as the individual scientists, such as rocket innovator Wernher von Braun. Our Russian allies, as well as the British and French to some degree, would soon be competing with us for these same scientific and intelligence prizes. This competition would become a major factor in seriously eroding our Military Government's highly publicized, carefully planned de-Nazification program to insure no important Nazi officials, or high ranking Nazi military or business leaders, held future positions of importance in government or business in Germany.

In consideration of the thousands of wounded German hospital patients, the city's senior military commander, General Von Hassbach, declared Göttingen to be an open city.[10] However, the Gauleiter, the chief Nazi party official of the district, was so infuriated by the General's action that he ordered the Gestapo, Germany's dreaded secret police force, to assassinate General Von Hassbach. Moreover, the Gauleiter also announced that anyone who cooperated with the American or Allied forces would also be murdered. The fact that a full general of the esteemed German Wehrmacht (regular army) could be assassinated was unimaginable and frightening to the German public.

But the similar threat to any citizen or German official who cooperated with our detachment created an enormous hurdle for us because we were required to appoint a new mayor, or Oberbürgermeister, as one of our first priorities. Our authority and ability to take control over the local government was dependent on being able to give orders indirectly,

---

9. *This laboratory was the center where Germany carried out the research and development plans of its pioneering supersonic jet plane.*

10. *Open City is a military term used in times of war, where a city official declares it is of no military value and will not be defended, and therefore should not be subjected to bombing or other military attack by an enemy.*

making them through the city's chief official, the mayor, who would then give them to the city's officials and services. However, when Captain White interviewed each of the five carefully screened potential candidates who possessed the necessary qualifications—experience and no serious Nazi background—everyone refused the appointment. The overwhelming fear of assassination by the Gestapo had had its desired effect.

We now had a big problem. We would have to be moving on in a few days, turning the Military Government responsibility over to a British Military Government team who were en route, but we were obligated to have a responsible Oberbürgermeister in charge of the city and its civilian inhabitants before we left. For we had just finally managed, with the help of a 2nd Div company, to round up all the vengeful, violent foreign workers, mostly Russians, who could not understand why we wanted them to stop shooting Germans.

Happily, Captain White was prepared for their refusals, for when the last rejection came, he assembled all of them in his office to hear his decision. He explained that his orders, and the welfare of Göttingen's citizen's, mandated the appointment of a competent non-Nazi mayor. He told them to discuss this subject among themselves in the room across the hall. And if at the end of 30 minutes no one had agreed to serve as the mayor, he would go over to the new camp where the Russian DP's were now being properly housed, and would select one of them to be the Oberbürgermeister of Göttingen.[11]

 Fifteen minutes later there was a knock on the door and all five mayoralty candidates filed slowly into the Captain's office. Then, Herr Dr. Schmidt, a respected minor judge, informed Captain White that he had agreed to accept the honor of being the new mayor, and the other four would serve as his advisors. While the threat he faced from the Gestapo was troubling, the thought of having a Russian DP as their new Oberbürgermeister was seen as a much greater danger to him and the Göttingen community.

---

11. *The Bürgermeister is the mayor of a town or other small community, while the mayor of a more populated city is known as an Oberbürgermeister.*

As General von Hassbach had previously been Hitler's Chief of Staff, only to fall out of favor when he was unsuccessful in leading the German armed forces to victory over the Russians, I thought he would be of special interest to the Army's and other U.S. intelligence agencies. Accordingly, I drove up to the impressive, white mansion on a hill overlooking the city where he was living, attended by his aide-de-camp, a very proper, straitlaced young Wehrmacht Captain. The general, dressed in full uniform, was a distinguished, fit-looking, rigid Prussian. His light hair had gray traces and his face was deeply lined. He was expecting me and formally handed me his Luger pistol. I drove him and his aide to V Corps headquarters. He was the only prisoner I personally took during the war.

A week later, I was in the outskirts of Leipzig, standing near the rubble of several bombed buildings, interrogating a captured German Captain. Suddenly, the piercing, shrill sound of an approaching shell riveted my attention. I kept looking directly at the German captain, not wanting to show any sign of fear or flight. I stood motionless, barely breathing, willing myself not to move or run. The falling shell suddenly became visible and dropped directly toward us, landing at our feet with an enormous thud, kicking up the debris in a showering spray. Involuntarily, I closed my eyes and tightened my lips, waiting for the explosion and death.

But there was no shattering blast or burning pain—only a puzzling, deathly quiet. I opened my eyes, not yet understanding what had happened or where I was. And suddenly, the realization shook me with a wave of disbelief. The shell hadn't exploded! It was a dud! Perhaps it was one of those shells made in one of Germany's forced foreign labor factories where sabotage was reported to have occurred. Whatever the cause, I was alive and very grateful. I said a silent, unspoken "Thank you, God." I looked over at the German Captain, still standing there stiff, silent, but obviously heavily shaken, too. "Captain," I said resuming my interrogation in my most casual voice and limited German. "Which of those panzer divisions we were talking about were SS?"

On April 18, orders arrived directing my unit to proceed immediately to Hof, a city situated in the Northeast corner of Bavaria, adjoining Czechoslovakia and the new Russian Zone of Occupation, where we

Russian military delgation in Hof. 1945, Arnold second from the left.

would meet up with a Russian military delegation, following Germany's official surrender on May 8, to toast our mutual victory with their dual purpose vodka—used both to operate the vehicle transporting them and as a stimulating refreshment when drained from its fuel tank. Hof had been a thriving city with a strategic location next to the borders of Prussia and Czechoslovakia. and was the long-planned, final destination of our detachment, making this transfer the end of our long journey through the four battle zones through which we had been operational in the European Theater and for which I would be awarded four battle stars on my discharge from the Army in the Spring of 1946.

I had found serving in a small, highly mobile Military Government team to be demanding, exciting, and personally fulfilling. Our activities had freed the American armed forces in Europe from having to deal with the urgent civil problems posed by the hundreds of thousands of German civilians and the tens of thousands of slave labor DP forced to work under inhumane conditions in Germany's cities and towns. This enabled our armed forces to concentrate their full attention and resources on winning the war. Moreover, I felt very fortunate that, unlike most soldiers in the infantry whose primary function and mission was to kill or capture enemy soldiers, my work provided a very important humane service—helping repair the war's destruction and restore food, water, public health, electrical, and other essential services to the civilian population. I believe these services were an important factor in preventing the development of any serious post-surrender Nazi insurgency as had been predicted and expected.

After a few days getting settled in Hof, I was busy tackling the Military Government's problems in this lively Bavarian city. We were supposed to stay in Hof for as long as I remained in the Army's Military Government, but I found myself with a new sense of proprietary responsibility and pride in making management decisions that would, hopefully, improve the basic infrastructure and essential services of the city, which had suffered extensive damage. I had been nomadic prior to my arrival in Hof, initiating quick-fix solutions to problems and then moving on. I was now able to take a more personal interest in helping to improve the health and lives of the more than 4,000 mistreated, malnourished, lice-ridden DP's (Displaced Persons) who had been forced to live and work in Hof's factories under pitiful conditions. I got broken water mains repaired and safe drinking water restored, first to the areas where American GI's were housed and then to the rest of the city's residents. I saw to the rebuilding of damaged railroad tracks and trains and the restoration of service to other communities in order to transport needed food and coal supplies.

BERLIN

Berlin 1945

But I was not destined to stay to complete many of the tasks I had begun. The Military Government HQ in Berlin had different plans for me. Three months after arriving in Hof, on July 10, I was ordered to report to the U.S. Group Control Council in Berlin where I was assigned for duty in the Information and Reports Office under Colonel Orlando Wilson, Director of the Public Safety Division. The Control Council consisted of senior representatives from the U.S., British, Russian, and French governments who were there to resolve major issues relating to the governance of partitioned Germany. The U.S. Public Safety Division was responsible for overseeing the public safety and internal security of the U.S. Zone as well as implementation of the U.S. Denazification programs. In civilian life, Col. Wilson had been Professor of Criminology at the University of California at Berkeley, and had earned national recognition for his creative, pioneering leadership as Berkeley's Chief of Police. Lt. Col. Minor Keith Wilson (no relation), one of Eliot Ness's chief undercover investigators, was Col. O.W. Wilson's executive officer and Chief of the Denazification Branch and had been instrumental in getting me assigned to work with him in this top Military Government organization. So, once again, my Cleveland experience was responsible for this new assignment and the opportunity to participate in an extraordinary historic adventure.

One of our first projects in Berlin was the identification and surveillance of all principal SS and Nazi personnel who might organize or lead a dangerous insurgency or terrorist movement against the American military occupation. A special counterinsurgency program had been initiated, requiring all potentially dangerous persons to carry special ID cards. These would make it impossible for them to obtain positions of trust or responsibility in government or business in which they could be dangerously empowered.

At my first meeting, the general in charge of this top secret undertaking had just finished reporting on the progress by the FBI in Washington, which had been entrusted with designing and producing the highly secure ID cards. It was also the first meeting for Jake Bean, the U.S. State Department representative, who had been listening intently to the report, but now he leaned forward and spoke up. "General," he said, "I know this is a very important project to protect us against potential German insurgents by making them carry special identity cards. But it's my understanding that all these former top Nazis and SS officials are scattered all over Germany, and they don't know where their former party and SS associates are. If we give them these ID cards, won't that provide them an easy way to establish their bona fides with one another and to organize against us?"

There was a sudden silence as all eyes turned to look at the general, who clearly was startled and visibly shaken. After a long thoughtful pause, the general slowly stood up, and announced in a crisp military order: "Gentlemen, this meeting and this project are now terminated."

In the course of writing my monthly report on Denazification and Public Safety for the Military Governor of the U.S. Zone, I periodically heard rumors of the incipient or active insurgent organizations of dedicated Nazi and SS officials who were plotting attacks on U.S. personnel or installations in Germany. These ranged from a guerilla organization called "The Werewolves," an assembly of armed SS and Nazi Party diehards in an inaccessible alpine fortress near Hitler's Berchtesgarten, to well armed, dedicated Party insurgent groups. None of these insurgent threats materialized to any significant extent, and the German civilians in the U.S. Zone of Occupation remained essentially peaceable and law-abiding. My personal view is that the essentially humane, constructive U.S. military government policies and programs in Germany, together with the generous economic assistance provided by the U.S. Marshall Plan, restored the economy and so improved the lives of virtually all civilians in Germany (and all of Western Europe) that there was no support for any serious insurgency movements. In addition, the decisive, shattering defeat of Germany's armed forces by the combined U.S., British and Russian armies and the capture of most SS armed divisions by Russian troops, as well as Hitler's suicide, served to significantly remove or diminish a major source of potential insurgency, as well as its leadership and resources.

The Denazification program was an integral part of the American Military Government's policy. It distinguished between "nominal " Party members and "active" members, the latter being those who had joined the Nazi Party prior to May 1, 1937 when the Party strictly limited membership to carefully screened, dedicated Germans. The program was designed to cleanse the government and German business enterprises of active Party members and prevent their holding any positions of responsibility and trust. Inherently, it was believed that the elimination of Nazis and Nazi influence was one of the prerequisites of the political and economic reconstruction of Germany.

But the implementation of the Denazification laws were quickly circumvented by claims that high ranking German government officials were "indispensable," as in the case of the Nazi official who had been in charge of the German railroads and had been dismissed because of his active Party membership. But the American general responsible for supplying U.S. troops in Germany with their material needs appealed the dismissal to the Military Governor of the American Occupation Zone, saying that this German was indispensable and the General could not be held responsible for supplying the U.S. forces if this particular German were not in charge of the railroads.

Although the Denazification officer concerned pointed out in his reply that the German railroads were only running at 20% of their capacity and that a less experienced but very competent and politically clean German could safely do the job. Nevertheless, the "indispensable" railroad official's dismissal was reversed. Ironically enough, the "indispensable" German died six months later of a heart attack.

As I mentioned in my account of the special U.S. civilian unit seeking information and German expertise on scientific and technological

Arnold in his office in Berlin. 1945.

discoveries when I was in Göttingen, the competition between the U.S. and Russia for German scientific intelligence and military talent was having an adverse effect on Denazification. In a letter I wrote home from Berlin in March, 1946, I reported: "Our Denazification program has taken a new turn and Keith and some of the others in our office feel that it'll now be the 'Program for the Reinstatement of Nazis and

Militarists in the Political, Social and Economic Life of Germany.'"
On January 1, 1946, I was promoted to Captain and I savored the
achievement as Colonel Orlando W. Wilson pinned the shiny twin bars
of a Captain on my khaki Eisenhower jacket. O.W. had been a wonderful boss—extremely bright, innovative, and with a very sharp mind who
respected intelligent opinions and questions and cut through reports
and discussions to the core issue. He later became an innovative and
nationally admired Superintendent of Chicago's troubled police department, which he reorganized, revitalized and equipped with state-of-the-
art communications capabilities and the reorganized department
won national recognition and admiration for its disciplined and
effective operations.

The end of the War in the Pacific brought a simultaneous, loud and insistent public demand to start bringing home the citizen warriors who
had been fighting the Germans and Japanese for the past four years,
and the War and Navy Departments responded with a point-based de-
mobilization program. Priorities for discharge were determined by the
total number of accumulated points each soldier, sailor and
airman received.

Going home in cattle cars. Whistle stop enroute to Le Havre.

I had no desire to remain in active service any longer than necessary, and I had earned enough points for early discharge. On 18 March 1946 I was commanding a contingent of 1,000 joyful, celebrating newly demobilized American soldiers traveling in former cattle-occupied railroad boxcars on a train headed for the French port of Le Havre for shipment home to the United States. On arrival, I would proceed to Ft. Devens, Massachusetts, where on 22 April 1946, orders would be issued granting me leave for 58 days to visit 1 Florentine Gardens, Springfield, Mass., and Cleveland, Ohio. At the end of my leave time, I would revert to inactive status and remain as a Captain, temporary AUS during the present emergency and for six months thereafter, after which I would become a member of the Army Reserve.

Arnold, the train commander.

TIME-OUT IN GENEVA
1946-47

Chapter 4

Why, then the world's my oyster
Which I with sword will open.
   William Shakespeare

The war and the Army had dominated my life so completely during the previous four years that I now found it very difficult to focus on, much less assess, what I wanted to do on my return to civilian status. I had no responsibilities or commitments to a waiting wife or children, nor any financial pressure requiring me to earn a living. The Army had taken care of all my needs, while the money it paid me had accumulated in a savings account and government bonds.

When I wrote my parents of my imminent discharge, I told them about my uncertainty about a future career, but mentioned my deep interest in the G.I. Bill of Rights (the Servicemen's' Readjustment Act of 1944), which provided veterans free education at the college or graduate level. This bill offered me an important interim opportunity for taking time-out and preparing for my future options in the two areas I found attractive and rewarding: government service and journalism. My letter also mentioned a new foreign-affairs graduate school at Yale that sounded particularly intriguing, and said that I had submitted an application to the Dean of Admissions, enclosing copies of my college records and government service background. But the dean's response had been negative, stating that my academic record led him to believe I lacked the study skills and related scholarly qualifications essential for their graduate study courses.

When I reported this to my father, his encouraging reply was quick, supportive and dismissive of the Dean's letter:

*"I think this is the first time you have been refused and told that you
were unable to do what you wanted to, and you are a little disappointed. I don't think you should be—this is really the first disappointment
and up to now you have had an easy life and been successful in getting
things you wanted.*

*"I am glad that you are frank with me and just remember I am just
an old companion—you don't have to mind me if you don't want
to. Maybe this is a good time to take inventory with yourself. Cheer
up—the world is still beautiful and you can make anything you want
to of yourself and you have the stuff that it takes to do it. Now is your
chance to decide on the road."*

By the time I reached the farm, however, I had made a decision. I
intended to pursue my interest in journalism and a course of graduate
study at the same time, while acquiring valuable and even adventurous foreign experience. I would achieve this by enrolling, under the
G.I. Bill, in the Graduate Institute of International Studies in Geneva,
Switzerland, one of the first educational institutions to specialize in international relations and part of the University of Geneva that had been
founded in 1559. At the same time, I would seek work as a "stringer,"
a part-time news representative, for U.S. news organizations that had
no regular bureau in Geneva or even in Switzerland.

My father approved of my new plan and, as French was the primary language spoken in Geneva, I thought it would be helpful to brush up on
my French. So I enrolled in Middlebury College's well-known summer
French language program. Moreover, before leaving for Switzerland, I
arranged to cover on-call news stories for Newsweek, The *New York
Times* Sunday travel section and the McGraw Hill News Service, which
served Business Week and McGraw Hill's numerous other specialty
business and industry publications.

In late September of 1948 I booked passage on the U.S. Line's Washington, the first large U.S. passenger ship to sail to Europe since the
end of the war. After a stopover in Paris, I finally arrived by train in
Geneva. After the widespread destruction and grim living conditions
I had encountered throughout most of Europe, I found Geneva—on
beautiful lake Geneva in one of the very few neutral and undamaged

European countries—a welcome, relaxing and ideal place in which to study and try to put my past and future life into perspective.

Arnold skiing in Cervinia, Italy.

In my first letter home, I wrote that housing was very tight and expensive, but I had finally found a room in an apartment conveniently near the Graduate Institute, although the rent was quite high, $36 a month. Food and the cost of living were also much more expensive than I had been led to believe, reporting: "Breakfast is generally around 50 or 60 cents for just coffee, rolls, butter and marmalade. Lunch (it's closer to our dinner) will average around a dollar or so, depending on whether or not you have a salad, wine or beer. If one eats in restaurants, he has to pay a minimum of $3 a day, but I have found a nearby pension where I have my dinner and supper for about $1.75 a day. I generally have a "Swiss" breakfast in my room, coffee and a couple of rolls and butter purchased the previous evening." Fortunately, the rate of exchange for Americans was rather favorable and I could cash up to $1,000 a month in travelers checks at the rate of 4.25 Swiss francs to the dollar. (If I were to buy Swiss francs with U.S. dollars rather than travelers checks, however, I would only receive 3.50 francs for each dollar, although I could not understand why the Swiss Banks approved of this.)

All my classes were at the Graduate Institute, where I found some 80 other American students, including not only veterans but also a contingent of Smith College students spending their junior year abroad. There were few lectures, but seminars were common. The Institute

encouraged students to read the books recommended for each course
and then demonstrate their knowledge in interactions with other students and faculty in seminars. The mix of these young Smith under-
graduates in the seminars with the older, weathered veterans was not
very productive of informed discussions. And scholarly debate was also
hampered by the often-volatile presence and defensive, impassioned
patriotic diatribes (often in poor, broken French) of students from
countries such as Yugoslavia, Romania, Albania, Hungry and Austria.
Nonetheless, I found the books enlightening, as were the differing,
strongly held views of my non-American classmates.

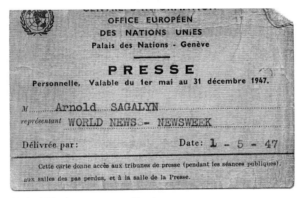

United Nations press accreditation.

With respect to my work as a journalist, Swiss law made it very difficult
for a foreigner to get a work permit. But as Geneva was now the European meeting center of the new United Nations, I got around the Swiss
permit problem by getting myself accredited as a UN journalist. This
enabled me to cover the numerous meetings and public hearings being held in Geneva on major postwar international political, trade and
other economic issues, most of which were of interest to the various
news publications I was representing. During the months that followed
I covered a wide range of events, including: 1) the preparatory UN
hearings to the 1949 revision in Stockholm of the Geneva Convention,
the core of humanitarian international laws governing the treatment
of civilians and prisoners in time of war[12] ; 2) meetings of the Palestine
Commission that would later result in the partition of the British Mandate of Palestine into Jewish and Arab states; 3) the historic, official

---

12. *These would be the first changes and first expansion of those laws since
1929 and would apply the lessons learned from World War II.*

termination of the UN's predecessor, the doomed League of Nations; and 4) a series of UN hearings to reduce barriers to international trade that resulted in the General Agreement on Tariffs and Trade (GATT). I also traveled to Bern and Zurich on assignments for Business Week and other McGraw Hill publications, and to the famed ski resort at St. Moritz, to write a story for The *New York Times* travel section on preparations for the 1949 Winter Olympics.

Sister Lenore in Geneva with a friend's son.

On the ship to Europe I had met Rodney Reilly, a Navy veteran who was also en route to study in Geneva on the G.I. Bill. He was an affable, warm and amusing fellow who was trying to escape going to work for his stern, conservative father—a small-town mid-western banker—and we had become good friends. When it became apparent that the small bedroom I was renting was inadequate, I joined forces with my new friend and together we planned to rent, from the University's professor of drama, a wonderful apartment in Geneva's old historic quarter. This apartment had a stage in its commodious living room. Henceforth, we agreed, when one of us would meet an attractive new girl we wanted to get to know better, we had an enticing invitational gambit—we'd invite her to "try out" for a part in a new show we planned to produce. During holiday breaks in fall and winter Rodney and I initially took

long skiing trips, along with other friends, to Zermatt, a beautiful resort town at the foot of the Matterhorn, Switzerland's highest mountain. Later we traveled to Cervinia, a new postwar resort on the Italian
side of the Matterhorn, where prices were much lower. Other times we
would go on walking trips in Gstaad and Davos, or boat trips on Lake
Geneva, or sun and swim at one of Lake Geneva's beaches.

One of the most valued events of my year in Geneva was the visit of
Lenore, my youngest sister. As I had left home when she was only
12, I had rarely seen and hardly known her during the later years she
was growing up. She was now at the London School of Economics,
and the heavy bombing of London had resulted in the strict rationing
or unavailability of most quality of life amenities. She had written to ask
if she came to Geneva, would I take her on a shopping trip to Italy. To
which I had happily agreed, as it was an opportunity to be both helpful
and to become better acquainted, which we did. This trip led to our
developing a very close and warm relationship.

I enjoyed living and studying in Geneva and working as a "stringer" for
U.S. publications, but as the summer was ending, I was making plans
to go home since my financial support from the G.I. Bill was ending. It
was time to go back to the USA and find a full-time job as a journalist,
my career choice. Out of the blue, a totally unexpected cable arrived
from London. The European head of the United Press (UP) wire service was inquiring if I would be interested in covering Switzerland for
the UP! The opportunity to stay on in Switzerland representing a major wire service, competing with the Associated Press (AP) and Reuters
wire services, was very exciting and challenging. But then, remembering the UP's well known reputation for paying the most minimum of
minimum wages, I calculated what I thought would be the absolutely
lowest amount I could possibly live on in Switzerland, which came to
$200 a month, and cabled this as an acceptance salary. The UP reply
was quick and brief: "Your request so far from reality no point further
discussion." Disappointed but not really surprised, I made a reservation
on a passenger ship home.

JOURNALISM YEARS
1947-52

Chapter 5

News is the first rough draft of history.
   Benjamin Bradlee

LIFE MAGAZINE

My year in Geneva with the various journalistic assignments I did for the McGraw Hill News Service and The *New York Times* travel section led to my decision to continue pursuing a journalistic career when I returned to the U.S. in the summer of 1946. My first preference was The *New York Times*, but I quickly discovered they had no current openings because their hiring policy was essentially restricted to the numerous former employees returning home after the war.

Hearing of an opening at Life magazine, I had a very successful interview there and was immediately hired as a reporter on the New York staff. I was soon accompanying Life photographers on a wide range of assignments. My very first assignment was to cover a devastating local snowstorm that had completely paralyzed vehicular and most pedestrian traffic in Manhattan. The photographer was Mark Kauffman, who had just returned from covering the war in China. This was the first time either of us had ever been in New York City. The memory of us— two newcomers to New York, trudging with great difficulty through the unplowed snowdrifts, and stopping the rare pedestrian to inquire where could we find Central Park, the Metropolitan Museum and other well-known destinations—still brings a wry smile at our ridiculous situation.

I found that there was an informal social culture among a large segment of Life's editorial staff and the photographers, many of whom were single, that involved meeting after work and socializing with one another in various bars and restaurants. During the following months I met and dined with most of the photographers who were based in or visiting

New York, including Robert Capa, the famous war photographer. Capa was an attractive, sophisticated-looking guy who was greatly admired and respected by his co-photographers, not only for his professional talent but also for his romantic appeal to and success with women. I would later become a very close friend of his younger brother, Cornell, who also distinguished himself as a Life magazine photographer and founder of the International Center of Photography.

My job as a reporter was to help plan the photographer's photo coverage, keep notes on all of his individual shots, write a report on the event for the writer and, when the story was scheduled to appear in Life, to check the story and captions for accuracy. The most memorable Life story I covered when I worked in New York involved a visit to photograph and interview Albert Einstein in Princeton, N.J. My photographer was "Eisie", the famous, extraordinarily talented, five-foot-four photojournalist, Alfred Eisenstaedt. Life was doing a story on the United World Federalists, a pro world-government group that Einstein was supporting, and the organization's President, Cord Meyer, who was accompanying us.

My first impression was a white haired man who impressed me by his quiet, innocent manner—I never met a man who conveyed such simplicity, an almost ethereal presence. The sight of Einstein and Eisenstaedt, two diminutive, essentially gentle former Germans, walking slowly around Einstein's house and conversing in German, was very moving and would have made a terrific photograph if I had had a camera. Meyer had been a decorated and badly wounded Marine officer in the Pacific and was now promoting world government. We would later learn that Meyer was secretly working for the CIA, a fact that quickly became known to many Washington "insiders."[13]

Not long after that, I was lucky to be assigned to the Time-Life news bureau in Chicago, headed by Hugh Moffett, a very bright, superior journalist and human being. In Chicago I was soon covering (for Time as well as Life magazines) a wide variety of often fascinating newsmak-

---

13. *His wife, the beautiful former Mary Pinchot, later had a liaison with President Kennedy and in 1964 was mysteriously murdered on the C&O Canal towpath in Georgetown.*

ers and events throughout the Midwest. I loved working in Chicago because it was such a lively, dynamic American city with a diverse, representative population, where the business and civic leaders demonstrated strong civic pride and responsibility.

Arnold at the University of Chicago for a Life magazine story.

One of my first assignments was to do a story on the University of Chicago's President Robert Hutchins' unique policy and practice of accepting students irrespective of age and awarding degrees on the basis of their demonstrated aptitude and knowledge. This was a highly unorthodox procedure at the time. To illustrate this, I collected the books that were supposed to contain all the knowledge a University of Chicago student was required to have in order to receive a BA degree. I had them arranged on the 10 shelves of a six-foot-tall bookcase, with each shelf visibly marked as belonging to a particular field of knowledge.

My accompanying Life photographer, Joe Scherschel, took pictures of the shelves. The subject matter and courses were: Social Sciences 1,2,3; Humanities 1,2,3; Biological Sciences; Physical Sciences; History of Western Civilization 011; Mathematics 1; Latin 1; English. A label on the edge of the shelves visibly marked each subject.

Not all assignments were routine, however, as I was soon to discover when I had to hire a small single-engine Cessna airplane to fly with my photographer to the mammoth annual Illinois State Fair in Springfield. The day was spent without incident, visiting and getting shots of some of the most interesting and colorful animal competitions, food awards, exhibits and harness races. But the sky had darkened by the time we took off to fly back to Chicago's Municipal Airport, then the city's only commercial airport and known as the world's busiest. (It would be renamed Midway two years later to honor those who had fought in WW II's seminal Battle of Midway.) Our flight was relatively smooth and uneventful until we approached Chicago when suddenly, without warning, our lights and entire electrical system went out. We were flying blind, without any radio communications with the control tower at the Airport. I went up to our pilot to discuss our situation and he reported there was nothing he could do except to continue toward the airport and hope for the best. I went back to my seat and told Joe we had a problem and we had to buckle up. And, if he thought it might help, to pray, as I then did.

When we saw the airport's lighted runways, and saw planes landing and taking off, I steeled myself and held my breath as our intrepid, ex-Navy aviator carefully and skillfully managed to slip in through the other planes that were in the air and taking off, and put us safely on the ground. It was as if it was just another routine landing on the deck of an aircraft carrier. I remember thinking that while my prayer was calming and not wasted, I felt sure that my lucky star had been shining down on us and this was just proof that my perennial good luck was still holding.

But I had no time to reflect about it, as the next day I had to leave early to cover a story for Time magazine on a small college in Olivet, Michigan, where the students were demonstrating against the firing of a popular professor who was too liberal for the newly installed, very conservative college president. This assignment has stuck in my memory because of the indignant college president's explanation to me for firing the professor, which ran in the next issue of Time: You can't criticize the college and expect to "continue to eat at its trough."

Arnold partying in Chicago.

The Chicago bureau in 1948 was an unusually exciting and journalistically fortuitous place to be for covering what turned out to be one of the most amazing political upsets in American political history. Starting with the early 1948 election polls, President Truman was written off by all the political polls, news pundits, and leading publications. A *New York Times* story was headlined: "Thomas E. Dewey's Election as President is a Foregone Conclusion." And the highly respected political pollster, Elmo Roper, was so confident that Truman's very low ratings in Roper polls and those of the other two major polls—Gallup and Crossley—would not change that he announced on September 9 that Dewey was leading by such a wide margin that there was no reason for him to publish another poll.

Life was so certain of Dewey's victory that, just before Election Day, it published an eight-page story on the presumptive president-elect Dewey with a full-page photograph of Governor and Mrs. Dewey, the caption describing Dewey as "the next President of the United States." And the nationally syndicated columnist Drew Pearson, as well as the highly respected Alsop brothers, wrote columns for publication on the day after the November 2 election based on their assumption that Dewey had won, speculating on his cabinet appointments and priority plans. Even his own Democratic Party leaders saw Truman's campaign for reelection as hopeless. This included Chicago's political boss, Jacob "Jake" Arvey, chairman of Cook County's Democratic party and an astute veteran politician. Up until Election Day, Arvey had told our bureau's political reporter that Truman had no chance of defeating New York's Republican Governor Tom Dewey.

I was one of the first reporters in the United States to learn that the Chicago Tribune was so positive that Dewey would be the next President it had gone to press on election night with its first edition carrying the now immortalized, boldfaced, banner headline on page one, "DEWEY DEFEATS TRUMAN." My coup came about because I was assigned to cover the election results of Illinois' incumbent Republican and very conservative U.S. Senator, C. "Curly" Wayland Brooks, who was considered a shoo-in against his Democratic opponent, Paul Douglas, a university professor. Thus, election night found me standing outside the Senator's hotel room with several other local reporters, awaiting the election results and Senator Brook's appearance and comments. His confidently jubilant campaign supporters were already celebrating his certain victory in a ballroom below. I was discussing the election with "Bazy" Miller, a favorite niece of the childless, formidable Robert McCormick, publisher of Chicago's biggest daily newspaper, the Chicago Tribune, when someone called over to her to pick up a telephone call in a nearby room. When she returned to join me several minutes later, she was giggling, and I asked her what was so funny. That call was from the circulation manager of the Tribune, she told me, and he had called to tell her that the Tribune had just printed its first edition with the headline "DEWEY DEFEATS TRUMAN," but now a new report indicated that the paper may have been too hasty in printing that headline.

As the evening wore on and fuller vote tallies came in, the radio network news broadcasts reported that Truman was ahead in 28 states with 303 electoral votes as opposed to Dewey's 16 states with only 189 electoral votes. He was beating Dewey in the popular vote by a margin of three million votes. Equally devastating for Republicans were the reports that Truman was carrying national and state Democratic candidates to victory as well, including Paul Douglas to the U.S. Senate and Adlai Stevenson to the Illinois governorship.

Senator Brooks was so devastated by the news of his defeat that he refused to emerge from his room to give us a statement. Finally, when his
administrative assistant came out to speak to us, he, too, was so upset
that he was visibly shaking and sputtering as he struggled to speak. And
when at last he did speak he blurted out bitterly and angrily, "I can't
believe that man Douglas, who has been poisoning the minds of school
children, is going to be Senator!!" Then, turning abruptly on his heels,
he walked back into the Senator Brook's room and slammed the
door shut.

The next day I accompanied our political reporter when he went to
interview "Jake" Arvey on the Democratic party's astounding victory,
and we found a greatly puzzled but happy Cook County Democratic
Chairman. What happened, we asked him? Arvey was very frank. "I just
don't know. I can't explain it," he confessed. "Last week I didn't think
we could elect a dogcatcher."

Truman's stunning victory had an enormous impact on my life, for a
few days later I had a call from New York telling me to start packing: I
was being transferred to the Washington Time-Life bureau where my
assignment would be to cover Truman and the White House for Life.
I had enjoyed my work and life in Chicago, but the D.C. assignment
was a promotion and, most important, an opportunity to have an inside
seat from which to observe the workings of the Federal government
and our elected representatives in the Executive branch and Congress.

I arrived in Washington a few days before I reported for work and was
successful in finding a pleasant, one-bedroom apartment in Georgetown that was convenient to the Time-Life office on 15th Street. After
checking in with Jim Shepley, the head of the Washington bureau, I set
out on my first assignment: to obtain accreditation and tickets for the
various parties and events that were scheduled in connection with President Truman's inauguration on January 20, 1949. Truman was first
sworn in as President after Roosevelt's death in a private ceremony at
the White House, some four years earlier on April 12, 1945. Now Truman, with his personal, dramatic and universally unexpected triumph
would experience all the pomp and circumstance previous presidents
had enjoyed. These would include a week of parties and receptions,
culminating in the oath of office on the west front of the Capitol facing

the Washington Monument and Lincoln Memorial, followed by the inaugural parade to the White House, which the overconfident Republicans had already expectantly planned for Governor Dewey.

Arnold in Time Life Washington office.

I was told that the person in charge of accreditation and tickets for the press was Sam Brightman, the PR representative of the Democratic National Committee, and was given directions on how to get there. I found Brightman standing in the middle of a large room surrounded by a small mob of press and radio news representatives, including photographers and cameramen. After I managed to push my way through to him, I told him I was from Life magazine and would like to get an accreditation pass and tickets for the various inaugural activities. Brightman looked startled and taken aback as he asked me in a rather strange, choked voice, "Who did you say you were with?" And when I told him again. "Life magazine," he jumped up on a heavy oak table and shouted at the top of his lungs, "Listen up, everybody!! Listen up!!!"

There was a sudden hush and then silence, and Brightman then continued to speak in the same loud, incredulous tone of voice. "This sonovabitch says he's from Life magazine and wants tickets to come to our inaugural parties!!" And in the dead quiet that prevailed, he shouted with a note of finality, "Over my dead body!!"

Surprised and shaken by this angry rejection on my first Washington assignment, I went back to the office and called Ed Thompson, the managing editor of Life, to report my experience and failure. Thompson was a seasoned, highly competent, well-liked editor. There was a brief pause before he spoke. Then in a matter-of-fact, reassuring tone, he replied, "That's all right, one of these days we're going to win an election." Despite the low esteem in which Life was held by many Democratic Party officials that year as a result of the blatant editorial favoritism toward Republicans shown by Henry Luce and his publications, I received the requisite press accreditation and tickets to Truman's inaugural events. (Later on when I became involved in Stevenson's Presidential campaigns, Sam Brightman and I would become good friends.)

It was pretty exciting to go to my first Presidential inaugural and to watch from nearby as Truman, dressed in a black morning coat and striped trousers, took the oath of office, administered by Chief Justice Frederick Vinson. I watched him as he delivered his speech from the West Portico of the Capitol. Then he drove off in a large, black open touring car, with Vice President Alben Barkley sitting next to him, similarly attired, both wearing top hats, while a protective covey of Secret Service agents walked and often ran alongside. The heavily guarded motorcade proceeded slowly past thousands of men, women, and children lining Pennsylvania Avenue, all the way to the White House.

Later that evening, I went to the more intimate Inaugural dinner in the ballroom of the venerable Mayflower Hotel on Connecticut Avenue, accompanied by Jim Whitimore, a young and talented Life photographer. I had previously scouted out the site of the Inaugural dinner with Jim and now we went up to the mezzanine, one floor above the Inaugural dining room, where there was a balcony that provided a clear view of the head table where Truman and his wife Bess sat. The various dignitaries and other guests were seated along a rectangular dining table that extended the length of the large room. During the next hour and a half Jim took shots of the President and Mrs. Truman as well as cabinet members and other prominent political personalities and captured the President's hilarious account to the audience's uproarious delight at his impersonation of NBC radio commentator H.V. Kaltenborn's insistent announcements of Dewey's victory.[14]

As I was taking notes on the people Whitimore was shooting, I noticed his camera kept returning to the couple in the right corner of the dining room table, seated immediately to the right and below Truman. I had recognized the man as Matt Connelley, Truman's appointments secretary, but did not know the attractive blonde next to him. I remember thinking Connelley looked as if he had been drinking too much and was being surprisingly intimate with her, when Jim unexpectedly came over to me and said, "Let's get out of here. I want to get back to the photo lab at the office." I looked at him in disbelief, saying we weren't finished yet, that there was a lot more shooting we should be doing. But Jim was very tense and insistent, so I followed him reluctantly as he walked quickly from the balcony to the elevator, carrying all his camera equipment in his large black leather bag. As the elevator door closed, I turned to him to ask what was going on, why was he so anxious to leave early. "You won't believe the picture I just got," he replied, his voice high and excited. "I've got to develop it to make sure," he said. Then, seeing that I wondered if he had lost his marbles, he explained, "Matt Connelly and his blonde were both so high that he had unbuttoned the top of her dress, had pulled out her breast and was fondling it!"

As soon as we got back to the office, Jim ran to the photo lab to develop that roll, and a few minutes later the telephone started to ring. As we were the only ones in the office that late, I picked up the phone. It was the head of the Secret Service detail covering the President that night, and as soon as he heard my voice he said. "We want that picture

_____

14. *Truman awakened at midnight and turned on the radio to hear Kaltenborn report that although Truman was 1,200,000 votes ahead in the popular vote, he was certain to lose. Truman went back to sleep, but woke up again at 4 a.m. to hear Kaltenborn say that while Truman was now 2,000,000 votes ahead, he was still going to lose.*

and the negative!" Taken aback by the unexpected call and feeling threatened by the hard finality in his voice, I was uncertain what I should say. So I tried to stall him. "What picture are you taking about?" I asked. "You know," he said. "We saw who Whitimore was shooting and we want it." I put the Secret Service caller off temporarily by telling him he to call back, because I would have to talk to Whitimore to find out just what he had actually shot, but he was in the dark room and currently unavailable.

I then walked to the photo lab and knocked on the door to the dark room where Jim was developing the roll and picture, and called out that I needed to talk to him. In a few minutes Jim came out with a big smile on his face as he said, "I got a great shot of Connelley holding the breast of his blonde and I had Truman in the shot, too." I congratulated him on getting the picture, but then broke the news about the Secret Service's call and their demand that we hand over both the developed photo and the negative.

We discussed what we should do, and noted that if we didn't give up the picture, we were going to have a hard time covering the President in the months ahead if we had the enmity of the Secret Service. But what finally proved decisive was the recognition that Life was a family magazine and would never run such a picture. So when the Secret Service agent called back, I told him we would give him the picture and the negative. (Today we would have taken our chances with the Secret Service's displeasure and the photograph would very likely have been published and syndicated in publications round the world).

In those days the White House press corps was very small—only about 10 regular reporters, representing the three main wire services (AP, UP and INS), the major Washington, New York and Baltimore newspapers, and NBC and CBS news—covered the White House on a daily, full-time basis. Most news publications and services only showed up at the White House when there was some important event or when a press conference was scheduled. In addition security threats and Presidential protective measures were amazingly light and low key. When Truman went out on his daily walks, only a few Secret Service agents accompanied him, and he often stopped to greet local pedestrians and out-of-town visitors. Later that year when Truman flew home to Indepen-

Arnold, 2nd from right, and other White House reporters in front of President Truman's residence in Independence, Missouri.

dence, Missouri, for the Christmas-New Year holiday, I was one of a very little core of Presidential Party reporters on the press plane that accompanied him. And the next morning I was one of only five reporters who joined him when he took his early morning walk, with only two Secret Service agents, one leading and the other trailing the small pedestrian Presidential procession. One of my missions when I was in Independence was to hand President Truman one of the first copies of the year-end issue of Time with his picture on its cover as 1948 Man of the Year, which the President accepted with a big grin, clearly reveling in the irony of the fact that Time and Life had shown strong, biased support for his Republican opponent, Governor Dewey.

The extremely light and casual protective security for President Truman changed dramatically the following year. Two Puerto Rican nationalists on November 1, 1950, tried to shoot their way into Blair House, where Truman was living while the White House was undergoing major repairs.[15] But from that time on, Presidents faced increasingly serious threats that demanded tougher, comprehensive protective measures. Although Congress would periodically approve strengthening the Secret Service's Presidential protective capabilities, their appropriations support tended to be inadequate to meet the measures required. It was

---

15. *Fortunately, the assassination attack was foiled by the return fire of the small detail of White House policemen guarding Blair House, which left two of the officers and one of the Puerto Ricans assassins dead.*

not until the Kennedy tragedy that the Congress would acknowledge that they, as well as the Secret Service, had a mandated obligation with the highest priority to provide the funding and related assistance to the Secret Service that was needed to protect the President (and the other designated protectees) against the deadly physical threats that had increased over the years.

While the daily activities of President Truman were not given the intensive press coverage so prevalent today, my assignments involved a wide and fascinating series of subjects and events ranging from the official signing of the North Atlantic Treaty Organization (NATO) to spending a day aboard a Turkish ship carrying a shipment of U.S. aid to Turkey as part of the Truman Doctrine, providing economic and military aid to Turkey and Greece (a forerunner of the massive Marshall Plan for economic and military assistance to 16 European countries that had suffered severely in World War II).

As an unattached bachelor, my social life was very active and I found myself in demand by old former Cleveland friends, such as Kay Halle, who had come to Washington during WW II to work for the clandestine U.S. foreign intelligence agency, O.S.S. Her cocktail hour salon attracted the Who's Who of Washington's political, literary and diplomatic circles. I also resumed my close friendship with Clayton Fritchey[16] and Dan Goldy, my former Cleveland roommate, who was now working at the Interior Department for the Assistant Secretary, Jebby Davidson, and would be my doubles partner at Al[17] and Jean Friendly's highly popular Georgetown tennis court weekends.

However, my assignment to Washington, as it had been to Chicago, came to an end when a telephone call from Time Inc. headquarters in New York informed me I was moving again, this time across the country to Los Angeles, where I would be covering the entire U.S. Northwest.

---

16. *Now working for George Marshall, Secretary of Defense, as Special Assistant and Director of Information*
17. *Editor of the Washington Post.*

The Los Angeles bureau was then headed by Elmer Lower, an experienced professional whose reputation as a demanding, but fair and considerate, boss proved merited. And, within a few days after my arrival, I was fortunate to find and get settled in a pool-house apartment, conveniently situated in nearby Brentwood. An important mission of the L.A. bureau was to cover Hollywood and its newsworthy "stars," and it was almost inevitable that one of my first assignments would be a Life story involving a Hollywood personality. As a number of Hollywood's stars were notorious for their tempestuous, uncooperative behavior, I was lucky that my assignee turned out to be Bill Holden, a warm, delightful, easy guy to work with. He was then an up-and-coming actor who had so far won lead roles in a series of minor films. Life's movie editor had marked him as a rising star and the following year his film career would take off when Hollywood's legendary screen writer and director, Billy Wilder, picked him to play opposite Gloria Swanson, cast as a former star of silent pictures, in the classic Hollywood film, Sunset Boulevard, which was nominated for eleven Academy Awards and won three.

Life was always looking for stories that offered an opportunity to put an attractive personality on the magazine's cover, for that would help increase the number of its news-stand sales. Prior to my arrival, Life had settled on doing the story of a new, highly photogenic resort surrounded by a beautiful mountain lake in Canada's British Columbia. As a young, good-looking, rising film star, Holden was seen as a "natural" for a Life cover, and arrangements had been made for Holden and his wife, Brenda Marshall,[18] to "vacation" at the resort. The key cover photograph would be of Bill Holden, athletic and bare-chested, water-skiing on the lake, with the resort and surrounding mountaintops providing a picturesque background. That was Life's plan.

Alan Grant, a Life photographer whose cover photos and other outstanding pictures of movie and news personalities had made him a star photographer in Hollywood, was assigned to shoot this story. I flew with him and the Holdens to Seattle, where we transferred to a small single engine plane equipped with pontoons for landing on a lake at the resort in British Columbia. Everything was planned for, except one thing: the capriciously variable weather in the high altitude in that part

---

18. *A film actress who had co-starred with Errol Flynn in several pictures.*

of British Columbia. When we arrived it was raining. And for the next several dismal days it was overcast and/or raining, dashing all hopes of getting a suitable cover picture. During those long waiting day- and night-time hours together in this new resort on a remote, isolated island where we were essentially the only guests, I had a chance to get to know Holden and his wife, Brenda, fairly well and to develop a warm friendship that would lead to a number of dinners and evenings together in their house back in L.A.

On the first day, I asked him how he got into acting, and he told me he grew up in South Pasadena, CA, and while attending the community college there, took an interest in radio plays. But when he graduated, his father wanted him to come into the family's agricultural fertilizer business, which was undergoing enormous growth after his father had taken over a number of the fertilizer businesses previously owned by Japanese who had been interned by the Federal government following Pearl Harbor. "This fertilizer business was a big business in California," he said. "And if I had gone to work for my father, I could have been the shit king of America!" he told me, smiling at the thought of that lost achievement. "But I was more interested in acting," he added with no regret.

Arnold, in plaid shirt, with Bill Holden, waiting for the sun to come out.

Bill was very good company during the long hours of waiting for the weather to improve. Finally, the continuum of overcast, sunless skies outside suddenly changed and the sun was miraculously shining on the fifth morning when we all raced happily out to our pre-planned positions—Bill to the dock for his water skis while Alan and I climbed into the motor boat that would be towing him. So the long-awaited photo of Holden water-skiing against that magnificent, sunlit British Columbia mountain background was successfully shot and would soon appear on the cover of Life.

Covering the entire West Coast for major news and other Life-worthy events often thrust me into dramatically different kinds of adventures and physical demands. Soon after I had returned to L.A. from my week with Bill Holden, I was flying with Life photographer Peter Stackpole to Missoula, Montana, to investigate and report on what would be become known as the worst disaster in the history of the Forest Service's elite smoke jumpers, which caused the tragic deaths of 13 Forest Service firefighters. These men had parachuted into Mann Gulch in the Helena National Forest to fight a wildfire that "blew up," trapping them in a valley of fire. When we got to Missoula's airport, the base of the Forest Service's airborne "smoke jumpers," we boarded a large tri-motored Ford airplane operated by the same company that provided the aircraft and pilots for the Forest Service's airborne firefighters, and were soon flying over the Mann Gulch, the deep ravine where the smoke jumpers had been dropped and perished. The slow, lumbering, but very stable Ford tri-motor planes were designed to circle and hover close to the forest, dropping firefighters, supplies or water to douse the fire, depending on the mission. Our plane provided a low, stable platform for my photographer to take pictures of the devastated, burned-out site.

The next day, led by an experienced Forest Service guide, we walked into Mann Gulch and reenacted on film the scene and itinerary of the firefighters who had been overtaken by the wildfire. As our guide explained it, pointing out the positions of the smoke jumpers and the rogue, out-of-control wildfire, in this type of fire the intense heat can create its own windstorm that "blows up" the flames from the ground to the top of the tall trees. At this point the fire had "crowned," and, propelled by the inferno's generated winds, had raced with the speed of an express train along the tops of the trees and across the deep gulch, trapping the fire fighters. At this completely unexpected development, I was told, all but one of the 16 Forest servicemen had panicked and had tried to run up the steep slopes of the deep ravine. Two managed to find a narrow crevice to escape through, while two others who got out were so badly burned they died in a hospital the next day. The foreman of the crew had kept his head and built a backfire in a wide circle around the area; then he lay down with his jump coat covering him and was the lone survivor inside Mann Gulch.

Although the deadly gulch was devoid of all living plants and beings, I was warned to avoid stepping in the burnt, still smoldering holes where something had once grown because, deep down, lethal red-hot embers still lurked. Scattered around the sides of the gulch were the black, pitiful remains of deer, small rabbits, and other wild animals that had also been trapped by the indiscriminate, remorseless wildfire.

In writing this, I checked several Google accounts to corroborate my memory of this forest fire tragedy and, finding some discrepancies, managed to locate and talk to a retired Forest Service veteran who had interrogated the surviving smoke jumpers. I asked him why the foreman had not instructed the others to follow his example, to lie down within the safety circle he had created. He replied that he had asked that very question of one of the surviving smoke jumpers, who told him that the roar of the intense fire was so loud that neither he nor any of the others standing near the foreman could understand what he was saying. "I could see his mouth moving but I couldn't understand a word of what he was saying. He was a very quiet, soft-spoken man by nature," he added. "And just then, one of the other men shouted, 'I'm getting out of here' and started running up the slope and the others instinctively started to run, too. There was no discipline then, it all broke down, and it was every man for himself."

Although working for Life and covering assignments throughout the West Coast had much compensation and could be very rewarding, both personally and professionally, I found Hollywood and lot of the people I had to deal with phony. And my earlier sense of feeling rootless, restless, and generally dissatisfied with my life was growing. My father's unexpected and unsettling death at the age of 67—June 1949, and my return to Springfield for his funeral precipitated an enormous turn around in my life and my future.

When I returned to Springfield, I discovered that my father, incomprehensibly to me, had died without a will. The legal result left his estate divided among all of us, without any indications of his plans or wishes as to the future management or disposition of the farm, Industrial Buildings, Holyoke Machine and his other business interests. Heretofore, my father had made all major decisions about the family businesses, so the new, divided ownership posed a difficult problem that threatened what had always been a strong, cohesive, and close family union. The root of the problem lay in the fact that only three members of the family —Lillian, Julie, and Irwin—were directly involved and employed in the family businesses, while neither of my other two sisters, Toby and Lenore, my brother Bobby, or I had any interest in becoming involved. In the long discussions with my mother and siblings, it became clear that those in and those not in the businesses had different, and seriously conflicting views and objectives. For example, Lillian, Julian, and Irwin (and Lillian's husband, Archie, who also worked for Industrial) thought they were entitled to certain expenses being paid for by Industrial or Holyoke. But Toby, Lenore, Bobby, and I saw these expense account expenditures as a form of compensation that was coming out of companies in which we had a legal interest but were not sharing.

While these considerations were rather petty, they symbolized the new reality--we were not all benefiting equally. My mother was only interested in our reaching an agreement that would satisfy all of us. As I was an outsider, but had been regularly communicating with each one, I was seen as more neutral and in a position to try to mediate our differences.

Fortunately, I recalled hearing about a similar family problem from Calvin Stillman, a close friend from Army days. Their solution was the result of hiring a bright, highly respected New York lawyer, Lloyd Garrison, who had successfully resolved Calvin's family dispute. After telling them about the Stillmans' success, my mother and all my brothers and sisters agreed to ask Garrison to meet with us and help us resolve our family's inheritance differences. He did and, after conducting a fairassessment and appraisal of the family businesses, he drew up a proposal for equitable buyouts for Toby, Lenore, and me, and annual income payments to my mother and Bobby. Everyone ended up satisfied and Lillian and Julian were able to take over ownership control of Industrial, while Irwin received ownership control of Holyoke Machine.[19]

My father's death and my extended visit home had a major impact in other important ways. One of them was that I decided to do something about my discontent with my nomadic, socially rootless personal life during the last three years. Accordingly, when I telephoned Time-Life headquarters in New York that I was planning to leave, they asked me to come to New York, where they offered me a job as the Time-Life Bureau chief in Ottawa, Canada's capital.

But Ottawa, Canada, at that time seemed a very unlikely place to find that someone special I was looking for to love and share my life, and I declined the posting and resigned.

MY TIME WITH THE TIMES: 1949-1952

I was still in New York rethinking what I wanted to do with my dissatisfied, directionless state of mind. As my interest in working for The *New York Times* had not completely diminished, I decided that this would be a good time to re-explore the possibility of working there and to remain in New York where I had friends. My luck and destiny converged again, for the recent skills I acquired working at Life were now available at the very time when the editor of the Sunday *New York Times*, Lester Markel, was looking for a new picture editor to brighten up the appearance of the Times' Magazine, Book Review, and other Sunday feature sections. I met with Markel, had a mutually satisfactory interview with him and started work a week later as Sunday Picture Editor for The *New York Times*.

---

19. *To prevent some outside minority Holyoke stockholders from acquiring Toby's and my personal Holyoke shares, Irwin promised Toby that in addition to the market value payment for selling her personal shares of Holyoke he would continue to send her annually the gift of a wheel of the delicious Vermont cheese she loved. It had previously been sent by Holyoke Machine to family members every Christmas. I was also put on the Vermont-cheese gift list and continue to receive it from Holyoke's current owner, Irwin's son Jimmy.*

One of my first actions was to hire George Tames—a local D.C. Photographer who worked on assignments for the Times' Washington Bureau and whose work had impressed me—as a full-time employee of the Sunday Times Washington office. At that time, the Washington Bureau had only two competent and heroic, Markel-harassed correspondents, Cabell Phillips and Nona Brown.

For the next two and a half years I devoted my efforts to satisfying Markel's objective of beefing up and expanding the use of the Sunday Times' photographic coverage. In addition to my duties as picture editor, I also filled in as copy editor for stories that ran in the weekly Sunday Magazine, an assignment that I was to discover could prove very hazardous.

The unexpected hazard came in the form of one of the magazine's most talented and respected writers, Gilbert Millstein, who covered theatre and entertainment topics. It was on a day when an unusual amount of advertising copy made it necessary to open up more space on the pages carrying a story he had written. To solve this space problem, I was given his copy and told to make the editorial cuts required. I hadn't been working on the Times very long and knew Millstein only casually as a highly charged and self-confident colleague who was regarded as one of the magazine's best, but touchiest, writers. So, while I was aware that the necessary cuts might not please him, I was completely unprepared for the fiery, outraged Gil Millstein who came storming into my office waving the revised pages of his article. He was so angry that he was sputtering as he confronted me at my desk, shouting, "What in hell do you think you're doing cutting my story! Who do you think you are?" I tried to appease him by explaining there was nothing wrong with his writing, that it was a great piece, but the unexpected need for advertising space required that cuts be made.

Millstein was so mad he was not listening to what I was saying. His face deeply flushed and his eyes glaring, he reached down and picked up a heavy glass inkwell sitting on my desk and raised it up over his head. For a moment I was sure he was going to hurl the inkwell at me, but a split second later, as he realized from my tightened facial muscles and widened eyes what I was expecting, his arm froze. I could see him struggling to think of the most insulting, devastating comment to express of the depth his contempt for my editing and me. And then a change in his expression signaled he had found it. "You! You! You! YOU belong on Madison Avenue!" he snarled almost spitting the words out. He then, reluctantly put the threatening inkwell back on my desk, turned and strode dramatically out of my office. In time I managed to establish a working rapport with him and never experienced that kind of unpleasant encounter with any other person at the Times. In fact, I made some very good friends there.

While Markel turned out to be a very contentious and difficult editor for many of the Sunday Department's employees, and for those daily Times staffers who would be called on to write special articles for the Sunday Magazine and Review of the Week sections, I developed a harmonious working relationship with him. I attribute a large part of my success to the fact that Times personnel confronted by his extremely unreasonable behavior, would quietly accept Markel's criticism of their work. I would argue vigorously with him and defend my work and decisions, and Markel seemed to respect me for that. I also found that working at the Times was especially rewarding because of the high quality of professionalism and sense of camaraderie among my co-workers. Dan Schwartz, Markel's deputy, who, despite the abuse he silently suffered from Markel, was a model of gentle supervision and support for every Sunday department employee. I also met two newly employed members of the Review of the Week Sunday section who became very good friends in Washington and who achieved outstanding journalistic acclaim as nationally respected columnists, Anthony Lewis and Joseph Kraft.

Again I had found that living alone in a dreary hotel room, and then in a small apartment, without anyone close or special in my limited social life, began to take its toll on my satisfaction with life after my workday ended. And my sense of restlessness returned. Moreover, while I had liked and felt journalistically fulfilled working at the Times with the many interesting, talented people there, I could not see myself settling down in New York or commuting by train to the suburbs for the next 20 or 30 years as many of my co-workers were expecting to do. More important was my lack of success in meeting or establishing any close, personal relationship with the woman missing in my life—someone who was attractive, intelligent, and compatible—in short, someone I would want to marry, have children with and settle down. Despite the exciting jobs and rewarding work I had had, I realized that I was living an essentially empty and incomplete existence.

But my run of luck, facilitated by the ties from my Cleveland years were to appear again when Clayton Fritchey telephoned me in early March 1952. He was now in Washington, serving as a special assistant and Director of Information for the Secretary of Defense, General George Marshall. He wanted me to come and help him at the Pentagon by taking on the task of Information Officer for the increasingly important U.S. -European alliance in the Cold War against Russia's Communist expansion.

MY STINT AT THE PENTAGON:
1952

I had essentially accomplished the mission Markel had given me at the Times and my work now was becoming rather routine and less interesting, so I was ready for a change and for a new challenge and, hopefully, adventure. When I called Clayton back to tell him I would be willing to leave the Times and join him in Washington, he told me he would be sending me a pre-requisite Federal Department of Defense employment application to fill out. He was confident that my previous experience in journalism and as a Federal public information officer would qualify me amply for the Pentagon position. In addition, the highly sensitive and classified nature of the NATO and Military Assistance information to which I would require access would necessitate a comprehensive background and character national security investigation, covering my past life. He was sure I would have no problem there and that my law enforcement and military service record should help facilitate and speed up my clearance.

Working at the Pentagon in the Office of the Secretary of Defense was a totally different and exciting experience, as well as a snapshot course on how an enormous, highly centralized government bureaucracy operates. My job as Information Officer for NATO turned out to be both challenging and adventurous, both aspects I found very appealing. My first assignment was to meet a group of ten visiting journalists from several European countries on their arrival in the U.S. and take them by private Air Force passenger plane, on an orientation trip covering the East Coast and the Midwest. We visited selected military and naval bases, the TVA, and various sites and cities chosen to acquaint them with America's industrial, cultural, and military capabilities, as well to give them a picture of how Americans live.

Another assignment and role was that of information officer for the Department of Defense (DOD) Military Assistance project, which had been established to supply military arms and equipment to strengthen the various NATO countries' defensive capabilities against Russian threats. My experience here would lead to my questioning 1) the competence of the major general, a reserve National Guard officer, who headed the program, and 2) the value of my own activities. It started when our 8:00 a.m. meeting at the Pentagon was being briefed on the status of various categories of Army, Navy and Air Force armaments and equipment which were being sent to our NATO ally, Italy. At the end of the report, the General nodded approvingly and asked if there were any questions, at which point the State Department representative spoke up. "General," he said, "We have just received some reliable and disturbing reports about the coming Italian national elections which indicate that the Communist party could win and control the government. So all these tanks, ships and aircraft we are sending them will end up in the hands of a Communist government." There was a sudden silence, broken by the heavy thud of the General's fist pounding the table and the angry, emphatic no-nonsense tone of his response: "Our job is to get this hardware into the hands of our clients. And if we have to worry about such extraneous political considerations, all I can say is that's a hell of a way to run a railroad! Now let's get on with the job of delivering this military materiel," he ordered, rising to his feet and indicating to the astonished committee members that the conversation and meeting were over.

When I first started my dual job as Information Officer for NATO and Military Assistance, I thought it would be very useful to learn more about the background of these two assignments, the major problems that had arisen, and the decisions that had been made to solve them. I thought that the best way to become informed and up-to-date would be to read through the Information Office's chronological files. Therefore, for the next few weeks, after I finished work and the rest of the staff had left, I spent my early evenings in the file room catching up on what had happened before I came. But my eager-beaver efforts to make myself better prepared to perform my job got an unexpected and unpleasant jolt when my immediate boss, a former CBS radio correspondent whom I had known in Geneva, surprised me one night in the file room and demanded to know what I was doing there. When I tried to explain that I was just trying to improve my capabilities for doing my job, he rejected my reasons and accused me of trying to get his job. My self-imposed studies had created suspicion and mistrust on his part and a mutual tension that made working together uncomfortable. So, when I lost my confidence and respect for the commanding General as well as the military assistance program, I thought I was getting the message that it was time for me to leave the Pentagon. Since Clayton had left DOD several weeks earlier to work for President Truman as an administrative assistant at the White House, I felt no further obligation to stay, and resigned that spring in 1952.

CAMPAIGNING FOR ADLAI STEVENSON 1952

Chapter 6

Let's talk sense to the American people. Let's tell them the truth, that there are no gains without pains, that we are now on the eve of great decisions, not easy decisions like resistance when you are attacked, but a long patient costly struggle which alone can assure triumph over the great enemies of man—war, poverty and tyranny—and the assault upon human dignity which is the most grievous consequences of each.

Adlai Stevenson, 1952 acceptance speech

In 1952, several days after Illinois Governor Adlai Stevenson was nominated as the Democratic Party's presidential candidate, Clayton Fritchey called me to say he was in Springfield, Illinois, and needed me out there to help him get Stevenson elected. The last time I had talked to Clayton he was leaving for Chicago on an assignment from President Truman to get a very reluctant Stevenson to accept the Democratic party's nomination. Truman viewed Stevenson, then Governor of Illinois, as the Democratic Party's best presidential candidate for the coming election. As Clayton explained his move to Springfield, right after his nomination Stevenson had met with the President in Washington to tell him he had no experience running a national campaign and needed help. Truman then assigned Clayton and David Bell, another personal assistant, to help him. Clayton was going to be a principal assistant to Stevenson's Campaign Manager, Wilson Wyatt, and would deal with the overall broad public information and public relations issues. I would work directly with him. Adlai's current press officer would continue to handle day-to-day press needs.

Democrats throughout the country were ecstatic about Adlai Stevenson. Mary McGrory echoed this in her *Washington Post* column right after his presidential acceptance speech at the Democratic Convention when she wrote: "Politically speaking, it was the Christmas morning of our lives." His candidacy brought many people into politics who previously considered it a corrupt and smarmy field. He was the personification of the best of the old fashioned highly educated WASP world. He was stylish, articulate and amiable. His wit was legend as was his elegant oratory and his ability to gather the devotion and respect from the best and the brightest to work for him, often at great financial sacrifice.

Adlai cared deeply about his mission and particularly about the way he would articulate it—often editing his speeches up until the very last minute. He had a gift with words and was an eloquent speaker. And he loved the attention of attractive women and he seemed irresistible to them. Fame rested lightly on his shoulders and he was at heart a no-nonsense man. I had enormous personal admiration for him. His acceptance speech at the Democratic Convention electrified the country--including me:

> *When the tumult and the shouting die, when the bands are gone and the lights are dimmed, there is the stark reality of responsibility in an hour of history haunted with those gaunt, grim specters of strife, dissension, and materialism at home, and ruthless, inscrutable, and hostile power abroad. The ordeal of the twentieth century – the bloodiest, most turbulent age of the Christian era – is far from over. Sacrifice, patience, understanding, and implacable purpose may be our lot for years to come. ... Let's talk sense to the American people! Let's tell them the truth, that there are no gains without pains, that we are now on the eve of great decisions.*

When I arrived in the quiet small town of Springfield, Illinois, Clayton led me to Stevenson's campaign headquarters, a white, unassuming, four-bedroom house close to the Governor's mansion where Stevenson and his core staff of Bill Blair, Carl McGowan, and Newton Minow were located. "The Governor has never experienced the staffing or housing requirements of a presidential campaign, and he thinks this house can take care of Wyatts's campaign staff. The downstairs rooms will serve as our offices, and we can all sleep in the bedrooms upstairs."

Seeing the astonished look on my face, Clayton explained with a straight face, "Adlai has never run a national operation before and he's very worried about the money. He wants to run a frugal campaign." Then he added matter-of-factly, "I think he's going to discover the reality very quickly," and led me to a small pine desk in the living room, "This will be your desk."

I sat down on a living-room chair with an embroidered seat and pulled out the top center drawer of the desk. It was jammed tight with unopened letters addressed to Governor Stevenson. I opened one: It was from a prominent Hollywood producer and enclosed a check for $10,000. I opened several more, all with personal congratulatory notes and containing campaign checks that had been sitting there. I quickly glanced at them to confirm their contents, before I put them back into their envelopes, put the envelopes back in the drawer, and closed the drawer. I would have to find out how long they had been there and get someone responsible to start processing, recording, and answering them.

It would not be long before the logistic and many other operational de-mands of managing a national presidential campaign brought increasing numbers of essential campaign staffers to Springfield. Wyatt had to rent a large block of rooms in a nearby hotel for offices. The unassuming white house was no longer big enough.

Stevenson's first campaign stop was a disaster. In addition to the extremely small gathering, the public address system wasn't working. The local campaign representatives and workers were insufficiently trained and equipped to turn out large enough crowds. My first major assignment was to prepare guidelines for advance personnel for future campaign appearances. They covered such basic needs as making sure there were sufficient amounts of campaign literature, buttons, and other campaign paraphernalia to hand out and ensuring there was not only a working public address system but an emergency backup as well. This was only the beginning of the innumerable Herculean tasks awaiting the relatively few—largely volunteer—members of Wyatt's personal staff, who had been brought to Stevenson's campaign headquarters to work on the first Democratic presidential campaign in 20 years in which an incumbent president was not the nominee of the party.

During the 20 years prior to Stevenson's 1952 campaign, Democratic presidential campaigns had had the tremendous advantage of possessing the invaluable experience and resources of the White House. Roosevelt and Truman's campaign resources included the advance planning, logistic, travel, traffic and crowd control, and protective capabilities of the Secret Service. In addition, they could draw on the resources of the cabinet secretaries and their satellite agencies in the research and preparation of reports on important domestic and foreign campaign issues, and even in writing position papers and speeches.

Unlike the well-funded campaign of the opposition Republican candidate, General Dwight Eisenhower, Stevenson's campaign staff was enormously handicapped and regularly frustrated by the volatility and inadequacy of its financial support. This critical, continuous shortage of funds was aggravated by the hostility and unreliable support of the chairman of the Democratic National Committee, which often resulted in frustrating situations where Stevenson's campaign staff could never be sure until the very last minute if there would be enough money available to buy national air time for a major speech.

One serious obstacle we discovered was that Stevenson's access to the public was severely limited by a widespread—virtually national— blackout by many newspapers and radio and TV stations of news about his campaign. His statements and positions on major issues seemed to be ignored. A Stevenson campaign team documented this by checking and comparing the relative amounts of space and time the respective newspaper and radio-TV news devoted to Stevenson and Eisenhower. Time and again Stevenson made a major campaign speech carried as a small paragraph on a hard-to-find inside page, while a minor Eisen-

Arnold Boglyn - a friend when a feller needed a friend

Adlai 2. Stevenson.

Adlai Stevenson campaigning.   *Photo by Cornell Capa*

hower statement was highlighted and run on page one. The immense
disparity in news coverage and the prevalent, strong pro-Republican
bias led Adlai to give a major campaign speech on "America's One
Party Press," and the inherent danger to a free Democratic society of
a press dominated by one political party. It is ironic that not only did
very few Americans ever hear or read about that speech and warning,
but ever since then, perhaps as a retaliatory, preemptive strike on the

part of conservatives, we keep hearing about the terrible "liberal" bias in today's news media.

The reality, of course, has always been that while there are certainly individual reporters and writers who may be "liberals," the far more important reality back in 1952 and I believe even more true and significant in 2008, is that the news media of America have been principally owned or controlled—and increasingly consolidated—by very conservative Americans. Moreover, the Right-leaning owners tend to see and operate their newspapers, radio, and TV stations as bottom-line dominated businesses, with little if any interest in a "well informed public." Their editorial policies and columnists reflect these conservative Republican-party views. While there may not be any direct orders handed down to the working reporters and managing staff, there's an old newspaper saying that is worth quoting here: "The milkman's horse doesn't have to be told where to stop." With the exception of the essentially unique family-owned "liberal" *New York Times* and *Washington Post*, there are very few influential news organizations now remaining in the U.S. that do not tend to reflect essentially the same asserted and widely supported conservative political views found on Murdoch's Wall Street Journal's editorial page or his Fox Network news and a multitude of other publications.

The so-called liberal *Washington Post* and *New York Times* are rarities and exist only because they are the very uncommon remainders of the once-upon-a-time, independent, family-owned newspapers that had flourished throughout the U.S. And the Post and Times exist only because they possess sufficient resources outside the meager earnings that can be derived from a newspaper alone today and because their owner families are willing, in effect, to subsidize their family-tradition newspapers through earnings from their more prosperous TV and other holdings.

A most important achievement and long-lasting consequence of Stevenson's '52 campaign was its impact on multitudes of well-educated, liberal-minded young Americans who had heretofore been turned off by politics and politicians. Stevenson's personality, politics and eloquent speeches attracted and magnetized them and motivated large numbers of them to become actively involved in political affairs—local, state, and

federal. Many of these Stevenson Democrats would become major appointees and stars in President John F. Kennedy's administration.

A special bonus of my experience was to meet and make new and lasting good friends with Stevenson aides like Bill Blair[20] and Newt Minow
and his wife Jo, as well as many other talented people who worked self-
lessly, harmoniously, and tirelessly together in a common cause. They
included very special people like Lou Cowan, who was Stevenson's TV
and radio advisor, a creative, successful TV and radio industry figure
who, with his wife Polly, would become two of the most wonderful
close friends I ever had.

Clayton Fritchey, my boss, was born a political optimist and throughout
the campaign he maintained not only a remarkably high level of energy
in his morning-to-late-at-night activities, but also his indomitable confidence in Adlai's victory. He was confidant and enthusiastic despite the
many discouraging campaign polls, for which he expressed strong disdain by pointing to the shameful 1948 predictions that Dewey would
demolish Truman. Thus when Election Day arrived with no more
campaign activities listed on that day's agenda, I expected I would have
a free, quiet day ahead. I had spent the previous day putting the finishing touches on the special elections communications room I had set up
to monitor the national election results as they became available, and
didn't expect anything important to happen until early evening when
the first results would come in.

When I met Clayton for breakfast, I mentioned that it was quite a
change to have nothing to do today and was very surprised when he
disagreed, saying, "You're mistaken. We have an important job to do
today." When I asked him what it was he said, "We have to prepare
and brief the Governor on the questions the reporters will be asking
after it's announced he's won the election." I looked at him closely,
trying to find some sign that he was joking, but his face and expression
only showed that he was really serious. He had convinced himself that
Stevenson was going to win the election. Thus we spent election day in

20. *Bill Blair became Ambassador to Denmark and the Phillipines during the
Kennedy Administration, and Newton Minow, Chairman of the Federal Communications Commission.*

Clayton's office, discussing and listing the most likely questions about Adlai's immediate personal plans and any announcements he might wish to make about cabinet or other top-level or personal staff appointments. I still have that list of questions. Then, after an early dinner Clayton, Wilson Wyatt and a couple of his top political advisors and I made our way up to the special communications room to await the traditionally early election results of a special Kentucky precinct which Wyatt had discovered had always voted for the winning Presidential candidate.

Thirty minutes after our arrival, Wyatt started to check his watch, waiting for the call from a man to whom he had given the number of a special telephone I had had installed. This fellow was to tell us the results of the voting in that Delphic, early closing Kentucky precinct. I was feeling very tense and the sudden, loud ring of that phone startled me. I turned to watch a very nervous Wyatt grab the phone and, pulling it up to his ear and mouth he uttered a sharp acknowledgement: "Wyatt!!" The rest of us maintained a dead silence as Wyatt listened for what seemed like an eternity, before he turned slowly toward us and, carefully putting the phone down, told us in a very sad voice, "It's all over."

ON THE AIR WITH TV & RADIO
1953-54

Chapter 7

*Television is and will be a main factor in influencing
the values and moral standards of society.*
  Pilkington Report, Great Britain,
  Committee on Broadcasting, 1960

After the disappointment and inevitable let-down following Stevenson's
defeat by Eisenhower, I returned to Washington and spent the next few
days trying to figure out my next step, beginning with finding a suffi-
ciently interesting, if not adventurous, new job that also offered a living
wage. So it was a very welcome surprise when Lou Cowan telephoned
me with an exciting job offer. He was starting a new NBC/TV talk
show in Washington, to be called "Meet the Veep," with Alben Barkley, Truman's recent Vice-President—formerly the veteran Democratic
senator from Kentucky and longtime Senate majority leader. Would I
be interested in producing the program and writing the script, and also
be his company's representative in Washington for contemplated, future TV-radio projects? My response was an immediate, "Yes, I would."

Four years earlier, I was part of a small Life magazine and NBC group
that teamed up in 1948 to televise the historic first televised Presidential convention, the GOP's in Philadelphia. Because the technology at
that time involved cameras that were so large and immobile, my job as
a reporter required me to bring the important political leaders we wanted to interview, such as Senator Robert Taft and Gov. Harold Stassen,
over to the fixed cameras with their fist-sized cables. (It was some years
before the cameras were small and light enough to be carried to the
interviewees.) Moreover, the number of Americans who owned TV sets
then was so small that appearing on TV was not seen as worthwhile to
many of the personalities in demand. An additional constraint in 1948

was the heat of the essential TV lights in a convention hall without air conditioning on one of the hottest summers on record. Despite the difficulties, I was impressed with the medium's enormous potential to reach and inform the public. Now I looked forward to returning to work with a much improved and mobile TV technology and a substantially larger, more receptive audience.

THE VICE PRESIDENT

Vice President Alben Barkley.

Meet the Veep was one of the first TV political talk shows. "The Veep" was the name Barkley's grandchildren gave him while he was Truman's Vice-President. Although he was much admired by the Democratic party, he was denied the nomination for President because of his advanced age—he was 70 years old. He returned to his home state of Kentucky, but found retirement dull, so I believe he relished the idea of the new radio show. I found him to be warm, homey, immensely likeable, and a joy to work with. He personified my image of the old-fashioned, Southern politician, born in a log cabin, who loved talking and mixing with people. He was a natural storyteller and had a treasury of gentle, delightful but effectively meaningful tales that carried a message.

I started each week's preparatory meeting by bringing him a bottle of his favorite bourbon, Wild Turkey. After he had downed a few leisurely shots of bourbon, and was "warmed up," I would start discussing with him that week's program and guest, usually a major political personage, such as Senator Robert Taft, the Republican majority leader in the Senate. Soon Barkley would be recounting one of his great stories, which I would record along with the many others I had previously heard. Later I would select one that seemed appropriate to insert into my scripted interview for that week's program.

One of my favorites was of the country preacher who was devoting his Sunday sermon on the evil of hatred, for the soul of anyone who hates his fellow man will be corroded. Then, looking over his attentive, assembled parishioners, he asked, "Tell me, is there anyone here in this great congregation, who can stand up and tell me that he does not hate anyone?" After a long silence, the preacher was about to give up when far back in the last pew he saw an extremely elderly figure with thinning white hair who was struggling to stand up. When the old gentleman was finally erect, holding on for support to the back of the pew in front of him, he called out in a trembling but triumphant voice, "I can!" Greatly pleased, the preacher asked him, "Tell me, my friend, and tell all your fellow parishioners here, how old you are?" And the white-haired old man replied in his quavering voice, "I'm 97." And the enraptured preacher turned and addressed the entire congregation saying, "Isn't that wonderful! This remarkable man has lived 97 years and can say he doesn't hate anyone in this world!" Then, turning back to the aged, hate-free parishioner, the preacher called out, "Tell me, and tell everyone here, how you have been able to live all these 97 years and say that you don't hate anybody?" Whereupon, the old man drew himself up straight and with a happy smile on his face replied in a clear, loud voice, "I outlived the sons-of-bitches!"

I quickly discovered that "The Veep" was very sensitive about how the public would respond to his folksy tales and, beginning with his very first TV show, he objected when I told him I wanted him to tell one of his "stories" at a designated point in the planned interview. "No," he would tell me. "I don't want everyone to think I'm just a jokester." And each time I would tell him, "Senator, you are not telling this story just to make a joke. You are telling it in the tradition of Abraham Lincoln, who told similar stories in order to make a very important, serious point more understandable." And each time Barkley would sit quietly for a few seconds, thinking it over, then he would relax, drop his objection and nod his approval of Lincoln technique.

Barkley loved being in politics, but he told me sadly that he was now out, and when I asked if he ever went back to the Senate to see his former associates, he shook his head slowly. "No," he replied. "No, I don't want them to think they can cast an old dog a bone." However, Meet the Veep created so much favorable publicity in his home state that he was encouraged to run again for the Senate in the next election and won handily. How fitting that a man who loved his public service so much would "die with his boots on." In 1956, while giving a speech at the 1956 Mock Convention held at Washington and Lee University in Virginia, he died of a massive heart attack moments after explaining he was now a freshman senator and therefore would not accept the invitation to sit in the front row of the Senate, declaring, "I'm glad to sit on the back row, for I would rather be a servant in the House of the Lord than to sit in the seats of the mighty."

Meet the Veep was followed by a weekly NBC national radio network news program, Report from the White House, in which a newsworthy Eisenhower cabinet member, provided to us regularly by the President's press secretary, Jim Haggerty, was interviewed by NBC veteran correspondent Ray Scherer[21] and senior White House reporter Merriam Smith of United Press. I produced the program and also wrote the

script for the questions Ray and Merriam asked. From time to time we included Ned Brooks, a respected Scripps-Howard Syndicate journalist, to enliven and provide variety to the interrogations.

At that time in Washington, the White House and top government officials generally paid little attention to what the media was reporting, except for nationally syndicated columnists and the network anchors. This would change when Kennedy

Ray Scherer, NBC correspondent.

became President, for he had many good friends in the Washington press corps and habitually read the news first thing in the morning. If he read or heard a critical story about a Federal department or agency, he would quickly pick up the phone and call the government official

21. *Ray and Maudie Scherer later became very close personal friends and country neighbors in Virginia's Rappahannock County.*

concerned to ask for an explanation. As a result of the President's interest, government and diplomatic officials and Washington's social hostesses started paying close attention to Washington journalists and what they were writing or saying, and media representatives suddenly found themselves courted and treated as VIPs.

When NBC did not renew Report From the White House, Lou Cowan asked if I would be interested in producing for NBC a new TV program entitled Conversation, which would initially air locally in New York, with Ben Grauer. Grauer was known for announcing the Sunday NBC Symphony radio and TV broadcasts and for serving as the host of NBC's annual New Year's eve live broadcasts from New York City's Times Square. Since I had no other Washington projects I would prefer to do, and Lou mentioned other TV and radio programs in the planning stage, I agreed to move to New York again and be the producer for Conversation.[22]

The concept of Conversation was to gather a small group of literate, witty personalities, and conduct a friendly, relaxed discussion on a selected topic in a living room setting. The participants would be good listeners and treat each other's views with civility. To my great distress, Ben Grauer turned out to be a terrible moderator— highly competitive, if not jealous of the others' intellectual capabilities. As a result, he tried to dominate the program and conversations, constantly intent on showing how smart and clever he was, and often interrupting a delightful or fascinating speaker to move the conversation onto a completely different subject. Unfortunately, we were stuck with him. Happily, we were rescued when the sponsor decided not to renew the program, and Lou managed to switch the program to NBC's national radio network and persuaded Clifton "Kip" Fadiman, a genial critic, writer, and raconteur, as well as editor of the very successful Book-of-the-Month Club, to serve as the host/moderator. Kip had previously achieved national acclaim as the moderator of Information Please, a popular, somewhat

---

22. *It wasn't until later that I learned that Lou Cowan was, in the words of Time magazine, the "most prolific independent radio and TV package producer in the business." This reputation began in 1940 with the long running program Quiz Kids, and continued to grow as he created some 40 shows for radio and TV, including Stop the Music and the $64,000 Question.*

intellectual radio quiz show in
which listeners called in questions
designed to outsmart a panel
of celebrities.

The program's frequent guests
included sophisticated, erudite
and entertaining luminaries such
as Marc Connelly, the multi-
talented critic, writer, director,
performer, lyricist, and producer,
and Bennett Cerf, whose puns
and performances as a TV panel-
ist delighted viewers of What's
My Line, who was also the highly
successful founder/publisher of

Clifton Fadiman, host of "Conversation."

Random House. I discovered that it was not easy to find accomplished
and articulate participants who not only had something especially interesting to say, but would also be supportive (and quiet) listeners who
did not intrude inappropriately when someone else was speaking. I discovered a large percentage of otherwise qualified would-be participants
had very strong opinions, as well as weak discipline, over their driving
desire to break in and present their own thoughts and views on the
current subject, or even introduce a completely different subject. Like
Grauer, they were not able to just sit quietly while someone else was
talking. So when I interviewed other potential guests to appear on the
program, I made sure they would be good listeners as well as articulate,
well-informed conversationalists.[23]

But Fadiman and the star conversationalists we had on the first show
were a joy and pleasure, with the result that the top entertainment publication, Variety, reported: "This week's premiere was a sheer delight
from opening to close. . . The foursome seemed to be having the time
of their lives, as bon mots, witticisms, gentle barbs and glib commen-

---

23. *These days, sad to say, virtually all the broadcast "talk" shows are loud,
uncivil shouting contests, where no one is allowed to finish more than a few sentences before being interrupted or shouted down by one of the other participants,
who most likely will also be interrupted.*

tary were scattered all over the place." (I was listed as the director while Lou Cowan was credited as producer.) I was very proud to learn later that Conversation, which Polly Cowan had taken over after I left, won the annual Peabody Award, the most prestigious award for achievement in international radio and television broadcasting.

Working with Lou Cowan and the friendship that I developed with him and his equally endearing and fantastic wife, Polly[24], was one of the most rewarding times of my life. Lou was an exceptionally talented and generous man and widely respected for his integrity, both in his private and business life. Consequently, it was one of the great tragedies and ironies of the times that, after he became President of the CBS Television Network, following the enormous success of his TV show, the $64,000 Question, a Congressional investigation revealed the mendacious, manipulative activities of Revlon, the program's sponsor, in controlling the quiz show's winners. The resulting scandal terminated Lou's TV program, ended his tenure as CBS president and cruelly wounded and scarred his remaining years.

A second ironic tragedy would be that the man who had pioneered and created so many entertaining TV programs would have his own and his wife's lives cut short by the very instrument of his success. A defective TV set started an electrical fire, which sent a fatal cloud of carbon dioxide up the stairs to the bedroom where Lou and Polly were sleeping.

---

24. *The friendship between the Sagalyns and the Cowans strengthened during summers at Martha's Vineyard where we both had friends in common. We followed with tremendous admiration Polly Cowan's incredibly courageous, dangerous civil rights activities in the "Wednesdays in Mississippi" trips she organized with the legendary Dorothy Height, President of the National Council of Negro Women. Started in 1964 to "create bridges of understanding across regional, racial and class lines," this civil rights project organized teams of Northern women of different races and faiths for weekly visits to Mississippi to develop working relationships with their Southern peers to advance social and racial justice, and later to start workshops to help poor black and white women learn how to help themselves and achieve economic self-sufficiency.*

LUMBERING IN OREGON:
1954-1957

Chapter 8

*A good man is the best friend, and therefore soonest to be chosen, longer
to be retained and, indeed, never to be parted with.*
    Jeremy Taylor

I loved working with Lou Cowan and enjoyed producing and writing
Meet the Veep and Report from the White House in Washington. I
was having a good time turning out the weekly TV (and later radio
network) program Conversation. But one overcast October morning in
1954 I woke up alone in my small, relatively dreary apartment to realize again that I did not enjoy living in New York City and I was lonely.
This was the same unhappy reality that led me to leave The *New York
Times* to work at the Pentagon in Washington.

Dan Goldy.

I talked with Dan Goldy, my former Cleveland roommate and close friend in Washington, who was a top assistant to the Assistant Secretary of Interior, C. Girard "Jebby" Davidson, and was now living in Portland, Oregon. Jebby had appointed Dan to be Regional Director for the Northwest of the Interior Department's new Bureau of Land Management, where he was responsible for managing Interior's millions of acres of Federal timber and grazing lands. When I mentioned my dissatisfaction with living in New York, Dan told me he was leaving his job at Interior and planning to go into the lumber business. He urged me to leave New York and join him as a partner in Oregon. "You'll love it here," he said, "There are a lot of wonderful people and attractive women I can introduce you to."

The timing was right and the prospect of starting a challenging new venture with Dan in Oregon was irresistible. "You're on," I told him. "I'm coming out to Oregon."

A friend is defined by Webster's Encyclopedic Dictionary as "a person attached to another by feelings of affection or personal regard" and Dan Goldy was certainly that and much more. We met in Cleveland in 1942, through a mutual friend, Henry Morgenthau (son of the then Secretary of the Treasury), who was working for Cleveland's Public Housing agency. Dan was at that time the deputy director of the Federal War Manpower Commission's regional office in Cleveland, and was looking for someone to share his downtown two-bedroom apartment. I found him to be extremely bright, articulate and with the capability to be a warm dependable friend. Fortuitously, I was then searching for lodgings closer in town, and as Dan and I seemed to hit it off, we decided to join forces and become roommates. The outbreak of WWII separated us. Dan was commissioned by the Navy and sent to Pearl Harbor, where he distinguished himself fighting bureaucratic waste and questionable practices by top Naval brass, while I ended up in the Army and service in Europe. We were fated to meet again and develop a lifetime friendship and partnership in Washington, D.C. and Portland, Oregon.

Although Dan became my closest, most trusted friend, in many ways we were very different. He was physically robust and exulted in outdoor activities, and spent as much time as possible at his ranch in

Bend, riding his horse over mountain trails or skiing down Oregon park slopes. He projected a commanding presence and enjoyed being the center of attention. He had thoughtful and strong opinions on almost every subject and was extremely articulate in expressing them and enjoyed debating those who did not agree. He was knowledgable about many subjects ranging from land management to international trade and his views were sought and respected. He was a trustworthy, reliable friend who could always be counted on to follow through.

The next two years in Oregon provided the relaxing environment, challenges and revitalization I needed to think more clearly and productively about myself, and what I wanted to do to fulfill my life. As part of this process, I devoted several months to learning about the lumber business for I was now a partner in Mountain Fir Lumber Company's mill in Grants Pass near the California border.

Mountain Fir Lumber Company mill, Independence, Oregon.

In Oregon I also became friends with Dick Neuberger, a nature and environmental writer and state senator, and his wife, Maurine, a state representative. As Democrats and liberals, these two people were a decided minority in the Oregon legislature. Dick was a natural politician who loved to interact with people and had decided to run in 1954 for the U.S. Senate against an entrenched Republican, Guy Cordon. In

Oregon in those days, the cost of conducting a political campaign for the U.S. Senate was relatively modest, but the difference in resources available to a Democrat like Dick were like night and day compared with those of the incumbent Republican U.S. Senator.

Senator elect Dick Neuberger checking election returns with Arnold.

Not only was Oregon largely a Republican state, but the Federal government's ownership and regulation of millions of acres vitally affected the state's economy and Dick's opponent was Chairman of the powerful Senate Interior Committee, which had oversight over many of these public lands. When Neuberger entered the Senate race, his announcement was met with incredulity and predictions of certain defeat. Aided by his wife Maurine and a tiny, dedicated, campaign staff, Neuberger and his supporters worked hard despite their limited resources. When the results of the ballots were announced, the incumbent Republican senator was called the winner. It was late at night and Dick and I were the only ones left as the rest of his campaign staff acknowledged it was all over and left. However, Dick did not concede and continued to make calls to the various precincts where he had not received the strong support he expected. But no one was answering. Suddenly he made a phone connection and was told the poll workers were so tired they had stopped counting and gone home. He was informed that a lot of uncounted ballots remained and the workers would return in the morning to finish counting. The final results weren't in yet and there was still a chance.

Dick and I stayed up all night and were among the first to get the tallies of the uncounted ballots, which gave him the additional votes needed to win the hotly contested Senate seat! It was a remarkable victory that brought Dick, Maurine and me, and his small campaign staff the exhilarating joy that comes only to those rare few who win an extremely lengthy and unexpected long-shot campaign, in this case a seat in the U.S. Senate. My first telephone call was to my close friend and mentor, Clayton Fritchey, then serving as the Deputy Chairman of the Democratic National Committee, to report the unexpected, but highly prized, much needed new Democratic vote in the precariously divided Senate.

Once elected, Neuberger brought to the Senate a pioneering voice for environmental protection, civil rights, conflict-of-interest laws, and reform to equalize the cost of Presidential and Congressional campaigns. We corresponded frequently until he died in office in 1960 from cancer. At his death, The *New York Times* wrote, "Perhaps the one thing on which political friends and foes of Senator Neuberger were able to agree was that he could not be ignored....", noting that he always took a position on a controversial subject—which could not and cannot be said for most U.S. Senators. His wife, Maurine, succeeded him as Senator, but after one term she refused to run again. telling me she hated the enormous amount of time and effort that had to be spent fund raising and campaigning instead of on important and more interesting national issues.

In 1956 when Stevenson decided to run again for President and it was too late to register him on Oregon's Presidential primary ballot, I helped organize and win another political long-shot: a statewide, write-in to contest the Democratic Party nomination of Tennessee Senator Estes Kefauver, who had built up a strong following and his name on Oregon's primary ballot. Stevenson's visit to Portland later provided an unforgettable experience when I accompanied him on a trip to nearby snow-covered Mt. Hood. The U.S. park ranger took us, along with Alf Corbett, head of Stevenson's Oregon citizens committee and a Magnum photographer on a sightseeing trip in a Snowcat, a heavy, enclosed tractor-driven vehicle. In the course of our sightseeing, a sudden wind sprang up, and in the blinding snow the Snowcat suddenly plunged down an unseen ravine and tumbled over several times before stopping at the bottom. While we were all shaken up, no one suffered any serious injuries. But a dramatic picture of the upset Snowcat and us trudging up the steep slope appeared in the national press and led to an anxious telephone call from my family to confirm that I had escaped unscathed.

Survivors of a Snowcat's 35 ft. plunge into a deep revine on Mt. Hood, Oregon. L. to R. Arnold, Forest Ranger and Adlai Stevenson. © Magnum

In Cleveland, Dan had met and married an attractive Women's Army Corps (WAC) Captain, Genevieve Rusttvelt ("Rusty"), and a great deal of my time was spent accompanying Dan and Rusty on trips visiting our lumber company's other two closer mills in Independence and Maupin. We were checking out available, potential tracts of privately owned or public tracts of timber that our mills could log and process in our mills. These sources were crucial for keeping our mills supplied since public timber sales by either the Interior Department's Bureau of Land Management or the Agriculture Department's Forest Service were always eagerly snapped up by competitive companies. Dan was constantly urging Joe, the chief executive of Mt. Fir Lumber, to buy and build up a large inventory of Douglas-fir and Ponderosa Pine trees, which our mills specialized in cutting to long dimensions. But he was unsuccessful since Joe could never understand that a much bigger profit was involved if we owned the timber that was cut in our mills. Trees were considered a nonrenewable commodity that received a special, low Federal tax depletion allowance, thus creating a bigger profit.

I was also an investor in oil and thermal energy ventures that were put together by "Jebby" Davidson, Dan's former boss at the Interior Department, who was now living in Portland with his second wife, Joan

Kaplan. (None of these ventures ever panned out.) Then Dan came up with a proposal for a new milling technique for producing high-value pine paneling from a low-valued species of tall, small-diameter pine, lodgepole pine, currently used primarily for telephone poles. This attracted the financial backing of Jack Kaplan, owner of Welch's Grape Juice and Jebby's father-in-law. We incorporated Western Forest Products, with me as secretary-treasurer, to carry out the lodgepole project, initially in Montana, which had very large tracts of lodgepole pine. After Jebby, Jack, Dan and I met with the U.S. Forest Service's regional director in Missoula to obtain his views and cooperation, Dan and I remained in Montana to scout out and identify the owners of large lodgepole timber holdings and a mill site in the Butte area that was accessible to competitive railroads. When Dan returned to Portland, I stayed on to spend the next week cruising the lodgepole pine tracts we had identified for potential acquisition.

During the many hundreds of miles I traveled, my most disappointing discovery was the abominable quality of food in Montana's small town restaurants. And when I finally decided I would just order eggs, thinking that was surely food they couldn't ruin, I learned I was wrong. I concluded that that no smart Montanans ate out. However, Montana's restaurants and lodgepole pine were to become moot when an associate of Dan's, who had been told about our venture, secretly tipped off and joined a rival Oregon timber company. Their competition for the limited, privately owned, lodgepole pine holdings caused the owners to raise the sales price so high that our venture became too risky to pursue.

I had been corresponding regularly with my mother and each winter I flew to a small resort in Arizona to visit her there where she found the climate beneficial for a respiratory ailment. Soon after the Montana venture collapsed and during a telephone conversation, my mother said she would like to visit me in Oregon. She had been worried about me, the last of her children to remain unmarried, and wanted to see where I was living. My move to Portland had been a welcome and relaxing change from New York and while I had still not met the woman with whom I wanted to share the rest of my life, I had made a lot of friends, largely through Dan or a former classmate and friend from Oberlin. In general, I was enjoying an agreeable social life. But I was delighted to see my mother and arranged to have her meet some of my friends and see the local "sights".

A few days after Mother's arrival, she complained about an eye problem, which was quickly diagnosed as a very serious detached retina. Treatment was still primitive and limited. A call to my sister Toby's husband, Malcolm, who was distinguishing himself as an eye surgeon in Springfield, led to quick action: I should immediately fly with my mother to Boston. There Dr. Stephen Schepens, who had pioneered a successful retina detachment procedure, had been alerted and would take care of her. The next day we were on a plane en route to Massachusetts General Hospital where Dr. Schepens operated on her and successfully reattached the torn retina, saving the sight in her eye.

When I returned to Portland, I was again forced to take stock of my own life and what I was accomplishing in Oregon. I had to acknowledge that despite the physical beauty of Oregon and the unique opportunities for enjoying its attractive quality of life—especially if one liked outdoor recreational activities such as skiing, hiking and riding—I found living in Portland pretty dull and lacking the stimulation and opportunities for adventure I had found in Cleveland and Washington. My good luck had not deserted me, for early in 1957 Clayton called me to return to Washington to join him and Phil Stern.

BACK TO JOURNALISM
1957-1960

Chapter 9

The basis of our government being the opinion of the people, the very first object should be to keep that right; and were it left to me to decide whether we should have a government without newspapers, or newspapers without a government, I should not hesitate a moment to prefer the latter.

Thomas Jefferson

NORTHERN VIRGINIA SUN

When I arrived in Washington in 1957, Clayton filled me in about the paper we were preparing to buy, the *Arlington Daily Sun*. It was a small newspaper—a circulation of only a few thousand with one employee—that was personally owned by the publisher of the nearby *Alexandria Gazette*, who was using the *Gazette*'s staff and press to publish the Sun. As a result of a successful lawsuit by the *Gazette*'s minority stockholders, the publisher had been ordered to stop using the *Gazette*'s staff, printers and press, forcing him to sell the Sun. Any prospective buyer would not only need a press and editorial, circulation, advertising and production staff but, most important, printers. Printers were virtually impossible to find in the Washington metropolitan area because of the pressing demands for skilled Linotype workers by the major Washington, D.C. newspapers, the *Washington Star*, *Washington Post*, *Times-Herald* and the *Daily News*.[1]

But we won't have this problem, Clayton informed me with a big grin and triumphant smile, over lunch in Georgetown. "We have an agreement with Bernie Bralove, who owns the Shoreham Hotel, to sell us

---

1. *The Linotype, which we acquired with the purchase of the print shop, was the standard method of printing at that time, and was a typesetting machine with a keyboard like a typewriter that enabled the printer to mechanically cast and assemble each line of type as one slug.*

a printing shop he owns here in Georgetown that comes with several printers. The purchase of the *Arlington Daily Sun*," he continued, "is being handled by the D.C. law firm of Hahn & Sundlun, who also represent Bralove. Gilbert Hahn, Jr., Bruce Sundlun and Bernard Bralove have all agreed to serve on our board of directors. It will officially become the *Northern Virginia Sun* to reflect its coverage of the fast-growing Virginia suburban region bordering Washington. A search is under way to find a home for the new Sun in the middle of Arlington, to buy a press and to start recruiting a news, advertising and circulation staff."

By this time, Clayton had become a major player in Washington. He not only was Deputy Chairman of the National Democratic Committee and had been Truman's choice to help Stevenson in his campaigns for President, he now had a widely read column syndicated by Newsday Syndicate which appeared regularly in the *Washington Post*. He was in demand socially, admired for his fierce independence and his witty conversation. He loved attractive women and they loved him back although he was by now a confirmed bachelor.[2] He was always a devoted friend and a constant mentor to me.

"Right now we have three partners, you, me and Phil Stern," he noted. Fritchey, when he was editor of the New Orleans Item, had developed close ties and a warm friendship with Edgar and Edith Stern, a prominent and wealthy New Orleans family. He had also become a mentor to their son, Philip. I first met Phil in 1949 when he was working for Senator Paul Douglas, and came to know and appreciate his talents. He was an accomplished writer who later authored several important non-fiction books. And later, he and his family became among our closest friends. After Clayton called me to join him on Adlai Stevenson's campaign staff, I persuaded him to bring Phil out to Springfield, too. Now, our joint Stevenson working relationship would serve to unite us to form the core of the Sun's leadership.

---

2. *He finally married Polly Wisner, one of Washington's most attractive grand dames who could hold her own against his stormy temper. She became our warm friend and confidant in dealing with Clayton.*

"We also need an additional partner with financial resources," Clayton mused, lowering his voice confidentially and leaning closer to me over the table. "Do you know anyone who might be interested?" I put down my coffee cup and looked up at the ceiling reflectively as I recalled a conversation I had had in Springfield, during the '52 Stevenson campaign, with George Ball, who had been head of Stevenson's Citizens Committee. "How about George Ball? He told me he wanted to write editorials and here is his chance," I replied with rising enthusiasm. "He'd make an ideal partner. I'll call him." Clayt nodded approvingly. George was a partner in a prestigious D.C. law firm and a good friend with whom I had worked on a personal project in Washington. He was delighted to become the fourth partner as this gave him his opportunity to write editorials, which he composed periodically. He wrote thoughtfully on a range of important foreign policy issues that I, as editor of the Sun's editorial page, was always delighted to read.

Northern Virginia Sun organizing Directors. From left: Arnold, George Ball, Bruce Sundlun, Bernie Bralove, Clayton Fritchey, Gilbert Hahn and Phil Stern.

Three years earlier the Supreme Court had ruled against segregation in public schools and ordered their desegregation and the Daily Sun had been a "voice for segregation" in supporting Virginia's fierce opposition to the Court's ruling. Virtually all of the state's conservative political leaders solidly opposed integration, most vociferously Senator Harry Byrd whose call for "massive resistance" helped lead to Virginia's closing down the state's public schools in defiance of the Court's order to desegregate them. The Sun was also known for its strongly conservative news bias, never covering or presenting the political opinions of those with whom it disagreed. As the new owners, we wanted the community to know that our paper would be different, that we would welcome and be open to all points of view. Announcing the purchase of the Daily Sun and introducing its new owners on April 1, 1957, we made the following statement and promise on that day's editorial page:

> *This paper will have its opinions. It will express those opinions on the editorial page but not in the news columns. We shall not restrict the editorial page of this newspaper merely to our own views.*
> *We shall welcome and encourage expressions of opinions from all citizens of Northern Virginia who have an honest interest in our community or national or international affairs. The Northern Virginia Sun will provide a forum in which men of good will can differ.*

Three weeks later the new *Northern Virginia Sun* was being published in its new plant and offices at 3409 Wilson Boulevard, Arlington, Va., on its own 96-page press, composed by its own printers, written and edited by its own news staff, and distributed by its own circulation department and news carriers. The replacement of the *Arlington Daily Sun*'s highly biased views and restricted news coverage by the *Northern Virginia Sun* was an earthshaking event in Arlington, Falls Church, Fairfax County and neighboring jurisdictions. Northern Virginia, unlike Richmond and other southern and rural areas of the state, had been growing rapidly and attracting more liberal-minded residents whose views and activities had been shut out of the old Sun. Now, the new *Northern Virginia Sun* with its large press and news staff intensively covering the activities of their local governments, schools and sports, and community and civic organizations afforded them a needed forum in which to express their views on issues that concerned them and their families.

Bringing the new Sun to Northern Virginia was a miraculous, as well as an incredibly exhausting feat. Sleepless nights and rushed days were spent finding a suitable building in Arlington to house not only the massive 96-page press and related composing room, but also the multitude of other news, circulation, advertising and other workers who first had to be found, screened, and hired. Then acquiring the numerous desks, chairs, typewriters and other office equipment and supplies and getting a multitude of telephone lines and phones installed. All that was accomplished in just three weeks!

The afternoon before the Sun's press was due to arrive, Phil, Clayt and I accompanied the advance man for the press to the Sun's new building. After examining the building and space planned for the huge press, he shook his head sorrowfully and informed us that the press was too big to get into the building. I was stunned and turned to John Beckham, our new general manager who had been manager of the print shop we purchased. He was now overseeing installation of the new press, "Didn't you measure the opening to be sure the press would go through?" I asked him incredulously.[3]

John looked stricken, the blood draining from his face as the enormity of this unforeseen disaster became apparent. "Well, I, ah, I eyed it carefully," his voice faltering as he stretched out both hands alongside his eyes as if he were measuring the entry space. "It certainly looked big enough to me. . . ." I broke in impatiently, "Get a measuring tape and let's be sure." A few minutes later, holding a measuring tape and with the press's advance man assisting him, his shoulders sagging in distress as the tape demonstrated the gap was three critical inches too short. There was a sudden silence and the early evening sky seemed to reflect the darkening sense of despair that enveloped us. No one spoke. What was there to say? Then something cut through my thoughts and an idea suddenly emerged. I turned to the advance man, " I saw a rental sign yesterday on a former Safeway store on Wilson Boulevard just a few blocks from here. Why don't we run up there and look at it to see if the press could be moved into it?" He nodded, "It's worth trying," he said and I drove him to the former grocery store in my 2-seater Mercedes with my other partners following me.

---

3. John was a "legacy" from Clayton's agreement with Bernie Bralove to sell his printing shop and the Sun would employ him as its general manager.

It was dark by now and I drove my car in front of the Safeway and aimed the headlights at the large plate-glass window, partly illuminating the adjacent parking lot as well. The advance man examined the window and large empty space, turned towards me with a happy smile on his face, "Yep, it'll fit in here fine." I then called the greatly surprised real estate broker at home to tell him we would sign an agreement for the building with him and also start moving in the next day. After that I reached our liaison representative with the telephone company to request his urgent assistance in switching all the designated telephone lines, while John made arrangements to move all of the office furniture, composing room and printing equipment to the new Wilson Boulevard building. The nature of the large open space initially necessitated putting all of the news, advertising, circulation, printing, and composing employees in the same room as the press. While very homey, this created a noisy environment for the non-press employees who had to work while the presses were running. The later installation of partitions greatly alleviated this condition.

Arnold, Phil and Clayton.

Responsibility for running the paper was divided among Clayton, Phil Stern, and myself. Phil was editor in charge of the news staff, Clayton the publisher in charge of advertising and circulation, while I, as associate publisher, was in charge of production, overseeing the press and composing room. I also served as editor of the editorial page. Living

up to these responsibilities required that Clayton, Phil, and I work
extra long hours daily, and often until late at night to carry out the
multitude of administrative tasks that demanded our attention.

Opening day at Northern Virginia Sun.

Once upon a time, before television, when newspapers were dominant
and widely read, every ambitious journalist was believed to dream
of owning his own small newspaper. I discovered that the touted joy
and benefits of ownership soon collide with the reality of the onerous
demands and long hours of running a small paper. This was especially
true in a metropolitan area where there are several, much bigger and
financially stronger competing newspapers. But as the three of us were
bachelors, it was relatively easy for us to take the long work hours in
stride, catching up on calls and innumerable unfinished tasks with
overtime spent at the paper.

However, I was not prepared for the task of insuring that a large, sec-
ondhand letter press will print out thousands of copies of that day's
newspaper in time to meet the circulation department's deadline--
only to have the press break down a few minutes after the day's run
starts, when the nearest available repair part is five hours away. Or for

the days when late-breaking stories delayed closing the final page one and you are waiting for the slow-moving linotype machines to print the last batch of type needed, only to have all the printers stop working, announcing it's their lunch time and walk off, despite your ardent pleas to wait 10 minutes to finish page one.

I just went through a frustrating week struggling with the mechanical vagaries of our rogue press and the lackadaisical arrogance of our printers, and I was feeling particularly beaten down, exhausted and very irritable that warm, summer evening in 1957. Everyone else had left and I was talking with Clayton in his office. Phil walked in with a wide grin on his face and announced that he and Helen "Leni" Burroughs Sedgewick, a young divorcée with three children, were getting married and wanted us to come to his wedding August 30th at her family's home in New Hampshire. I was completely surprised and my body and mind were still sluggish and deeply weary from the stressful effects of that week's challenges. My first reaction was to ask Phil, "How can you possibly take the time off to get married?" Fortunately, my mind cleared enough to respond instead: "Congratulations, and thank you, of course I'll come." But Phil's surprise announcement had a momentous effect, like having a bucket of cold water thrown in your face. It triggered the realization that if he could stop working long enough to get married, then so could I.

TIME OUT FOR MARRIAGE

When one loves somebody, everything is clear—where to go, what to do—it takes care of itself and one doesn't have to ask anybody about anything.
   Maxim Gorky

This announcement exposed my failure to find the woman I had been searching for the past 10 years. I was now 39. If I wanted to have a family and a more fulfilling life, I had better start working on this goal beginning right now. So I was in a receptive frame of mind when Ted Miller, a young Washington area lawyer I had met in Portland, Oregon, telephoned me that he had a very attractive young woman lawyer he wanted me to meet that day. In the past I gave this type of call low priority. Instead I questioned him at length about her. He told me he had met Louise at law school and how beautiful and interesting she was, that her husband had died two years ago leaving her with 2-year-old twin girls and a third daughter on the way. I found myself undaunted, saying yes, I'd like to meet her. Then, when he called me back to report she wasn't feeling well enough to meet as she was still recovering from a bout with Asian flu and was going home early.

I did not leave it that way and forget about her, which was my normal tendency. Instead, I telephoned Miller the next day to ask him to try to set up another meeting. When he called back to report that Louise wanted to postpone our getting together until she had fully recovered, he told me he had persuaded her to meet briefly that afternoon near her office on 15th Street, NW, for tea at 4 p.m. If I could just drop by casually around 4:15 p.m., he would introduce us and then leave.

Ted's scheme worked. By the time I had finished tea I knew she was the special woman I had been waiting for. We had so much to talk about and learn about one another that I drove her home to Hollin Hills, due south of Alexandria. I was introduced to Dana and Laurie, her twins, Rita and her large, vigilant French poodle, Pedo, as well as Louise's housekeeper-nanny who looked after the children while Louise was at work. There was a lot to learn about each other and a great deal of catching up for both of us until one evening when we had stopped by my apartment at the Arlington Towers, overlooking the Potomac River. Louise suddenly asked me the big question. "Are you really serious about me and want to get married, because if not I don't want to waste any more of my time." I looked at her intently, trying to gauge her seriousness and at the same time assess my own feelings. We were both very quiet while I thought about her, about me, and about us. It had only been a few very heady, wonderful and fully absorbing weeks, so there were many important unknowns. But the one most important fact was that I felt confident that she was the one and only one I had ever met for whom I felt this fulfilling sense of loving warmth and attraction. From her captivating blue eyes down to her fabulous, shapely legs and ankles, I loved not only the way she looked, but also what she had to say when she articulated and defended her views.

During those short but intensely concentrated weeks, we spent every hour together after work until late in the evening when I drove from Hollin Hills back to my Arlington apartment. I had learned enough to be certain that in all the important areas that matter in a happy marriage, she was the woman I loved, the lifetime mate for me. We basically shared the same opinions and tastes with respect to the kinds of people, places, and things involved in our everyday lives. She had an inner strength and integrity that I found admirable, as well as an ability to think creatively and rationally and to interact with people with sensitivity and wisdom. She also had an appealing and wonderful talent for friendship. And she had demonstrated an extraordinary ability to manage successfully her work as a lawyer and that of a loving, capable mother with three small children.

I wanted Clayton to meet her and arranged to have lunch at the Rive Gauche in Georgetown. He brought along Kay Halle, which turned out to be a disaster. Kay turned her back on Louise and talked only to Clayton and me during the entire lunch, leaving me furious and embarrassed by Kay's unforgivable rudeness. Clayton had been completely captivated by Louise, as I hoped and expected, and he told me later how angry he had been with Kay. He had chewed her out for her disgraceful behavior, which apparently reflected her displeasure at the likelihood she could no longer depend on my availably as an extra man and an escort to social events. After that lunch I decided against introducing Louise to any more of my friends, as I did not want to risk subjecting her to the remotest possibility of anyone else's hostility or disapproval. Besides, I had made up my mind and no one was going to change it. Furthermore, the long drive back to my apartment every night was taking its toll on my sleep and ability to function effectively the next day at my job.

"Yes, I am very serious and I want to marry you," I said with a mixture of resolve, love and relief. Louise's tense face relaxed and with a happy smile as she replied, "I want you to know I can promise you only two things: I'm very good at wrapping packages and I can give good parties." And those two talents were later demonstrated on many important occasions. They have been useful and important talents during the 52 years of our happy, successful marriage.

We discussed how best to tell the children about a new father, inform-ing our respective families and gaining their support for the marriage. Louise told me that her mother and father had not approved of her first husband and marriage to him had led to estrangement from her parents. After his sudden death from a heart attack in 1955, relations remained somewhat strained. She believed the children would not be a problem, as they had become used to me and wanted to have a father as their friends did. She felt confident that her parents were anxious to have full reconciliation and would welcome me as help-ing bring that about. But she was not ready to let her parents know about marriage just yet. I, too, wanted time to prepare my mother and siblings, although I was sure they would be relieved to know I was getting married at long last (even adding a family) and that they would be overjoyed, especially when they met Louise.

As for the children, we both felt it important that this big change in their lives would be best if it took place when we could all be together and start our new life as a family in a new house. To avoid any anxiet-ies on our part about whether either of our families might disapprove of their new in-law, we agreed we should get married right away in a private ceremony and keep our marriage a secret until we had first met with each other's parent(s) and we had found a house and were ready to move.

Through quiet inquiries, we learned of a rabbi who could marry us in a private ceremony in his home in Park Fairfax. We obtained the necessary civil license and one week later on November 22, 1957, Louise and I were in my Mercedes, with the top down and a warm, friendly sun overhead, headed for the rabbi's residence. Suddenly, I felt Louise's hand grabbing my right arm and simultaneously heard her alarmed shout, "Stop the car!" Glancing quickly at her to see if she had been stung or otherwise injured by something, I pulled over to the side of the road and turned to ask her what was wrong. "What am I doing?" she shouted. "I must be out of my mind! I've only known you for three weeks, and here I am going to entrust my children to you." I had prepared for a possible emergency and had put a small silver flask filled with a very good Courvoisier in the glove compartment that morning. I now took it out, unscrewed the cap, and handed her the flask, "Here, take a big sip. You'll feel better."

She looked at me, her eyes wide and anxious and then took a long sip. We sat there for a few minutes while the brandy took effect and her coloring came back and her tension eased as she regained her composure. "It's going to be all right," I assured her starting the car and resuming our drive. The only attendant was the Rabbi's wife and after the brief, simple marriage ceremony and the Rabbi's blessing, I kissed the bride. We were now man and wife officially, and we drove to a nearby Hot Shoppe where I treated Louise to our wedding lunch, a Mighty Mo hamburger with relish and mustard. Looking back over 52 successful years of marriage, it's hard to believe that it all began after knowing each other only three weeks.

Arnold and Louise at her parents' Thanksgiving. 1960.

Louise and the girls had been planning to go to New York for Thanksgiving at her parents' apartment at 927 Fifth Avenue. She called them to ask if she could invite a friend for the Thanksgiving dinner, to which they readily agreed. Thanksgiving morning I traveled to New York with Louise and the children, checked into a nearby hotel, and walked over to the Edelman's apartment at the appropriate time to join them for dinner. Louise introduced me to her parents and her brother, Dick, a good looking young man with a friendly smile and cheerful outlook. Louise's mother and father were very cordial and polite as they listened, clearly with deep interest, to her account of how we had met through a mutual friend who had been a classmate at Law School. And then to my description of my job at the *Northern Virginia Sun*. Dick asked where I had grown up and gone to school, after which the conversation became more general and relaxed as her parents switched their focus and full attention to their rarely seen granddaughters, who all gave star performances charming their grandparents and uncle, talking about their activities in Hollin Hills.

The following week Louise learned of an attractive 18th century house with a swimming pool and coach house at 224 South Lee Street in the Old Town part of Alexandria, overlooking the Potomac. The house had been owned by George Washington's mentor, George Johnson. On first sight we were both enthused and in agreement that this was the new home we were looking for and it met our mutual goals: mine as a local publisher to be a resident of Northern Virginia; Louise's to be close to Washington and interesting jobs with flexible working hours. With our children, families, and close friends now informed of our marriage, we moved into 224 South Lee Street as the Sagalyn family.

The first night in residence came the first challenge to test our marriage. Pedo, Louise's beautiful, white-furred, well-mannered standard poodle, who had followed Louise up the stairs to our bedroom, jumped up on the king-size bed and promptly stretched out in repose. I turned to face Louise, and in a firm, determined tone said. "Pedo can't sleep on the bed with us. He has to sleep outside." And Louise, in an equally firm and determined tone responded that Pedo had always slept on her bed and she didn't see any reason why that had to change now. I looked at her set lips and unwavering eyes in disbelief, quickly followed by a mounting feeling of anger and realized we were facing a crisis. "Either he goes or I do," I heard myself saying. A long anxious silence ensued as Pedo, sensing the tension and the hostility directed at him, raised his statuesque head and looked inquiringly at the two of us. It was clear that Louise was carefully pondering what I had just said, and that she was seriously debating an answer. It was equally clear to me that this could go the wrong way for me and that my rival Pedo might win out. Louise then turned to look over at Pedo and I knew she had made up her mind. I held my breath as she walked over to the bed, stroked Pedo lovingly and then, taking his collar, pulled him gently off the bed and into the hall outside our bedroom, slowly closing the door after him. I had won, I exulted joyfully, but silently, knowing it had been a close call.

We were lucky to find Lena Gaarn Larsen, a beautiful, competent Danish au-pair who would take care of Rita, who was only one-and-a-half, and the twins Dana and Laurie, while Louise and I were at work, and later when we went on our three-week honeymoon to Round Hill, Jamaica, and Havana, Cuba. During those three weeks we had the relaxed time to get to know one another's feelings and views better, as we talked about a wide range of important likes and dislikes, on personal as well as broader social, cultural, political and other issues.

I was very pleased that my first impressions of Louise as the long-sought lover, mother, and partner I wanted to share my life with were confirmed. And in the following days, months and years it became increasingly assuring that we shared essentially the same opinions on virtually everything important that arose in our marriage. This included how to raise the children, and their education, social life and the development of their talents. I learned we both agreed on the kind of houses, friends, social, cultural and entertainment activities, as well as the political views and leaders we favored. It became a family joke that the only strong disagreements that developed were in a car where we each had strong, different opinions on the right route to take to reach our destination.

BACK TO THE SUN

When I returned to work at the Sun after our honeymoon, I was secretly disappointed to find that the composing room, press and editorial page had all managed very well without me. But I was also happily reassured that I could now devote the necessary time to my new, more important and fulfilling priority, Louise and my new family.

The new Sun filled a long-standing communications void in the fast-growing Northern Virginia area. Thousands of new residents, often Federal employees with higher educational backgrounds without the traditional Virginian's ultra conservative social and political views,

Arnold and Phil celebrating Northern Virginia Sun's First birthday.

welcomed the Sun. They were pleased with the new daily's extensive coverage of their local government, schools, sports and civic organizations, along with its inclusive editorial approach and news columns. This journalistic adventure was reflected in the enthusiasm, upbeat air of trail-blazing excitement and high spirits among our talented young reporters and writers. Many of them had never worked on a daily newspaper, and they gained great experience that benefited their careers. Among them were Marianne Means, who would later be a national columnist for the Hearst Syndicate; Helen Dewar, who became the Congressional reporter for the *Washington Post*; and "Scotty" Fitzgerald Lanahan, the daughter of F. Scott Fitzgerald, whose elegantly written, subtle articles skillfully skewered many of the area's most pompous political figures with their own words.

From its very first days, the news side of the Sun excelled and was very well managed, but the business aspects were plagued from the start. Beginning with the hiring of the Sun's general manager, John Beckham, whose costly failure to measure the opening of the original building forced us to abandon the site of the Sun's planned quarters and move into another space. The next calamity was the loss of the business records of the predecessor Daily Sun when they were destroyed by its bookkeeper, probably out of a misplaced sense of loyalty to her former employer. As a result, we were never able to justify our own books and never knew whether our own balance sheet was accurate. While Clayt and I, and to some extent Phil, had worked on the news side of news publications, none of us had any previous experience with the business side, and this deficiency was to take its toll. Clayton, who had become the editor of a large Baltimore daily paper in his early 20s, had no experience publishing a newspaper, nor much respect for the business side and businessmen. I recall painfully his comment when we first started and were discussing the need for the paper to be profitable, "It shouldn't be hard to make money. After all, we're only competing against businessmen," he opined.

I had no experience in newspaper publishing or other relevant business either, but it was becoming clear that Clayton's plan to focus on building circulation and his belief that significantly high circulation would produce substantially higher advertising revenue wasn't working. We had increased the Sun's circulation from just a few thousand to 25,000 in one year.[4] In addition we were printing a "shopper" (a free paper filled with paid advertising) that was delivered to virtually every home in Northern Virginia. Yet that was not enough to make the paper financially solvent. One reason, we unhappily learned, was the inefficient, high cost of delivering the Sun to its 25,000 daily subscribers who were spread over a broad geographical area including Arlington County, Falls Church, Fairfax County and Alexandria. Instead of concentrating on building circulation street by street, block by block and saturating every street and neighborhood—simplifying delivery for the circulation department and individual carriers before moving on to the next neighborhood to repeat the same concentration process—the Sun's rush to get a big total number led to a nightmare delivery system with customers through many widely scattered neighborhoods in Northern Virginia.

---

4. *We were the fastest growing daily in the US that year.*

An even more crucial economic factor proved to be our failure to attract ads from the traditional, large newspaper advertisers, the region's department and grocery store chains. We discovered too late that their policy was to advertise in papers that could reach their customers not only in Northern Virginia but those shopping in their stores in the District of Columbia and suburban Maryland as well. Despite its already significant and growing circulation in Northern Virginia, these critical advertisers had no interest in advertising in our or any other paper that did not circulate in all three metropolitan areas.

Initially, George, Phil, and I had made equal investments of capital to start the paper, and to meet the Sun's earlier financial requirements. Clayton's contributions were his services as Publisher, although he also received a salary. While Phil and I as full-time working partners were also entitled to salaries, they were not paid to us but instead credited to us as invested capital. But as the growing disparity between the Sun's income and debt grew increasingly wider, the demands for additional capital contributions began to exceed our resources.[5] Eventually, Phil called on the resources of his parents to meet the Sun's payroll and bills. His appeals for additional funds were usually accompanied by sincerely optimistic reports by Clayton on the paper's progress in circulation and community support, and his upbeat predictions of improvements in advertising revenue.

Clayton's original model for the Sun's success had been based on Newsday, an independent daily paper on Long Island. Founded at the beginning of World War II, Newsday benefited from this flood of new residents who moved out from the city during and after the war, who provided a large, loyal and local readership for the new paper. The nearby location of an airplane manufacturing plant and other factories attracted thousands of workers and service businesses, which brought the paper advertising revenue. The war restrictions on newsprint also helped spur Newsday's growth as it was allocated sufficient newsprint to meet its large press runs, while the established N.Y. papers were

---

5. *From the start, the Sun was always short of money requiring George, Phil and me to contribute more to meet payroll, Initially, I had sufficient capital to help make up the deficits. However, eventually George and I had to pass on further contributions.*

unable to expand their circulation into Long Island because government regulations froze their newsprint supply to their pre-war circulation levels.

However, unlike Newsday's readers, the *Northern Virginia Sun*'s readers turned out to have no sense of loyalty to the Sun, because they did not regard their residence in Northern Virginia their permanent "home." A large proportion were on temporary assignment to one of the military services, the State Department, foreign embassies, or other organizations involved with the current Federal administration or Congress, and they tended to vote and think of their homes as being in another state. The large number of transient residents resulted in such a large turnover and loss of readers that the Sun had to get two new subscribers every year for each one dropped, just to stay even. This widespread feeling that Northern Virginia was not their real home also applied to residents who continued to live there for many years, and it seriously impeded any feeling of loyalty to or participation in their community, and any loyalty to the Sun as their community paper.

By 1959, the printers we had acquired with the print shop were proving insufficient and incapable of producing enough type to meet our press deadline. Like all Linotype printers in the Washington area, ours were members of the powerful Typographical Union, which had required us to sign a contract with the same hiring conditions as they had with the Star, Post and other Washington papers many times our size. When we tried to hire additional printers, the union informed us that our contract not only mandated that for every printer we hired we would also have to hire two additional floormen we didn't need (the composing room workers who placed the finished printers' type in the pages that would then be put on the press). But no extra printers were available, even if we were willing to pay for the unnecessary floormen.

The pressroom's deadline was 12 noon, the same time as the beginning of the printers' normal lunch hour. I tried without success to persuade our printers to postpone their lunch until 1 p.m., which would enable them to produce enough type to close the last page and meet our noon deadline. But the printers felt no loyalty to the paper and our calls to the Typographical Union for help were ignored. The only way we could see to overcome this problem was to get an AP or UP wire service automatic printer that would punch out news items on type we could then use to close page one. However, the Typographical Union vehemently opposed all automated typesetting machines as a threat to their members' jobs and they refused to permit us to use the AP or UP wire services. We were stuck and our frustration grew as we kept missing our press deadline, causing the circulation department to fail to deliver the Sun to our news carriers on time. These delays resulted in angry telephone calls from the irate parents of our teenage carriers, and equally unhappy calls about the late deliveries from our subscribers. My name on the masthead led some subscribers to telephone their complaints to me at my home. The most memorable of these calls came at 10 p.m., when a woman's furious voice demanded that I personally deliver that day's very late Sun to her house some 20 miles distant in Fairfax County. The next day, I suggested to Clayton that we change the name of the Sun to the "Northern Virginia Moon."

In a crisis meeting, Clayton announced that he had arranged to get an automated typesetter wire service installed and discussed with the Sun's department heads the various protective measures we needed to take in the likely event that the union would order all of our printers to walk out, which it promptly did when the installation was made. To our astonishment and outrage, the Typographical Union's strike was soon followed by retaliatory action and punitive measures by the Teamsters Union and the Newspaper Guild, neither of whom had any members or were in any way associated with the Sun. Declaring their brotherly support for the striking printers' union, both of the other two unions proceeded to sabotage the Sun's operations. The Teamsters physically threatened our circulation drivers and put sugar in their vehicles' gas tanks, while the Newspaper Guild systematically telephoned and warned the parents of our young carriers to stop them from delivering the Sun.

I had been a member in good standing of the Newspaper Guild when I worked for the Cleveland Press, and had supported the rights of all unions to organize and protect the rights of their members. But the arrogant, ruthless, and uncaring behavior of the Printer's Union, and the intimidating actions of the uninvolved Teamsters and newspaper unions left in me a very bitter taste of disillusionment. (The Typographical Union's strike ended up before the U.S. Labor Relations Board, which ultimately ruled in our favor.)

The reality of Clayton's vision of the Sun as a viable suburban daily, similar to Newsday, was an unending river of red ink. It was now clear to me and my partners that there was no future for the Sun as a daily, providing its readers not only with local news, but also with a window on the important national and world happenings as well, as Newsday did. And while it might have thrived as a weekly or bi-weekly newspaper, none of us found that limited scope personally appealing.

Kennedy's election in 1960 resulted in Phil, Clayton, George Ball and I joining his new administration. Since Phil's family were by this time the major investors in the Sun, their business advisors arranged to sell the paper to a New Jersey publisher.

BUILDING A FAMILY
1957

Chapter 10

All happy families resemble one another...
Leo Tolstoy

Learning to be a first-time father to three new daughters, as well as
a first-time husband at the age of 39, proved to be a sensitive, challenging and demanding on-the-job learning experience. Almost every
day brought a new test. As a relatively untried husband and parent,
I felt I had to prove myself worthy of my wife's and the children's
trust. Our mutual need to get to know and adjust to one another was

Arnold and Louise with Rita, Laurie and Dana, 1962.

facilitated by the fact that the girls never really knew or remembered John London, their birth father. Dana and Laurie were only two, and Louise was still pregnant with Rita when he died. And all three girls had periodically expressed a strong desire to have a real father, as their friends did. Consequently, it was only a matter of time and patience and Dana, Laurie and Rita soon demonstrated an affectionate willingness to welcome me as their new father.

Looking back now, I realize this getting to-know-and-trust-one-another period was to be expected. Happily, Louise was always there to help me understand what they were going through, and to let me know when I should devote my full attention to their concerns. I was also helped by their inherent capacity to receive and return my growing love and affection.

Time and doing things together that we all enjoyed brought us all closer. When Lisbeth was born five years after our marriage, May 17, 1962, she provided Dana, Laurie and Rita with a new "doll" to take care of. The arrival of a baby sister helped unify the family and diffuse any earlier tensions. When that happened, it seemed the right time for me to discuss with Louise, and then get Dana's, Laurie's and Rita's approval, of my formally adopting them, keeping their London surname as their middle name and making us a united family in name as well.

I had now achieved my long-sought goal—to find someone I cared for and loved enough to share my life and have a family to raise, giving me the sense of meaning and purpose that made my existence worthwhile.

BY OUR HOUSES YE SHALL KNOW US

Where thou art, that, is Home.
  Emily Dickinson

The 7 houses we have acquired and lived in over the 52 years of our marriage tend to characterize us and describe how we wanted to live as a married couple and a family. Our first was an 18th century Federal house in Old Town Alexandria, overlooking the Potomac River, next, was a rambling former farm house on Albermarle Street, with a tennis court, swimming pool, tree house and outdoor trampoline (where our children all grew up). Then a historic house with a boxwood garden and lap pool in Georgetown. Home is now a scenic, multi-windowed Watergate apartment overlooking Washington's Potomac River. Included were our get-away, vacation homes on Martha's Vineyard, Rappahannock County, Va., and our Berkshires retreat on the border of Richmond, MA, and Canaan, N.Y., where a devastating tornado couldn't stop us from rebuilding. Each was a special, warm, refuge with wonderful, fond memories of our times as a family, living together on stress less vacations and other special occasions, to play or just relax, where we could see and catch up with one another and old friends.

The roll call of these houses might seem as though we had endless funds to invest in how we lived. The truth is that we were lucky to buy and sell at just the right time so we could parlay each sale into larger down payments. I take minimal credit for this success. It was Louise's acute real estate knowledge that made it happen. She is fond of saying it all began with her first time purchase of a row house in Old Town Alexandria for $12,500 in 1953! From there to Hollin Hills and then to our first house together back in Old Town. The Vineyard houses were bought with inherited money and when we sold them, the income from the proceeds financed our vacations for the next decade, then our house in the Berkshires. Donald Brown deserves praise for the creative financing of Whippoorwill Farm where we did not even have to pay for the down payment.

This was the odyssey of our houses.

OLD TOWN ALEXANDRIA[6]

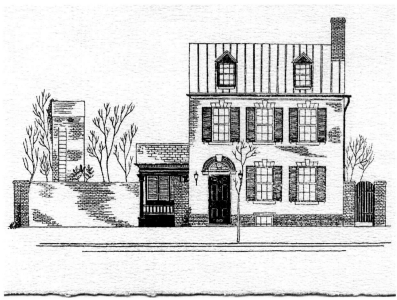

224 South Lee Street, Alexandria Virginia.

When we started the *Northern Virginia Sun*, it was agreed that to give the newspaper creditability, Phil Stern and I, as co-publishers and the freedom to move there, should be residents of Northern Virginia. Both of us independently found houses we liked in the historic early 18th century community known as Old Town Alexandria, located on the Virginia side of the Potomac River, directly across from the District of Columbia.

Ours was an historic, 18th century Colonial house at 224 South Lee Street overlooking the Potomac River that had been the residence of George Johnson, George Washington's mentor and as a prominent member of the Virginia House of Burgesses who delivered one of Patrick Henry famous speeches when the latter was too ill to deliver it personally. The double living rooms, large paneled library and fan-

---

6. *In 1958, Old Town was just beginning gentrification. It had a true Southern population, some poor pockets, some wealthy and all of it was segregated. There were few restaurants, fewer upscale stores, and no public schools, which were closed after the 1954 Brown vs The Board of Education Supreme Court decision outlawing school segregation.*

tastic kitchen—it's spacious brick fireplace was capable of cooking an entire wild boar or large pig hanging from two high swinging iron bars—made it wonderful for entertaining. An oven in the fireplace was a Colonial heritage with a ready supply of hot water, running from a large water tank in the attic through a copper pipe inside the brick chimney that was heated by the log fire, made for table conversation.

Altogether, it provided an especially warm and inviting place for living and entertaining, while its swimming pool, coach house and adjacent garden was a wonderful play area for the girls and their friends. These included the children of my partner, Phil Stern, who like me was the beneficiary of three young children from his wife Leni's earlier marriage. They lived only a few blocks away in a magnificent 18th century house and surrounding gardens. Our children became life-long friends as did Leni and Louise. As a gift to our daughters, Leni, a talented painter with a wonderful sense of color, painted a series of whimsical, enchanting murals along the staircase wall bordering the staircase to the girl's bedrooms.

Louise left her job as legal counsel to Panhandle Eastern Pipeline, a major energy corporation, to spend more time with the three girls during their early, formative years. Then, after our life had settled down, we had the help of a series of competent, reliable, Danish, Swedish and other au pair young women to look after the children. This enabled Louise to work out legal assignments with flexible hours, which permitted her to be home early when the children returned from school.

She found these jobs at startup Federal agencies such as Head Start at the Office of Economic Opportunity, and later working on various Presidential Commissions, including The Presidential Commission on Crime in the District of Columbia, where she wrote The Commission's report on the Juvenile Court, and on the Kerner Commission on Civil Disorders. Following these projects, she would start several not-for-profit and for-profit enterprises.

With Lisbeth's arrival on May 17, 1962, Louise and I recognized that our only available bedroom space for Lisbeth was unsuitable, as was Virginia's segregated local school situation. These two problems, combined with my new job in the District, now made a compelling case for moving into Washington. Louise started to look for a new house in the Northwest Washington–Chevy Chase residential area, where many of our friends who had also joined the new Kennedy Administration had recently moved because of the good public schools, attractive housing and tree-lined neighborhoods.

A few weeks after Louise started house hunting, she called me, very excited, at my office to report she had just seen a terrific house with a lot of land, just above Cleveland Park. Our friends, Aggie and Al Wolf, looked at it, and while they had decided it wasn't rural enough for them, they had thought it might be just right for us. Louise said it was a terrific house and property, and just perfect for us. However, some other house hunters had expressed an interest, and she didn't believe it would be available very long. Could I go with her to see it during my lunch hour?

I drove to the address, 3006 Albemarle Street, NW, just off Connecticut Avenue and immediately adjacent to Rock Creek Park. The house was a large, rambling, former farmhouse with five bedrooms and a rear-screened porch, set in a large garden area a good distance back from the street. It was screened from the street by trees and thick shrubbery, next to a deep, thickly wooded ravine, and sited on a large, triple lot with tall birch trees that abutted the park.

Family on the steps of 3006 Albemarle Street ,NW, Washington, DC.

Louise and I looked at each other and we both nodded in agreement. Yes, it was just what we both were looking for, and we immediately signed a full purchase contract for the property. As it turned out, we signed just in time, for an hour later an earlier couple had returned to sign a purchase agreement.

3006 ALBEMARLE STREET

Prior to moving into the house, we had an architect draw up plans to enlarge the narrow windows in the front and rear of the living room, to run from the ceiling to the floor. The rear windows were set in French doors opening on a new rear balcony overlooking the garden and Rock Creek Park. A new baseboard heating system was also to be installed to compensate for the extra heating required with the additional window openings.

Unfortunately, our new architect, Mr. Wright, turned out to be our Mr. Wrong, for he forgot to tell our heating contractor about the plans for the new windows, so the resultant heating system proved extremely inadequate. To this day I still have memories of sitting in front of a log fire in our living room fireplace, huddled in heavy sweaters and wrapped in blankets, during the many cold winters that followed.

But we had lucked out when we moved into our Albemarle Street house and Forest Hills neighborhood, and during the next 23 years Louise and I watched our children grow up in an extraordinarily comfortable house and environment with attractive supportive neighbors, with whom we made many warm, lifetime friendships. Our large, surrounding gardens enabled us to enjoy such amenities as a swimming pool, tree house and an outdoor trampoline that became a neighborhood playground for the girls and their friends. In addition, only a few hundred feet away, was a tennis court, which we shared with our immediate neighbors and warm friends, Don and Ann Brown, and Jimmy and Ginger Newmyer.

The tennis court was symbolic of the active civic and cooperative spirit of our new neighbors, dramatically demonstrated one morning when our peaceful breakfast was disturbed by the noise of bulldozers and

Tree house in Albemarle Street garden. 1964. L to R, Dana, Rita, Laurie, Lisbeth, Louise and Arnold.

chain saws clearing the adjoining, forested deep ravine. At the time we purchased our house we had expressed interest in buying this adjacent lot to protect ourselves against an unwelcome, disruptive neighbor, but our real estate broker dissuaded us. The abrupt steep slopes and very rugged, unattractive nature of the terrain made it unsuitable for building a house or other residential use. To our deep horror, we discovered that the land had been sold to a public works contractor for use as a dump for debris from streets being repaired and there was nothing we could do to stop them. But some months later, when the deep gap of the former empty ravine had been largely filled with all kinds of trash, the Browns and Newmeyers discovered that the contractor-owner was going to sell the land to a developer who had submitted plans to build several houses on the lot. The three families joined forces and succeeded in getting the DC government to reject a permit for a multi-building project on the ground that it was unsuitable for our residential neighborhood.

Louise and I, and the Browns and Newmeyers, now discussed our common interest in buying the lot, and building a tennis court. With the street contractor having no further use of the lot, and no other likelihood of finding a buyer for the debris-filled land, the lot's owner would be happy to sell it to us. To minimize the cost of the lot, re-grading the land, and building the tennis court, Donald came up with the idea of selling the lot fronting on Albemarle Street to a developer to build a single attractive house. To entice a buyer, it was agreed to offer the occupant a lifetime, equitable use of the court. And so it happened that Brock Adams, an ardent tennis player and U.S. Senator from the state of Washington, became our neighbor and co-user of the tennis court, which all of us played on happily virtually daily, and with double matches and occasional tournaments, with many of our neighbors and other friends.

Remembering my own, decidedly favorable, Springfield public school experience, I was a strong advocate for public school for our daughters, and when we moved that fall of 1962, we enrolled Dana, Laurie and Rita in the nearby, well-regarded Ben Murch public elementary school. Unhappily Ben Murch turned out to be a full-scale disaster, as it had an excessively rigid, inflexible instruction system, as well as poor teachers. Moreover, there was a breakdown in class discipline that made the daily fighting and escapades among some of their classmates much more fascinating and entertaining to our girls than their academic studies. The next year saw Dana and Rita in the nearby, private Sheridan school, and Laurie attending the Georgetown Day School, and soon Dana, Rita and Lisbeth would all end up at the Quaker Sidwell Friends School.

The Albemarle Street community was a particularly healthy and stable environment for adolescents growing up during the turbulent, '60s and '70s, which witnessed not only enormous social, cultural and political change resulting from the civil and women's rights, and Beatles music/Woodstock rebellions, but also the Vietnam war protests that led to a multitude of college and high school students experimenting with marihuana, cocaine and other dangerous drugs.[7]

As Dana, Laurie and Rita were by nature creative and artistic, as were their friends, they had little direct interest in the Vietnam protests. However, they were influenced by the social and cultural changes arising out of them, such as: maturing girls and boys tended to stop dating one another, and instead to socialize in groups; and because of the pill, couples who formerly would marry, now saw no need to make such a commitment, but began living together and thus maintained their independence. There was a new radical rebellion against parental authority that exceeded the natural, rite-of-passage testing of parental authority. It was inevitable in the '60s and '70s that these changes would impact on the lives of most impressionable teenagers— and parents—and Dana, Laurie and Rita and their circle of friends were no exception.

Then there was the family summer trip to Europe in 1970, when Louise and I had flown to Nice accompanied by Lisbeth, who was only eight. The other three girls were also in Europe, but on different itineraries. Although the plan was for us to eventually all meet up in Rome, working out the various timetables and coordinating when and where we would all meet had not been easy. In Nice, Louise and I rented a car to drive to Italy, where we visited Louise's brother Dick and his family, who had rented a large, attractive villa in Rapallo on the Italian Riviera.

I've never forgotten that drive because a few hundred yards before we exited the very long, underground tunnel connecting France and Italy, our car ran out of gas! It was only then that we discovered our rental car had a defective gas gauge that was still showing plenty of

---

7. *Even the very proper Sidwell Friends students were not immune. When Louise and I learned that one of Dana's friends was shooting heroin, Louise called on Sidwell's principal, Bob Smith, to organize an educational, drug- preventive program for both the faculty and students. However, Smith was a Quaker, and told her he couldn't do anything until there was a consensus, whereupon Louise persuaded Gene Gordon, a prominent psychiatrist and close friend, to undertake this project.*

fuel. Fortunately, after escaping the danger and horror of the speeding passing cars behind us, we found a gas station just a short walk from where our car had stopped, but unfortunately, they were just closing for lunch and would not wait on us until after their sacred mid day break.

Far more stressful for Louise and me, was the breakdown in our communications and near-failure to rendezvous as planned with both Rita and Laurie. Laurie had been hitchhiking in Ireland with Ray Scherer's niece, and she planned to join Louise, Lisbeth and me in Rapallo, Italy. We arranged to rendezvous at the train station there, but when we arrived at the station, we discovered to our great distress that there was another local station, and we were anxious when Laurie's train pulled in whether she, unknowingly, might continue to the second stop. But fate was kind that day, for Laurie had believed we would be meeting her at the train's next stop, and she just happened to be looking casually out the window on the side where we were standing and spotted us just in time to get off.

Our communications problems were not over. Rita was with a Choate summer school trip that ended up in London. We pre-arranged a flight to Rome, where we would meet her plane at the airport. But as that date drew near, our worries began when we tried unsuccessfully to telephone Rita in London to confirm her flight and arrival time in Rome. When the Choate representative told us they had lost contact with her, our anxiety level rose precipitously. But the day of her flight, we had no alternative to going out to the airport, sustained by our basic faith in Rita's smarts and capability. However, Louise and my angst level increased dramatically as we watched the passengers unload with no sign of Rita. And just as we had given up hope, a straggling passenger appeared at the plane's exit staircase, wearing a big wide smile—it was Rita!

Our parental stress was dramatically tested in a different way when our entire immediate family went on to Venice, where we were booked into the Hotel Danielli, a 5-star posh hotel. That summer in Italy, when we were with Dana, Laurie and Rita, their striking, shabby and at times challenging and inappropriate attire had manifested their teenage rebellion, but until Venice it was not a big problem. But in this hotel, everyone would be expected to be properly, elegantly dressed for dinner. As we stood with Lisbeth waiting outside the formal, elaborate dining room, we were completely uncertain what Dana's, Laurie's and Rita's reactions would be when they came down for dinner in their normal, near ragged-looking blue jeans that first night.

Suddenly the girls were approaching and to our enormous surprise all three appeared, handsomely, attractively "dressed-to-the-nines" and we all walked nonchalantly into the dining room to our table. They had assessed the situation themselves and had availed themselves of the glamorous bathtubs and scents in their room and dressed in their finest outfits. There was no discussion of the proper dress subject that night or any other night we were in Venice. We were fortunate that our older daughters' rebellion was mainly manifested in the relatively mild testing of Louise and my parental authority and more traditional cultural mores.

When I proposed marriage to Louise, she had told me that as my wife, she could promise two things I could count on: she knew how to give good parties; and she was very good at wrapping presents. And she never disappointed me in either of these important domestic areas. But Louise also was constantly surprising me with her incredible reservoir of talents and continual achievements as a wonderful, compassionate, caring, and resourceful wife and mother. Although I knew she was bright and intellectually knowledgeable, I also discovered her extraordinary talent and capability to make and be a devoted, reliable friend to me, and to a multitude of friends dating back to childhood, and to a continuing stream of new ones.

At a time when most women were expected to stay home and dedicate their lives to motherhood and their husband's needs and career, Louise was breaking out of this mold to became a pioneer, and showing our daughters that women could not only be good mothers and wives, but also lead highly satisfying, rewarding, productive personal lives in both the public and private sectors.

OUR FIRST VACATION HOUSE:
MARTHA'S VINEYARD

Our first few summers we arranged to stay for a month at my family's
farm in the Berkshires, where we lived in the Barn House next to the
dam.[8] But after discovering we both preferred to find a vacation place
of our own near the sea, we rented a house in Wellfleet, Cape Cod,
where we joined the Paul Warnkes and Burke Marshalls and had a
delightful and satisfying family summer vacation. However, when we
discussed looking for a place to buy there, we were concerned that the
Cape Cod area was so popular that it soon would be too crowded and
lose its appeal as a quiet, relaxing place.

Dana, Laurie, Michelle, Rita, cousin Rita, Adine, & Avital, on the lake at the Farm.

Before we were married, Louise had summered with friends on Martha's Vineyard, and had loved its isolation, small population, many
scenic beaches. She proposed we rent a house there for the next

---

8. *One of the rewards of summering at our farm was introducing Louise, Dana,
Laurie and Rita to their new Sagalyn relatives and vice versa. For I had always
been regarded as the lone and seemingly dedicated bachelor of our family, so
my brothers, sisters and their children were especially thrilled by my marriage to
Louise, and immediately enchanted by her and their new cousins. The following
several summers brought us all together again and firmly cemented the mutual
warmth and affection of the new family ties.*

summer, which we did, first in Gay Head with the Abe and Toni Chayes family, and then returned the next summer to Chilmark. We loved the Vineyard, enjoying its recreational and social activities as a family, in a relaxed setting and atmosphere where the children would be away from the pressures of school and grades, and Louise and I free from work and other daily city pressures. We were also delighted to discover that among the few Washingtonians summering there were some close friends, including Phil and Leni Stern, Tony and Linda Lewis, and Anita and Gene Gordon. As their children and our children were good friends, they were an added attraction and provided welcome summer playmates. We also had an opportunity to catch up with Lou and Polly Cowen and their friends, Judy and Dooley Rosenwald.

Vineyard houses and land to buy were scarce and in demand. It was only after a few years of rental houses, and an urgent early morning call one January from our real estate agent to fly up that day, that we finally purchased a large rambling, early colonial house in the East Chop part of Oak Bluffs, overlooking Vineyard Haven Sound.[9]

Our property included two small cottages just below the main house, as well as a converted boathouse on the Sound. We rented our two cottages and boathouse only to close friends, including the Donald Browns and Paul Warnkes, who all became devoted Vineyard summer residents. When a beach cottage on the Vineyard Haven Sound just below us became available (reached by a private dirt road just beyond the Vineyard Haven bridge), we bought and enlarged it, drilling pilings into the ground and constructing a large family room, master bedroom and bath, and a large, wide adjacent wooden deck that extended to within 10 feet of the water. I can still recall vividly lying on our bed in the quiet of the night, and the only sound was the lulling, lapping of the waves outside as I fell asleep.

We built a long, sturdy wooden pier out into the Sound, from which we could swim, and dock our new Boston Whaler, which we used to

---

9. *The house of our next door neighbor on the main road, we quickly learned, was that of Gloria Swanson, the movie star and reputed girlfriend of Joseph Kennedy, father of President Jack Kennedy.*

Our 1st Martha's Vineyard house. overlooking Vineyard Haven Harbor.

take shopping for groceries in Vineyard Haven and pick up our mail at the Post Office there. We also had a little Sunfish we all learned to sail around the Sound. When our new beachfront quarters were

Beach cottage on the Harbour.

finished, we sold the large colonial house and the two cottages. We all loved and looked forward every year to spending the summer in our idyllic Vineyard home, swimming, sailing, playing tennis and catching up with summer friends. Particularly memorable were the glorious evening clambakes and other cookouts on the beach where we gathered with old and new summering friends from Washington, New York and Boston.

WHIPPOORWILL FARM

While our Vineyard house proved to be a wonderful and many ways perfect solution to our family's summer vacation needs, the children's growing-up, highly active teen-age years, and pressures of school during the other months led to us discussing the value of a family weekend retreat that was conveniently close to our Albemarle Street house. As we had visited friends who had attractive getaway homes in the relatively nearby Maryland/Delaware Eastern Shore, that area became our first choice, we made arrangements to drive out there to look at some available properties.

We were just finishing breakfast on the clear, sunny spring Saturday scheduled for our Eastern Shore visit, when suddenly a jarring, arresting vision of my sitting frustrated, in virtually endless, unmoving, homeward-bound traffic approaching the heavily congested, lone Bay Bridge over Chesapeake Bay, made me put down my cup of hot chocolate and exclaim to Louise, "That damn Bay Bridge! It's a nightmare! It takes forever to cross weekends and I don't want to have to deal with that problem every time we go out there." There was dead silence, and then Louise asked resignedly, "How about a place in Virginia?"

I remembered a friend, Ed Harris, who had retired from the St. Louis Post Dispatch and was living and working as a real estate broker in Virginia's rural beautiful Rappahannock County among the Blue Ridge Mountains. With Louise's agreement, I telephoned him and learned he had just completed the sale of a former dairy farm on the outskirts of "Little Washington", the county seat. However, a separate, scenic, hillside 250-acre segment of the farm situated adjacent to the Rush River was available for sale. Saying it provided ample acreage on which we could build a house with spectacular views of the surrounding Rappahannock countryside, he encouraged us to drive out and look at it.

Two hours later we were meeting with Ed, who then showed us the hillside, which we walked with increasing delight at the fabulous views as the land sloped sharply down to the Rush River. Before we left to return to Washington, we had picked out a dramatic site with sweeping vistas, where we could build quickly and inexpensively a prefab A-frame weekend house. We signed a purchase contract for "250 acres, more or less," and we then spent nearly every weekend relaxing and enjoying this remarkably picturesque county's many rewards, including getting to know many of the colorful local people.

Lisbeth in front of the Washington, Virginia A-Frame on the Rush River.

During the next few years we were increasingly aware of the influx of new arrivals, including people we knew, who were also seeking a weekend second home. All of them attracted by Rappahannock County's stunning views, tranquility, superior outdoor recreational features, and it's easy accessibility to our Washington. One Saturday morning as we were enroute to our A-frame house, Louise read to me

Our Whippoorwill House

a story in the *Washington Post* about metropolitan Washington's fast-growing expansion into the area's rural communities, and the terrible environmental impact and destructive consequences when uncaring, insensitive developers moved in. Louise was concerned that it was only a question of time before developers came to Rappahannock, but she believed such development could be done in a restrained, sensitive and tasteful manner that would preserve the essence and beauty of the area without raping the land. She was intent on demonstrating how this could be done. Her vision and determination led her to find Whippoorwill Farm, a 1,000-acre working apple and peach farm a short walk to Little Washington. She organized a partnership that included Peter Labovitz, a developer who had taught planning at Harvard, Donald Brown and his JBG partners, Ben Jacobs and Joe Gildenhorn, and Rita Salzman, an interested friend to purchase it in 1971. As a result of Donald's expertise, the property was virtually cost free due to a very low-rate Federal farm loan and the sale of a small section of the land to Bob and Merci Eichholz that covered the down payment. Later, they sold the lumber to pay off the mortgage.

Peter's sensitive, environmentally friendly development plan laid out plots of either a minimum of 25 or 50 acres depending on the degree of slope of the land. The plan included the construction of a 40-acre lake, where we could swim, go boating and fish for sizable bass and other natural fish stocked by the state. Louise and I then sold our A-frame house and surrounding acreage on the Rush River,[10] and moved to a former, dilapidated, 18th century, stone farm house.

---

10. *The sale of the A-Frame revealed our acreage deficient by 50 acres. Approaching our lawyer, Jim Bill Fletcher, he pointed out that as he had also been Mrs, Cheatham's lawyer, and in true country fashion, he declared he could not possibly help to rectify the situation!*

Situated in our selected, designated plot, we completely rebuilt it with the help of Ellen Kurzman, a friend and talented architect, into an attractive, comfortable vacation cottage. It had a screened porch overlooking the lake I called "Lake Louise" and Peter's family called "Peter's Pond". I have fond memories of the many wonderful weekends and longer times we enjoyed there.

Donald and his JBG partners built a large, comfortable, carpeted "log cabin" just above the lake. Louise and her partners were content to keep Whippoorwill as a green, largely forested park-like, environmental jewel. And when it was finally sold nearly 35 years later, it was to a buyer who was committed to keeping the land free of any future inferior development.

Lisbeth riding Debby in a Rappahannock Point-to-Point race.

Lisbeth now began riding and acquired Debby her own jumper pony. With the help of a wonderful, lovely man, and talented trainer, Moody Aylor. Lisbeth developed into a competent rider, winning blue ribbons in local shows. As the youngest member of the Rappahannock Hunt, she rode and jumped over farm walls and fences with the more senior members of the Hunt as they chased a wild fox over the notoriously rugged Rappahannock countryside.

Lisbeth also competed in Rappahannock's spirited point-to-point pair races. I nervously held my breath as she raced Debby, jumping over the high barriers along the racecourse, until she safely crossed over the last hurdle and passed the finish line. Unfortunately, I was allergic to longhaired animals, making me acutely uncomfortable as tears blinded my eyes whenever I was close to Debby, and this became a fact of life with which I learned to live.

Another dominant feature of our family's weekend activities became the operations and stocking of The Country Store of Washington, VA, a partnership and joint venture that Louise and Sharon Labovitz started in Little Washington. Originally a somewhat decrepit looking building which held a weekend antique store in the center of town stocked with a small, miscellaneous array of undistinguished country antiques, their vision was to convert it into an attractive, inviting show case of high-quality crafts and collectible country antiques. The Sagalyn and Labovitz families joined forces on weekends to scout the

The Country Store of Washington, VA. (Currently, The Inn at Little Washington)

nearby Virginia and Amish Pennsylvania country auctions to purchase antiques and other stock for the store. Louise and I also filled crates of antiques to send back from the English countryside on trips abroad.

To attract customers, Louise and Sharon began staging and publicizing special country events, such as how to make Ukrainian Easter Eggs, and press newly harvested apples into tasteful cider. The soon started to attract hundreds, (and on one weekend, several thousands) of visitors from the big city to Little Washington and The Country Store of Washington, VA.

As a result, Peter and I found ourselves spending and enjoying an increasing part of the weekends helping our wives run The Country Store by taking over such important, strategic problems as picking up and hauling supplies and stock, and sweeping the floors at the close of day.

The severe gas shortages in the '70s drastically reduced the number of people driving out from the metropolitan Washington area to see the countryside and shop at the store. Louise and Sharon then conceived the idea of installing a restaurant in their building that would be a destination to attract customers to the combination restaurant and store. Their search led them to two young men operating a catering business in nearby Orange County, Patrick O'Connell and Reinhardt Lynch. After satisfying themselves on the high quality of their food, Louise and Sharon offered to share enough of the store's space to open a restaurant in their building. Louise also agreed to lend them the money they needed to set up the restaurant.

As Louise and Sharon had started to switch the sales of most of The Country Store's merchandise into a mail-order catalogue operation, reducing the amount of the building's space they needed, they agreed to give Patrick and Reinhardt an option to buy the entire building in five years. Named the Inn at Little Washington, the new restaurant became widely acclaimed by critics as one of the best restaurants in the U.S. But before the restaurant became famous, the boys created a difficult and extremely ugly situation that made the arrangement too uncomfortable to continue. That persuaded Louise and Sharon to allow them to buy the building immediately. Soon after the sale, Patrick and Reinhardt quickly rewrote the history of the Inn at Little Washington. In interviews with the press, restaurant and food critics, they stated they had started in an empty "former garage", obliterating completely the previous existence of The Country Store, and Louise's and Sharon's enabling role and financial assistance.[11]

GOOD BYE TO THE VINEYARD

Our quiet, tranquil summer vacations in Martha Vineyard changed dramatically when a multitude of press and radio–TV news media flooded into Martha's Vineyard following the July 19,1969, tragic accident of Senator Ted Kennedy when, in driving his car off a bridge in nearby Chappaquiddick and after swimming ashore, he failed to notify authorities about a young female passenger whose submerged body was found the next day. The resultant deluge of news and feature stories also included accounts of the island's beauty and attractive beaches, quickly attracting hordes of curious sightseers. Widely publicized promotional advertisements by the island's steamship authority offered special day trips from the main island. Before long, these "day-trippers" and their rented motor bikes were clogging the island's few, narrow paved roads making normal travel to the grocery store, post office or the beaches a nightmare for regular summer residents.

One of the main attractions of Martha's Vineyard for us had been that almost none of the summer residents were from Washington, so that our vacations were a real change in our social life. However, the enormous notoriety the island had received led to the "discovery" of the Vineyard by numerous other Washington residents, who ended up renting and buying summer vacation homes there. As a result we now kept running into people we knew from Washington who wanted to socialize with us and/or our children, asking what parties or beaches we were going to so we could meet.

The ultimate breaking point that caused us to sell our Vineyard house came later, when the now grown up Dana and Laurie had moved to New York to work, and announced they wouldn't be coming to the Vineyard. They discovered their friends in New York would all be going to the Hampton beaches during the summer, and this develop-

---

11. *The New Yorker (3/29/99) did a feature story,"The Inn Crowd" describing how the boys created dissention in the town of Washington with some of their unsavory behavior.*

ment and the venality of the Oak Bluff's tax office would precipitate the sale of our Vineyard summer home.

The following summers, we rented a series of houses at Nantucket, but found all of them too expensive and disappointing by comparison with what we had become used to at Martha's Vineyard. Instead, we decided to shift our vacations to Europe, principally Italy, France, and England.

WALKWAYS & WALKING VACATIONS

Hiking in the Dordognes, France.

In the 1980s our vacations changed into joining small groups on 7-10 day country walking trips in England, Italy and France. Louise, with the help of several friends, including Nancy "Bitsy" Folger, Ann Hoopes, Anita Jones, Edie Schafer and Joan Shorey, started Walkways, a nonprofit organization that promoted walking for fitness, health and recreation. Active vacations were part of the message. Organizations were developing that permitted travelers to walk from town to town free of backpacks while luggage was transported to the next town by station wagon. We were among their most ardent customers in this novel travel company nitch.

WalkWays published a monthly magazine on walking which I served as its editor. Walkways was a pioneer organization with a successful mission that ultimately encouraged American women and men to start a regular walking regime for fitness and health, including walking to work. An almanac on walking resources and a catalogue of walking accessories were also published. Walkways vision and efforts helped persuade reticent shoe manufacturers that women—who, they told us, cared only about fashionable shoes—would also be interested in walking shoes that were comfortable as well as stylish.

MOVE TO GEORGETOWN

1985 was a memorable year, triggered by the loss of one of our garden's magnificent oaks. The next day at breakfast Louise shared her sequential ruminations: "We have been living in our Albermarle Street house for 23 years, and not only do all of our kitchen appliances need replacement, but the house itself looks tired and needs refurbishing. But I've done this house twice before, and I just don't want to do it again. Furthermore, all our children are launched and the house is too big, what do you think about our looking for a new house?"

I was a little taken aback, but then I thought about the other enormous changes that had occurred during the past few years, such as Dana, Laurie and Rita growing up and moving out, and Lisbeth away at school, and how at times both of us felt we were rattling around in a half empty house. I could see why she was restless and wanting a change. But it was also true that I loved this commodious, comfortable old farmhouse, with its tennis court, swimming pool, and with lots of land and privacy adjoining Rock Creek Park. However, as I was sure she would never find anything I would like that was comparable to Albermarle Street, and to which I would agree, I said "Sure, go ahead and look."

As the weeks went by, she had looked at a lot of other houses, and from time to time I would go with her to look at a possibility. But there was nothing that rang a bell for both of us. Summer was almost here and we had made plans to vacation in Europe, when late one morning Louise telephoned, very excited. She had just seen the most perfect house. It was a stunning, two-story, brick house with a very large old-boxwood garden and with parking on the southwest corner of N and 30th streets in Georgetown. Its former owner, Helen Burgess had just died, and Louise's friend, Edie Schafer, was an agent for the broker selling the house and had persuaded Louise to see it.[12] "It was fantastic!" Louise told me, and I had to see it before the estate signed a contract with another prospective buyer. We were on our way to Nantucket for the Clare and Harris Wofford's wedding for their daughter Susie, and Louise urged me to stop by on the way to the airport.

Louise and Edie were waiting anxiously for me when I arrived at the Georgetown house, and hustled me though the front door into an ante room with fading wallpaper, and then into an enormous 40-foot long magnificent living room with a large marble central fireplace in the middle of a wall of bookcases. The entire rear wall consisted of floor to ceiling thick, sliding glass doors that opened onto a large garden dominated by a massive maize of boxwoods that stretched to a distant brick wall that enclosed the garden on three sides and served as boundary lines between our Southern neighbor and the Bradlee house.

It had been raining earlier and as I walked down the maize of Boxwood bushes, my light, summer suit was soaked by the wet, heavy Boxwood branches, which dampened my spirits as I would be wet on the airplane flight we were about to take. As Mrs. Burgess had been living in a rest home the last five years of her life there had not been much upkeep.

My overall impression was I was in a tired, depressing dwelling. My feeling was reinforced by the fading wall-paper in the hall, the living room's withering once beautiful silk drapes and the now darkened ceiling in the dining room by the years of black smoke from the many candles that had provided the room's only illumination. I did not like

---

12. *It was an 18th century structure that had been the coach house of George-town's historic Laird-Dunlop Manor House, the residence of Robert Todd Lincoln, President Lincoln's son. Helen Burgess, a granddaughter of J.P. Morgan, had bought and greatly enlarged it into its current form, as a large, magnificent house in which to live. The adjacent Manor House was the residence of Ben Bradlee, the former executive editor of The Washington Post.*

the patchwork repairs favored by a frugal Mrs. Burgess, such as the strips of scotch tape on cracked windows and the bare electric wiring that ran across a kitchen wall.

Louise and Edie were waiting for me near the front door when I had finished my personal tour of the house, and Louise's first words were. "Well, what do you think?" I knew she was going to be deeply disappointed, but I thought it best to be completely frank. "It's a disaster. I 'd never live here," I replied. And as I learned the next day that another couple we knew who had also been looking at the Coach House had signed a contract that same day; its availability had now become moot.

However, fate had intervened. Several weeks later Louise had a call from Edie. The couple who had signed the contract for the Coach House had discovered that a scenic easement Mrs. Burgess had put on the house, prevented them from making some planned changes that were critical to their family's space needs. As a result, the Coach House was back on the market again. And when Louise rushed to tell me about this new development and pleaded with me to reconsider our buying the house, I felt rather guilty about the abruptness and finality of my very brief inspection of the Georgetown house, and I knew how strongly she believed this particular house was the right one for us. In reviewing my initial, unfavorable impression, I recognized that my criticism of the poor maintenance, and cheerless condition of the rooms involved superficial aspects that Louise could easily rectify. And my previous reaction and assessment may not have been just, inasmuch as they did not deal with or represent the overall value of this unique historic house.

In fairness to Louise, I believed I needed to make a more thorough inspection and evaluation of the property and the pros and cons of living in Georgetown. Apart from my negative reaction, I had also been concerned about Georgetown's poor nighttime reputation arising from the numerous late-night bars and restaurants that attracted hordes of partying and often rowdy Georgetown college and other area youths. For many of these who emerged from the bars late at night, would often end up, intoxicated, carousing and disturbing the neighborhood peace.

To ascertain the gravity of reports of public safety problems, I spent a couple of weekend nights checking out the Coach House neighborhood and talking to the 2nd District police officials responsible for policing Georgetown, and satisfied myself that the police department was handling these problems generally satisfactorily. As a result, I told Louise I was agreeable if she wanted to put in a bid for this Georgetown house.

As we had made plans to leave in a few days for a vacation in Europe, we gave Edie our telephone number and cable address where she could reach us let us know whether our bid was accepted. In anticipation of this, we also selected a real estate broker to initiate the sale of our Albemarle Street house, and the day after our arrival at our destination in France we received a cable informing us our bid had been accepted.

The Georgetown house at 1248 30th Street, NW.

I loved living in our Albemarle Street house with its many amenities and our wonderful neighbors and friends. But I quickly discovered our elegant, compact, yet spacious Georgetown house with its large handsome garden and two, attached accessible garages at each end, all enclosed by high, attractive brick walls, better met our new reduced needs as a family of only two. Also, our accessible location on the SW corner of 30th and N Streets NW immediately introduced us to the special charms and many rewards of living in the Georgetown community. Especially notable was its friendly and cohesive small village aspects, a neighborly community where you walked everywhere and quickly met other residents when you shopped at nearby stores, or dined at one of the many restaurants.

Dana.

However, the reaction of my nephew Rafe, the first family member to visit us in our new house before the renovations, was of disbelief and disapproval. "How could you possibly have given up your Albemarle Street house for this?" he exclaimed. Perhaps understandable in light of his history of house-sitting at Albemarle Street, playing on our tennis court and swimming in our pool with his friends while we were in Martha's Vineyard. Happily, our daughters' responses were mostly laudatory. When Dana first saw our new house she said "I would have killed to have lived in Georgetown while I was a teenager." The girls all loved visiting the Georgetown house, and agreed with Dana when she said, "I don't have any of that old baggage here. I'm starting fresh, as an adult, so it's more fun and I look forward to coming back."

But Dana was suffering from depressive illness, a serious, ancient malady, previously known as melancholia, that had claimed Abraham Lincoln, Beethoven and Winston Churchill among it's many victims. Over the past years this debilitating mental illness took its toll, stifling any interest or enjoyment in activities that had once given her pleasure. She was consumed with an overwhelming sense of helplessness, hopelessness and pain. The existence of a stigma had led the general public—and even medical professionals—to believe this suffering was all in the victim's head, and wasn't a real illness with physical pain. And the stigma continues today, inhibiting parents and young people to seek help. The widely-held public myth that depression victims do not experience physical suffering has been disproved in recent years by scientific studies and publicized by the revelations of physical suffering experienced by American luminaries who have gone public. The distinguished author, William Styron, vividly described his pain as comparable to that of a "crushed knee".

One of the common symptoms of a depressive person is a sense of personal guilt and lack of self worth helps explain why Dana refused medical treatment. But 25 years ago when Louise and I sought medical assistance, we were frustrated by the incredibly limited scientific knowledge that existed about mental disorders and effective methods of treatment. Since the pioneering National Institute of Mental Health had only been created in 1948, the treatment of mental disorders was still in a relatively early research stage. Before long we discovered there was a scarcity of effective treatment. When we finally found a highly recommended psychiatrist with the requisite experience, however, Dana's strong aversion to anyone she believed wanted to control her mind made her hostile to psychiatric help. Although she would show up promptly for the appointment, she would spend the entire time in complete silence, all efforts to engage her in conversation. Later we heard of another practitioner who had had unusual success in prescribing a new, anti-depressant medication, we were elated when we were able persuade a reluctant Dana to make an appointment.

Unfortunately, to our great disappointment, Dana experienced an adverse reaction to the promising medication, and she refused all further medical treatment. Dana had been working as an elementary school teacher in New York City, loving being with young children, and she was reciprocally loved by them, as was attested by the letters we received from their parents. Therefore, she was devastated when she received a letter from the school principal informing her that he was terminating her employment. He would later explain that her work had been exemplary, but he had been led to believe she had only been interested in a temporarily teaching assignment.

The telephone call came the Labor Day weekend from the hotel where Dana had checked in the day before, informing us that Dana had taken an overdose of sleeping pills. She left individual letters addressed to Louise and me and to each of her three sisters, explaining her suicide as an act of her love for each us. And she left a carefully wrapped Christmas gift for us and for each sister. Dana was beautiful, she was smart and she was talented. She was 33 years old.

Now, twenty three years later, it is very hard and painful to re-read her long, handwritten, 11- page letter that begins, "Dear Mom and Dad," and asks us "Try to understand there wasn't an alternative. My only hesitation was the devastating effect this would have on you all . . . Do I blame anyone for my unhappiness? Absolutely, positively not. You mustn't feel guilty. . .there's nothing you could have done to prevent my death."

Despite Dana's letters that she alone was responsible for her death, we were completely shattered - individually and as a family. Each of us could not help asking if there hadn't been more, something, anything that could have been done to prevent it.

Fortunately, our friends and neighbors rallied to our support to console us. It took a long time, but we finally emerged from our grief and decided to establish a memorial in the mental health field to promote more scientific research into depressive illness and its effective treatment.

Within a few months, and with the support of friends we had raised significant funds. We consulted with Dr. Frederick Goodwin, the Director of the National Institute of Mental Health, and himself a leading authority on depressive illness, on how best to devote Dana's memorial fund to help other young victims of depressive illness.

Goodwin offered to help organize and participate in a 2-way education and discussion program on depressive illness that would be beamed from Washington via the college TV network. The National Alliance for the Mentally Ill (NAMI), was at the time a small grassroots organization whose volunteer citizen advocates were dedicated primarily to helping people with schizophrenia. We were impressed with their record of achievement. NAMI agreed to take on the project focusing on depression in young people and developed the discussion forum on depressive illness for the college TV network. It was a great success and helped to push NAMI into the field of depression. Today, NAMI has field offices all over the country assisting families coping with mental illness. It plays a major role in advocating in the public sector for improvements in the mental health field.

CRIME IN GEORGETOWN

In light of my earlier concern about public safety problems in Georgetown, and my own background in this area, I decided to become actively involved in reducing crime and improving the security in my new community. My first step was to talk with the police lieutenant at the 2nd District headquarters who was responsible for maintaining liaison with the Georgetown community, and obtain his views relative to Georgetown safety problems. I also wanted to know what his experience had been in obtaining the support of Georgetown residents in helping the police prevent street robberies, physical assaults, house and car thefts and other serious offenses that had become a real problem.

After I mentioned my criminal investigation background, he became very frank about Georgetown's vulnerability to criminal predators, largely attracted by the multitude of visitors with money in their pockets and seeking entertainment in the numerous bars and restaurants, he told me that when they exit the late-night bars and restaurants, they usually tend to be carefree and frequently intoxicated, making inviting and easy targets for the lurking criminals-in-waiting. As a result, Georgetown residents who happen to be on the street at night will also be potential crime victims. However, as the police department was overloaded and undermanned and received many calls for assistance at this time of night in other parts of the city as well, especially on weekends. There wasn't very much more they could do to alleviate this problem.

When I asked him what success the police department had in organizing the Georgetown community's awareness and support of crime prevention programs, he just shook his head, saying, we've found it's impossible to organize Georgetown residents. My follow-up investigation revealed that the community's representative organization, the Georgetown Citizens Association, CAG, was poorly funded, with one very part-time employee to assist an apathetic membership and leadership that were tiptoeing around their community's vulnerability to its growing crime and public safety problems. And I saw no signs of change on the horizon. Fortunately help was on the way. A strong, effective civic-minded Ev (Clyde) Shorey and his dynamic wife, Joan, who had been in Louise's class at Vassar, moved into Georgetown, and very soon after we joined forces to make Georgetown a safer and better place to live, work and visit.

Everett and Joan Shorey.

Invigorating the Citizens Association and its leadership with fresh talent capable of building up CAG's membership base and motivating them to participate more fully in measures that strengthened Georgetown's public safety was a high priority. I joined CAG, and, took over the chairmanship of the Committee on Crime and Public Safety. Previously it had been the policy of CAG"s leadership to regard the activities of the business community and Georgetown University as inimical to those of the residential community. This friction had led the 2nd District police commander to avoid responding to any major requests for police assistance unless there was agreement from all three parties.

Louise, Joan, Ev and I all believed it was in the residents best interest to work together with the business association and Georgetown University officials on issues we could agree on, particularly on crime and public safety. As chairman of CAG's Crime and Public Safety Committee, one of my first calls was to my counterpart crime committee chairman of the Business Association recommending we attend each other's meetings with the view to working out disagreements on subjects needing special police assistance. Halloween was a problem for the entire Georgetown community as huge, unruly Halloween night crowds swarmed into downtown Georgetown. The violent behavior of some drunken celebrants had resulted in serious injuries and even a fatality. Working together we were able to get the police department to annually assign a large contingent of additional uniformed officers to control the streets. The extra police details, along with curfews on serving liquor and blocking traffic were successful in ending the violence and the disorderly Halloween mobs.

At the same time, I believed we should move ahead on the critical crime problems by developing a long-term community crime prevention program that would cooperatively complement the police. As this would require statistical crime reports and analyses that would show where, when and why the most serious crimes were occurring in Georgetown, we commissioned a greatly respected, crime research and analysis organization directed by Jerry Wilson, a friend and the former distinguished Washington police chief. Their illuminating report on Georgetown's criminal "hot spots, pinpointed the time and specific street locations where serious violent and property crimes were taking place. The identification of these "hot spots" were invaluable in planning and executing effective counter-measures.

Recognizing that we could not expect extra help from the 2nd District's overburdened police resources, we concluded that our only alternative was to create our own security guard force. Hired and paid by CAG from contributions by residents, they wore a police-type uniform, patrolled a specific beat of several blocks unarmed, but carried a cell phone to call 911 in the event they saw a crime being committed or otherwise needed help. Residents who contributed to the guard program were given their neighborhood guard's telephone number, and could call a guard to walk them home from their parked car, or walk a guest to or from his/her car.

On his part, Ev's reputation and outstanding record of integrity, reliability and accomplishments found him taking on the duties of Treasurer of the Citizen's Association, and straightening out it's tough, neglected financial problems. In June 1993 he was elected President of CAG, and I was elected Vice-President. One of our most important achievements was to organize an annual fund-raising campaign that brought in enough money to hire a competent full-time executive director to manage CAG.

Joan turned her considerable people talent to developing a Neighborhood Watch program. She organized block meetings and appointed block captains dedicated to significantly improving the security of Georgetown's residents and visitors. To educate and sensitize Georgetown residents about the local crime threats and obtain their support of the block program, I produced a short video, filmed by my nephew Dan Sagalyn, entitled "Georgetown at Risk," which was shown at block meetings. Within a relatively short time, Joan organized an astounding more than 80 blocks in Georgetown, each one led by a civic minded citizen block captain.

In 1998, I was awarded the Citizens Association prestigious Peter Belin Award, given " in recognition of his distinguished contributions to the Georgetown community." Four years later, Ev and Joan's outstanding services to Georgetown would be heralded when they jointly received the Belin Award.

THE MYSTERY OF THE SAGALYN NAME PRONUNCIATION

A rose by any other name would smell as sweet.
  Gertrude Stein

After more than 50 years of witnessing the bewilderment and speculative theories as to why my family pronounces the Sagalyn family name with the emphasis on the first syllable, Sag-al-lyn, while all my nieces, nephews and cousins emphasize the second syllable, Sa-gal-lyn. I want to take advantage of this opportunity to apologize to all Sagalyn family members for the mystery and confusion I never intended or expected, and explain how it came about.

From the time I was born in 1918, the Sagalyn name had been pronounced by emphasizing the second, middle syllable, Sa-gal-lyn, although my father tended to give a softer sa-gaul-lyn sound to the name. As my father was a very prominent businessman and supported numerous civic and charitable enterprises, the Sagalyn name was well known, highly respected and readily recognized when spoken with the emphasis on the second syllable.

So the pronunciation was never a topic of debate in Massachusetts, but in college it was sometimes mispronounced in strange and unusual ways. This was largely resolved when my classmates tagged me with the convenient nickname of "Sag." (One Wesleyan classmate, seeking to be funny or more creative started to call me "Four Quarts." Baffled, I fell into his carefully planned trap when I stopped and questioned him the second time he had greeted me as "Four Quarts." "What's this 'Four Quarts'?" I asked him. "How did you ever come up with that name?" "Don't you see, four quarts, that's a gallon, he replied with a big grin.)

My first real problem with the Sagalyn pronunciation occurred after I started working for Eliot Ness in Cleveland, and my job as his personal aide required me to make and receive a steady volume of telephone calls. To my great surprise when I gave the caller my full name, Arnold Sagalyn, I would tend to receive a puzzled reply of "Who?" and then hear astounding variations of Sagalyn, most often sounding like "Scallion." The problem, I thought, was the combination of Arnold and Sagalyn, where my emphasis of Arnold on the first syllable, Arn-old, followed by the emphasis on the second syllable in Sa-gal-lyn made the combination appear to merge, making it very difficult for the other persons to understand what I was saying. As a result, I was exasperated and frustrated, as I would have to keep repeating my name over and over again, while the person I was speaking to would keep repeating back some strange variations that bore no resemblance to Arnold Sagalyn. After several weeks of these frequent, and very time-consuming telephone dialogues, I telephoned my father in Springfield to share my problem with him and to suggest a possible solution.

The basic difficulty, I told him, is that unlike back home people out here tend to emphasize a name's first syllable. For example, if your name is Robinson, Rob gets the emphasis. As a result, our pronunciation seems to be hard for them to understand. However, I told him, I discovered that if I stressed the first part of our name, Sag-al-lyn, there was no problem. There was a brief chuckle from my father. "I'm sorry you are having this problem," he said. No one pronounces our name correctly anyway. So if your pronunciation makes it easier for people there to understand you, go ahead and say it that way. It is still spelled the same." And that is how the different pronunciation of Sagalyn started.[13]

But as often happens when you do something that seems a good solution for a current and one-time situation, there are sometimes unexpected consequences that cannot be easily reversed and can come back to plague you. Curiously enough, I had naively made an earlier name change blooper as a spur of the moment lark, believing it would remain a private joke and no one would ever notice it. It occurred when I was helping write my high school graduation yearbook in 1935, and it, too, came back to haunt me. My job was to select apt and often humorous quotations to accompany each graduating student's record of activities, affiliated clubs etc. In the process, I noticed that most of my classmates had middle names, and I did not, so I impulsively decided to give myself a middle name and selected James, perhaps because I thought it sounded dignified. And my new middle name, I thought, would exist only in the school's 1935 yearbook.

I gave it no further attention until I had to send a transcript of my school grades to Wesleyan soon after my high school graduation and I discovered the school had inserted my recently created middle name, James, in my record of grades. I really didn't like my invented middle name, but I recognized I had unwittingly created a permanent type of parasite that would become part of my name officially on all my future college records and follow me in future military documents when I enlisted in the Army. But my luck was still with me, the U.S. Army only recorded middle initials, causing James to disappear, to be replaced instead by the initial "J". And now I became Pvt. Arnold J. Sagalyn. And after the war, I was able to drop the middle initial J as well, becoming just plain old Arnold Sagalyn when I started fresh again in my journalism years.

---

13. *My Sagalyn pronunciation problem and occasional query about the name's origin led me to raise this latter question with my father my next visit home. He told me that his forebears had been traders who had traveled all over the Far East, as well as Eastern Europe, and the Sagalyn name had arisen out of their far-flung travels.*

But foolish mistakes often have a life of their own. Many years later, I obtained through the Freedom of Information Act, copies of my FBI and Secret Service investigative background and security reports. Alongside my name, Arnold (NMI) Sagalyn, would always appear the words, "aka Arnold J. Sagalyn."

However, the first syllable emphasis on the Sagalyn name that began with Eliot Ness was to continue, despite later attempts to return to the Massachusetts pronunciation with the emphasis on the second syllable. So many of my friends and associates in Cleveland—including Clayton Fritchey, Keith Wilson, Kay Halle and Dan Goldy—were to continue as close friends in my later years and activities. Thus, I found reverting to the original pronunciation of Sagalyn too complicated and awkward. But on frequent occasions when I'm in the Berkshires, or other places where Sagalyn relatives live, when I give my name I will emphasize the middle syllable of Sagalyn and readily acknowledge that to be the correct pronunciation if asked.

This name pronunciation confusion arose again when my nephews Rafe and Danny came to Washington and their jobs and acquaintances interacted with mine. People in town are often puzzled and question us about our family relationship. From time to time, I take the time to explain why we pronounce our family name differently.

Regrettably, I've learned that some things cannot be easily solved by trying to cut the Gordian knot that sticks to the pronunciation of a name. Happily, however, the Washington Sagalyns have managed to take in stride the two interchangeable pronunciations of Sagalyn, acknowledging the difference in pronunciation as the occasion arises. No matter how it's pronounced, we are the same close Sagalyn family and over the years our family ties, periodic social gatherings and reciprocal feelings of mutual love and affection have remained warm and strong.

RETURN TO GOVERNMENT SERVICE
1961-1968

Chapter 11

Don't let it be forgot
That once there was a spot—
For one brief shining moment
That was known as Camelot
> Alan Lerner

TREASURY

John F. Kennedy's dynamic, youthful style and his exciting victory over Vice-President Richard Nixon in the 1960 presidential campaign had immediately stirred my strong interest in returning to government service. When I told Clayton, Phil and George of my intention, I was not surprised to learn that each one was already exploring working for Kennedy.[14]

Ideally, I wanted to find a job for which offered new, challenging experiences. I began my search by focusing on two areas where I had creditable experience--public information and law enforcement, quickly concluding the law enforcement area was much more interesting and adventurous, in light of my experience with Eliot Ness. To assist my search, I consulted the Plum Book, published by the Government Printing Office after each presidential election, with listings of the executive branch "Schedule C" policy and supporting positions.

---

14. *Clayton became Public Affairs Advisor to Adlai Stevenson, the new U.S. Ambassador to the United Nations, Phil Stern was appointed a Deputy Assistant Secretary for Public Affairs in the State Department, and George Ball joined the Kennedy Administration as Under Secretary at the State Department.*

Although the Justice Department would appear the logical place to start looking, I knew they would prefer applicants with a law degree. However, the Treasury Department had wide-ranging domestic and international law enforcement responsibilities and employed thousands of criminal investigators. Besides, Eliot Ness had had a very successful and adventurous career as a Treasury agent in what was now known as the Alcohol and Tobacco Tax Division of its Internal Revenue Service, which made the thought of working in the Treasury especially appealing.

When I opened the Plum Book, I turned immediately to the Treasury Department listings. My eyes suddenly lit up, and I felt a stab of excitement as I saw it: "Assistant to the Secretary for Enforcement." I read that the position's responsibility was to advise the Secretary on law enforcement policy and coordinate the criminal investigative operations of Treasury's seven separate law enforcement agencies: the U.S. Secret Service; the Bureau of Narcotics; the Investigations and Enforcement Division of the Bureau of Customs; the Intelligence, Inspection and Alcohol and Tobacco Tax Divisions of the Internal Revenue Service; and the Intelligence Division of the U.S. Coast Guard. The position also had responsibility for directing the training of Treasury's 4,000 criminal investigators.

This was a perfect job--one I never even dreamed existed. Moreover, it somehow seemed fitting and predestined that this position would have oversight over Eliot Ness' former agency. I saw only one significant problem: getting in to see and then to convince Kennedy's new Treasury Secretary, Douglas Dillon, that he should hire me. My luck was clearly holding up. I was told this appointment would be made by Secretary Dillon's principal Undersecretary of Treasury, Henry "Joe" Fowler, whom I knew as a friend and neighbor in Old Town Alexandria. More important, Louise had previously worked with him to elect Democratic candidates in Virginia.

I received a quick appointment with Fowler, who greeted me warmly, and listened intently as I described my strong interest in the Treasury enforcement appointment and handed him my resume. After reading through it carefully, he questioned me at length and in detail about my work--first with Eliot Ness in Cleveland and Washington, then my experience during World War II as a military government officer establishing law and order in newly captured German towns and cities. Later, my work in the Public Safety Branch, Office of Military Government for Germany, U.S. Headquarters in Berlin, which was responsible for overseeing and reorganizing Germany's criminal and security police organizations.

At the end of our interview, Fowler commented favorably on my qualifications for the Treasury enforcement position, but he explained that the appointment would be contingent on my successful completion of various professional, political, character and security prerequisite requirements. These included letters of recommendation and support from highly reputable law enforcement professionals; testimonials to my good character, habits and loyalty to America from former employers, associates, and other creditable persons who knew me well— and political support.

I knew I had to provide these supportive testimonials and assembled them in a special folder as they arrived. I focused my attention on completing the critical Federal Employment Form 57 Application, The Form 57 was a comprehensive and detailed questionnaire covering my whole life's history, starting with my date and place of birth and continuing with my education, all my previous jobs, employers and residences, foreign and domestic. As the sensitivity of the Treasury position required me to posess a top-secret security clearance, I had to undergo a "full-field" background and security investigation by Federal investigators of my character and loyalty to the US. Their probe routinely verified the accuracy of every item and statement on the Form 57 questionnairea, and in the process they interviewed past and current classmates, friends, neighbors, employers and associates concerning my conduct, character, loyalty to the United States, reputation and personal habits, such as excessive drinking and gambling.

 Fortunately, the onerous task of filling out this exhaustive multipage Form 57 and remembering accurately long-ago dates and addresses, was facilitated enormously having been through a similar background and security vetting by the Army's Counter Intelligence Corps (CIC) nine years earlier, in1952, when I worked for Clayton Fritchey at the Pentagon. I was lucky because, unlike virtually all other Federal agencies who were dependent on the FBI to conduct their Form 57 employment investigations, the Treasury Department used the Secret Service to vet it's own employees.[15]

Arnold's swearing in: Arnold, Laurie, Louise, Dana, Rita and Treasury Undersecretary, Henry "Joe" Fowler.

On April 5, 1961, my official appointment as Director of Law Enforcement Coordination[16] was announced in a Treasury press release, and was followed by a swearing-in ceremony conducted by Undersecretary Fowler, with my proud mother, Louise, my daughters, and a

---

15. *This was critical in my case, because as a naive, young reporter on the Cleveland Press, I had incurred the enmity of the FBI's Director, J. Edgar Hoover when, as a reporter on the Cleveland Press,I had written on spec an article that questioned the wisdom of the FBI policy of reassigning FBI agents every one or two years. That incident was to cause potential trouble for me in later years. See chapter 12.*

16. *A memorandum from Secretary Dillon's office stated a change in my position's title from Assistant to the Secretary for Enforcement to Direct or of Law Enforcement Coordination, was a difference in name only, and that all of the previous position's functions and responsibilities would remain the same. It noted I would continue to "represent the Office of the Secretary in operational aspects of all Treasury law enforcement activities."*

number of friends, in attendance. Looking back at that event all these many years later, I must admit no one there was prouder than I was. Part of that was the realization that just 22 years after starting my job with Eliot Ness, I was now responsible for the training and coordination of the operations of the criminal investigators of his former Federal employer, the Alcohol and Tobacco Tax Division of Treasury's Internal Revenue Service - as well as Treasury's other six criminal investigative agencies.

I had received a temporary Treasury consulting appointment a few weeks earlier in anticipation of my successful completion of the investigations and was assigned a small office on the top floor of the main Treasury building, where I could read unclassified briefing materials which were supplemented by oral briefings. As a result, transition into my official duties went very smoothly, and I was well-prepared to chair my first Treasury Enforcement Board meeting with all seven of the department's criminal investigative agencies.

Treasury Department ID.

After the swearing in, I was thoroughly delighted with my new office located in the lower Northwest corner of the Treasury building at 1500 Pennsylvania Avenue and adjacent to the White House. It was a spacious, impressive room with high ceilings and towering marble pillars, while the high, narrow, barred windows facing Pennsylvania Avenue filtered in the outdoor light. A large American flag stood behind my massive, highly polished desk, and hanging on the wall behind me were an extraordinary display of contraband objects that had been seized by Treasury agents. They ranged from menacing-looking machine guns, sawed-off shotguns, and automatic rifles to large rugs and colorful porcelain jars that had been decorated with unlawful, reproductions of various denominations of U.S. currency.

Sitting immediately outside my office in a small modest entry room, was my inherited, guardian secretary and absolute jewel, Mrs. Florence Bridges, and nearby was the desk of my experienced and aimable deputy, Fred Douglas, a former Secret Service agent. Both had served in their current positions for many years, and were familiar with the operations and the principal officers of the various Treasury law enforcement agencies. They would prove incredibly resourceful and invaluable in helping me carry out my duties and responsibilities.

INTERPOL

Virtually every day brought new challenging events and tasks, and none was more intriguing than the telephone call I received one bright, sunny June morning from Assistant Secretary Gilmore Flues, informing me that I would be a member of the U.S. delegation to the annual meeting of the International Criminal Police Organization (Interpol), which would be held in Madrid that Fall. Flues, a holdover from the Eisenhower administration, who had direct supervision over the Secret Service and Bureau of Narcotics and administrative oversight over many of my activities, would be serving as Chairman of the U.S. delegation, as he had been the previous years. What little I had previously known about Interpol had come principally from fanciful detective and mystery novels. Therefore, I found the prospect of actually attending Interpol's annual meeting as an official U.S. delegate very exciting.

Founded in 1923 by delegates from 20 primarily European countries to combat international crime, It's constitution restricts Interpol activities to common law crimes in all countries and prohibits it to intervene or undertake any activities of a political, military, religious or racial nature. By choice, neither Russia nor any of the Communist block countries were members ,and by 1961 Interpol had grown into an international depository for criminal files and fingerprints, and served as a criminal information clearing house and control center, with a police telecommunications network serving 83 sovereign member countries. At that time, it was based in Paris and it's Secretariat and Secretary General were all employees of France's criminal police, La Sûreté.

Interpol members comprised its General Assembly, the supreme governing body, which met annually in a different member country, and elected Interpol's officers, who constituted its Executive Committee, and were responsible for implementing the General Assembly's decisions and maintaining close contact with the Secretary General. Contrary to most fictional accounts, Interpol's employees had no international legal authority to investigate a crime or make an arrest. Instead, it relied on the indigenous law enforcement forces of its network of National Central Bureaus, which each member country was required to establish. Membership in Interpol was restricted to sovereign nations, each of whom designated a representative.

When the U.S. became a member in 1938, the Justice Department was designated as its representative and appointed its FBI Director, J. Edgar Hoover to serve in this capacity. He severed his relations with Interpol in 1950, following a bitter dispute. However, several of Treasury's law enforcement agencies had offices in London, Paris, and Rome, and they continued to maintain an informal relationship with Interpol. Then, in 1958 the U.S. enabling act was amended to authorize the Justice Department to designate the Treasury Department as U.S. Representative to Interpol. (Currently , this representative authority is back in the Justice Department.)

The week before I was scheduled to accompany Flues to Madrid, I was stunned when informed that Flues had to cancel his trip, and I would be taking his place as chairman of the U.S. delegation to Interpol. As the delegation's chairman, I would have to write a report to the State Department on the highlights of the meeting, including the major decisions made by the General Assembly. The other members of the U.S. Delegation primarily were representatives of those Treasury Law Enforcement Agencies that had international regulatory responsibilities, and they included Charles Siragusa, the highly competent and charismatic Deputy Commissioner of the Bureau of Narcotics, with a legendary record of top Mafioso convictions; Paul Paterni the Deputy Chief of the Secret Service, whose main concern was the increasing foreign counterfeiting of U.S. currency; Philip Nichols. Jr., the Director of the Bureau of Customs; Al Long the Internal Revenue Service's Director of Intelligence, and Byron Engle, the Director of the Office of Public Safety, of the U.S. Agency for International Development.

They would devote most of their time in committee meetings, talking business and developing new working relationships with key law enforcement officials of the various countries.

I, on the other hand, focused my attention on educating myself about Interpol's organization and operations, and in the course of becoming acquainted with it's the Secretary General, I learned that the General Assembly would be electing its new officers on it's last day, including three vice- presidents (VPs) representing the world's major geographical regions, each serving the Executive Committee during a 3-year term. The first VP to be chosen would represent North and South America, and the Commissioner of The Royal Canadian Mounted Police (RCMP), Canada's national police force, was running unopposed for this vice-presidency.

At the first meeting of our delegation there was strong sentiment that this office should rightly be held by the United States, but nothing more was said about this and I felt it was inappropriate for me to propose myself as the U.S. candidate. Therefore, I was very surprised the next day when I was told that Charlie Siragusa and Byron Engle had teamed up together to campaign for my election and were hard at work systematically soliciting the support of the delegates the 83 member countries. Although I had been introduced to Siragusa at my first meeting of the Treasury Enforcement Board, and had heard about his numerous achievements, I knew very little else about him. And I had only met Engle in Madrid at our delegation's first meeting, but I soon would got to know him very well when our work paths crossed and we became good friends.

I did not take this electioneering news very seriously, as I understood Canada's RCMP candidate already had a big lead. If I had known them as well as I did later, I would have understood that Charlie and Byron were forces to contend with. It was their firm belief that the U.S. merited the VP office and its membership on Interpol's Executive Committee and they were confident they could persuade a majority of Interpol members to vote for the U.S. candidate. But I was fully occupied with my various duties as chairman of the delegation and not fully aware of their campaign. Therefore, when election day came and the voting took place, I was bowled over and temporarily speechless when the vote tally of the first vice-presidency position, North and South America, was announced with my name as the winner. As the first of the three vice-presidents elected, I would be the senior VP, and when the General Assembly met in Helsinki in 1963, I would preside over the Assembly in the absence of Interpol's president.[17]

The United States Representative

International Criminal Police Organization (Interpol)

and Mrs. Arnold Sagalyn

send Greetings of the Season

and Best Wishes for the New Year

Protocol Christmas card sent to Interpol representatives.

As my election to the vice-presidency simultaneously made me a member of Interpol's Executive Committee, I was obliged to travel to Paris every Spring for committee meetings. Fortunately, Louise was able to accompany me on some of these trips to Paris and to annual General Assembly conclaves in the Fall. Accordingly, I arranged to take some of my vacation leave at the conclusion of these Interpol meetings, and Louise and I vacationed in various parts of Europe with friends, usually Abe and Toni Chayes. We still reminisce about the memorable culinary tours of multi-starred restaurants, the tasting trips to notable vineyards and other unforgettable joyous times and places. One hilarious incident occurred when we checked into a hotel in Athens. I wanted to make a courtesy call to the head of the Greek National Criminal Police, my Interpol associate. Unfortunately, I did not have his telephone number, so I called the hotel operator and asked her how to reach him. She said "Just a minute please." The next thing I heard was a masculine voice identifying himself as the hotel manager and then asking, "Why are you want to talk to the head of criminal police? Do you have a dead body in your room?" He sounded much relieved when I indicated my real purpose.

---

17. *Interpol's president, Sir Richard Jackson, Assistant Commissioner(Crime) at Scotland Yard had to return to London following the sensational Great Train Robbery, in which a large criminal gang ambushed the Glasgow-London mail-train carrying more than $50 million worth of British currency.*

These combination Interpol-vacation sojourns started propitiously the following year, when Louise accompanied me to the Fall meeting of the General Assembly in Copenhagen. This second trip turned out to be a glorious visit, because my old friend, Bill Blair, who was now the new Ambassador to Denmark, had invited us to his spectacular wedding, a glittery, star-studded social event which was held that same week in a magnificent historic cathedral. Blair also gave a special reception at the American Embassy, in my honor as Chairman of the U.S. Delegation and Vice President to Interpol.

Interpol meeting in Brazil, 1964.

That event gave me invaluable insights into the traditional punctuality of the Danes, as well as experiencing a deep personal embarrassment. The Embassy invitation had stated the reception time as 6 p.m. But used to the flexibility of arrival times at Washington's social events we innocently arrived at 6:10 , only to be shocked and dismayed to discover most of the Danish officials and the other invitees had already entered the American Embassy door promptly at 6:00 p.m. Even more distressing was to discover all of them had already passed through the official greeting line, where we were expected to greet them. Otherwise, it was a very lovely reception.

Apart from Treasury's Customs, Narcotics, Secret Service and Internal Revenue agencies, and the FBI and Justice Department, virtually no other Federal, state and local law enforcement organizations knew very much about Interpol or its services. Then one day I had a call from State Department informing me that this lack of knowledge was causing some serious problems. From time to time, individual U.S. police departments were receiving requests from foreign police agencies for assistance in apprehending U.S. citizens traveling abroad, who allegedly had defrauded commercial establishments or foreign nationals. In some cases the accused U.S. citizens had been arrested and held for deportation by the police department, only to learn belatedly that the U.S. had no treaty with the country authorizing the arrest and deportation for the alleged crime. Could I help prevent these?

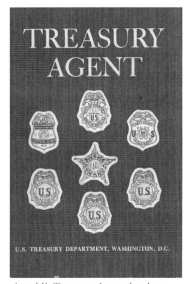

Arnold's Treasury Agents brochure.

Since my office also served as the U.S. National Central Bureau (NCB), the U.S. clearing house for all communications between foreign Interpol members and U.S. police agencies, I wrote an article on Interpol's role published in Police Chief, the publication of the principal U.S. police association, the International Association of Chiefs of Police, which was widely read by local and state law enforcement officials. It addressed this extradition problem and the proper international procedures for assuring that any request relating to a criminal offense was covered by an existing treaty between the U.S. and the foreign country concerned.

One immediate result was a large Increase in Interpol related correspondence that overloaded my and Fred Douglas's capability to give them the time and attention needed, especially those that sometimes involved highly sensitive domestic and foreign policy issues. I concluded the time had come to appoint a full-time person to run the NCB. As I believed Andrew Tartaglino, a senior Bureau of Narcotics agent, who I worked with on Interpol matters, had the experience and good judgment needed. I called Henry Giordano the Commissioner of the Bureau of Narcotic, who agreed to Andy's long-term loan to my office to run the NCB.

The variety and challenges of my Treasury liaison activities resulted in a continuously interesting agenda that made me look forward every day to solving complicated law enforcement policy and management problems. There were frequent meetings with top Justice Department officials on important criminal justice issues and I developed and enjoyed a cordial, cooperative working relationships with a wide range of Justice Department officials, particularly those in the Criminal Division. Many of these meetings related to organized crime, as Treasury agents had been primarily responsible for producing the evidence needed to successfully prosecute Justice's major organized crime cases. Inasmuch as FBI's director, J. Edgar Hoover, had long denied the very existence of the Mafia in the U.S., it was only after our Bureau of Narcotics had turned over to the FBI its notorious Mafia informant, Joe Valachi, that Hoover and the FBI officially discovered the Cosa Nostra.

But my liaison responsibilities extended beyond the Criminal Division to other sections of Justice. One day I had a call from my good friend Burke Marshall, the Assistant Attorney General, Civil Rights, who was one of the brightest stars at Justice and for whom I had huge respect. Burke was on a mission to desegregate the closed, all-white profile of the FBI and Secret Service, and his monthly telephone calls to me followed a fixed pattern of questions and answers that were especially memorable. Just before noon the last day of every month my phone would ring and I would hear Burke's soft, polite voice, "Arnold, this is Burke. I am calling to find out how many Negro agents the Secret Service hired this month?"[18] To which I invariably replied, "Burke, I talked to Chief Rowley about this earlier this week and he told me

---

18. *Negro is a term referring to people of Black ancestry. Prior to the shift in the lexicon of American and worldwide classification of race and ethnicity in the late 1960s, the appellation was accepted as a normal neutral formal term both by those of Black African descent as well as non-African blacks. Now it is often considered an ethnic slur, although the term is considered archaic and is not common as a racist slur. The term is still used in some contexts for historical reasons such as in the name of the United Negro College Fund.*

he's working hard on this problem, but all the qualified Negro candidates have prison records that disqualify them. I told Rowley that all young Negroes who usually have few places to meet and socialize except on their local street corners, have arrest records for either 'loitering,' or for 'failing to obey' a police officer to move along. These are not serious offenses and shouldn't count against hiring them." Then I would ask him, "Burke, how many Negro FBI agents has Mr. Hoover hired this month?" And every month, Burke would routinely reply, "The Director has told me he has increased the number of Negro agents 100%." And each time I would respond, "Does that mean he has one black agent now, or two?" Then there would be a brief pause after which Burke would repeat in his soft, ever so polite tone, "The Director has told me he has increased the number of Negro agents 100%."

I also developed a close working relationship with Courtney Evans. Assistant Director of the FBI's Special Investigative Division, which began when we both were appointed to serve along with a senior State Department representative, as an oversight committee for the Office of Public Safety (OPS) in the U.S. Agency for International Development (AID). Originally established by President Eisenhower to train foreign police forces in Latin America, it was revitalized by President Kennedy to train civilian police forces in friendly Third World governments to help them counter Communist subversion and insurgency. This program trained newly created civilian police forces who lived in and among local communities, and would also provide needed and more humane public protection. These police forces would be under the direct control of the president, or other civilian chief executive and thus provide a power base separate and independent from the military forces. The introduction of civilian policemen was seen as winning the support of the civilian population that traditionally had been policed by the country's military forces who, tended to respond to civilian disorders with brutal repressive force, using their indiscriminating, deadly military weapons .

Robert Kennedy, the Attorney General, and Averell Harriman, Under Secretary of State for Political Affairs, both took an active interest in this OPS program, which was directed by Byron Engle. I had originally met him when he was a member of the U.S. delegation to the

Interpol meeting in Madrid and he had been enormously helpful in my Interpol election to be Vice President, and we would become good friends. As Director of the OPS project, Byron established an international police training school in a large building near Key Bridge in Georgetown that had formerly housed the city's street cars. I later gave a regular lecture there on the U.S. police system for senior foreign police officials.[19]

I sometimes explained my unique law enforcement position to visitors foreign to Washington and the ways of our government as being the only one in the Office of the Secretary of the Treasury who had nothing to do with money unless it was counterfeit. One time however, my job thrust me into a situations that was concerned with money and would have international consequences. A telephone call I had from the Director of the Intelligence Division of the Internal Revenue Service, Al Long, who asked me to persuade Treasury Secretary Douglas Dillon to terminate the printing and usage of all high denomination currency above $100. The IRS felt that this might be an effective way of preventing their use in evading income taxes. As Long explained it, the large denomination currency, such as the $1,000 and $5,000 bills, were enabling many large tax evaders to easily conceal and carry out of the country huge amounts of money without detection or reporting it to the Treasury.

I told him I would look into it and checked with knowledgeable Treasury and outside sources about the feasibility and consequences of withdrawing these high denominations from circulation. I discovered that while these large bills had once been important and necessary in auctions and other business activities, the development and wide acceptance of bank letters of credit, and more recently credit cards, greatly diminished the need for $1,000 and larger value currency . My study also revealed that the U.S. was the only remaining large, industrial country that still issued bills of such high denominations.

---

19. *In 1974, following contentious reports that a police trainer in Latin America had been teaching torture techniques in an interrogation course, Congress killed the OPS Aid program and prohibited U.S. Training assistance to foreign countries. However, OPS's policing and counterinsurgency missions were reportedly taken over by other U.S. agencies.*

I wrote a memorandum to Secretary Dillon reporting Long's request, and my findings and recommendation that he terminate their future issuance. While these high denomination bills would remain legal tender and be honored by the banks, they would be withdrawn by the Federal Reserve Banks when they routinely came in, and would not be recirculated for future use. The signed endorsement and approval of all the heads of the Treasury divisions concerned were attached. My findings also included the fact that the Treasury would benefit financially, as many of these large bills over the years had likely been destroyed or otherwise lost so they would no longer represent a retrievable charge against the Treasury.

Shortly after that, I had a call reporting that the Secretary had approved my memorandum, but he wanted Mr. Long to send a memorandum for the file documenting the tax violation basis for his action. I immediately called Long to report the good news and the Secretary's request . Al expressed his delight, thanked me for my help and assured me he would get the memo to me right away. A week went by, with no memo. After the second week, I called him to ask what happened to his memo. There was a long silence, and then with great embarrassment, he informed me that while the Intelligence Division knew these income tax violations were occurring with the aid of the large thousands of dollars denominations, his staff were unable to document this. But the secretary's approval had already been processed, and the high denomination bills were withdrawn from circulation.

I became involved in another intriguing IRS intelligence project, following a telephone call from Assistant Secretary Stan Surrey, a brilliant Harvard financial economist, who now was in charge of Treasury's tax policy. I had previously enjoyed working with him on a high profile tax-evasion case that was stymied by our failure to gain access to the secret Swiss bank account of a targeted a prominent American business allegedly in violation of US laws . Stan now asked me if I could fly out to Las Vegas to check on the operations and progress of a special IRS undercover unit, whose mission was to obtain the evidence needed to prove the gambling casinos were regularly "skimming" the profits of their daily receipts to avoid paying the requisite U.S. income tax.

When I arrived at the city's airport. I was met by head of the IRS detail, who immediately led me off to an isolated area where he quietly briefed me on IRS's difficult operating conditions. Any time we want to talk, he told me, we had to go outdoors, because the hotel and all the public rooms, were likely to be "bugged". The casino operators did this routinely to protect themselves against anyone planning to rob them. They also picked up a lot of valuable information that could be useful for other protective and, reportedly, blackmail purposes. During the next few days I discovered the casinos had such intensive and effective security that they succeeded in defeating, at least temporarily Surrey's and IRS's tax enforcement efforts in Las Vegas. The trip was a very educational and enlightening introduction to the Las Vegas gambling world.

One of my life's most fearful-for-my -family experiences was the Cuban missile crisis that lasted two weeks in October 1962 and brought the United States and Russia to the terrifying brink of nuclear war. (The Soviet Army Chief of Operations was quoted as saying, "Nuclear catastrophe was hanging by a thread. . . and we weren't counting days or hours, but minutes.") This emotional reign of terror was triggered when CIA aerial photos on Oct. 15 revealed that the Soviet Union was constructing nuclear missile sites in Cuba, only 90 miles from Florida, to defend the island against a future attack by the U.S.

After tense meetings with his national security advisors, President Kennedy spoke to the nation on October 22 informing them of the Soviet nuclear missiles in Cuba that were capable of hitting Washington and any other city in the Southeastern part of the United States. Kennedy said he was ordering a naval quarantine of Cuba to prevent the Russians from bringing in military weapons and supplies, and he demanded the removal of the Soviet missiles and sites. And he warned Krushschev that any nuclear missile launched from Cuba would result in a "full retaliatory response upon the Soviet Union." But the resultant messages exchanged between Kennedy and the Soviet Premier Krushchev brought increasing tensions and confusion each passing day as they failed to clarify each other's intentions. And the knowledge that Russia's had medium size missiles that were capable of hitting Washington heightened the enormous concern that dominated our conversations when we met talked with our friends, for this threat of an imminent nuclear catastrophe was hard to ignore.

And this hovering Armageddon seemed to be confirmed when a call from Treasury's Administrative Assistant Secretary, Art Weatherbee informed me, in confidence, to be ready on two hour's notice to accompany Secretary Dillon by helicopter to the government's secret emergency underground headquarters in West Virginia, which I had previously visited on a national, emergency, evacuation drill. What about my family ?, I asked. And what do I tell them?

"Oh, I have good news for you on that," Weatherbee said. "Unlike the other government agencies, the Treasury Department has made arrangements for your family to be housed in a mountain community only a couple of hours drive from Washington. Tell your wife to pack a car with enough clothes and provisions to last a few weeks and to be ready to leave on two hours notice. That same call will give her specific instructions on how to get there."

I stood there in shock, almost paralyzed as his words and their meaning sank in. "You're telling me I shall be leaving my family behind, and that my wife will be taking our children out of school to drive them to some unknown place in the mountains to live for a few weeks, or even longer, where they don't have any friends or know anyone ? That's not the America I know and believe in. I'm not deserting my family! Tell the Secretary I can't go with him and I'll just have to take my chances here."

Happily, six days later, on October 28 , Kennedy and Krushschev each issued statements of a settlement: Kennedy promised not to invade Cuba and to remove U.S. nuclear missiles from Turkey, near the Soviet borders; while Krushchev in turn agreed to dismantle the missile sites in Cuba and turn back his ships carrying military supplies to Cuba. This agreement led to a warm-up in the Cold War between them. But it had been a very last-minute, close call and in some respects, a miracle that a nuclear war was avoided.[20]

20. *It may be helpful to know this background of the U.S. and Cuban hostile rela-tions. In February 1961, shortly after his inauguration, Kennedy approved a CIA*

November 22, 1963, was a day that began very happily. Louise and I were looking forward to our dinner-dance that evening to celebrate our 5th wedding anniversary. But that day was fated to end dramatically, and to change our lives, along with those of millions of other people in and outside of the United States.

After a routine morning of meetings with my deputy, Fred Douglas, and Pat O'Connoll, the Director of the Law Enforcement Training School, I walked across 15th Street to grab a quick lunch at the bar of a restaurant in the Hotel Washington. I just finished my usual toasted chicken, lettuce, and tomato sandwich when the speaker over the bar, broadcasting a local radio news program was interrupted with a news flash from Dallas, Texas. "President Kennedy has been shot!," the commentator announced and had been rushed to a hospital. But no further details about his condition were available.

I slid off my stool in a stunned daze, quickly paid my bill and rushed back to the Treasury Department, heading for the office of the Chief of the Secret Service, Jim Rowley. He was alone, sitting silently at his desk, his face deeply drawn and gray, conversing on the telephone when I walked in. I sat down in a chair in front of him, tense and anxious as I waited until he finished, wanting to know what had gone wrong. Where had the Secret Service's protective shield failed? I was very familiar

---

plan to support an invasion of Cuba by Cuban exiles in the U.S. and whose training in Guatemala President Eisenhower had earlier approved. The plan and its execution in April 1961 were ill-fated, as news of the exiles preparations leaked, and when the invasion force, Brigade 2506, landed on the beaches of Cuba's Bay of Pigs on April 17, they were strafed by Cuban air force planes, that also sank two of the exile's escort ship and destroyed half of their air support, leaving Castro's fighter planes in control of the skies. By the end of the next day, they were being attacked and overwhelmed by 20,000 of Castro's troops and April 19 brought the end of the invasion, with the surrender of almost 1,200 Brigade members, more than 100 killed and an unknown number had escaped by sea.

The Brigade prisoners were kept in prison for 20 months, and the U.S. Negotiated a deal with Castro that resulted in Attorney General Robert Kennedy personally soliciting pharmaceutical companies and baby food manufacturers and shipping to Cuba $53 million worth of baby food and drugs, all of which were in great short supply in Cuba.

Source: John F. Kennedy Presidential Library and Museum.

with the worrisome, inadequate resources the Secret Service had been struggling with to ensure the safety of the President and Vice President, in light of the increasingly dangerous nature of the threats against presidents since the unsuccessful attack against President Truman. The Service's bare bones budget had prevented it from hiring and training urgently needed additional protective agents.

I first became aware of Congress' low priority for the protection of the President soon after I started work. Chief Rowley telephoned me one morning to tell me the high, iron protective fence encircling the White House and its surrounding grounds was in such weakened condition that he was fearful that a small group of sightseeing tourists leaning against it could cause it to collapse. Rowley said he had been unsuccessful in getting the funds or other assistance needed to repair the fence. He asked for my assistance and I was able to obtain the funds needed. Not long after, Rowley called me for help again. Increased security threats, together with more traveling by the President to other large cities, had created a serious vulnerability and he had an insufficient number of trained protective personnel to cover and safeguard the President's route in crowded, built-up urban areas.

A vital protective procedure on such trips was to vet the occupants of all the buildings along the scheduled route and station an armed, trained agent to keep a close watch on the windows of every building overlooking the presidential motorcade as it passed. During an event, the agents needed to make certain every window already checked and declared secure, remained closed and could not pose a threat from an assassin's rifle. Rowley said he did not have enough protective personnel required for these essential surveillance assignments. To help him, I asked the chief executive of each of the other Treasury enforcement agencies to assign to the Secret Service on temporary presidential protection duty each month, a designated number of experienced, armed criminal investigators, to be available on call. By drawing on the Treasury's overall criminal investigative resources, I was able to provide Chief Rowley with up to 30 additional trained, skilled T-men to augment his critically shorthanded presidential protective details. And through personal contacts at the Defense Department, I arranged to obtain more qualified, experienced military intelligence personnel, when extra help was urgently needed.

As I sat there in Rowley's office I remember thinking how terrible and ironic it was that earlier that year, Treasury had asked Congress for additional Secret Service funds to hire the agents desperately needed to protect the President. But this request had been turned down by the House Committee, with the incredible explanation that the law authorizing the Secret Service to protect the President only stated it "may" protect the President. Therefore, it was not "mandatory" to protect him, and Congress had other, more important priorities!

"What went wrong? How did we lose the President?," I asked Rowley when he ended his call. He told me there were three factors that might have prevented the tragedy. First, Kennedy had been complaining about too much protection and had refused some of the protective measures the Secret Service detail had wanted to impose, beginning with the bulletproof plastic roof on the president's car. The roof had been removed. Second, there was a special step built into the back of the Presidential car directly behind where he sat for a Secret Service agent to stand shielding the President. That day he ordered the agent who would have taken the bullet to stand down.

Third, it was a standard requirement that the agent driving the President be young, with very quick reflexes. His instructions mandated that if he saw or heard anything out of the ordinary that might signal a danger, he was to hit the accelerator and move the President's car out of the area as fast as possible. However, that day the regular Secret Service agent assigned to drive the President had reported sick, and had been replaced by a middle-aged agent. The consequence was that when the first Nonlethal shot was fired, instead of speeding the President to safety, the driver had turned his head to look behind him to see what was happening. That delay left the President vulnerable to the second shot, which turned out to be fatal.

Looking back nearly 40 years later, I wonder why a protective agent had not spotted the window opened by Oswald to fire his rifle and taken immediate, counter measures that would have prevented the killing? Had the chronic shortage of Secret Service agents left these particular windows unwatched? I don't know the answer. I was not involved in the follow-up investigation by the Warren Commission, and I was too traumatized then to even think about such details. For as I sat there on that terrible November day with Chief Rowley, my mind and focus was on only one all-important question. Would President Kennedy survive?

Rowley and I were probably the first persons in Washington to learn of the President's death when Rowley received the devastating telephone call he had been waiting for from his agent at the Dallas hospital. That news would not be made public pending the completion of a number of urgent decisions and tasks, ranging from the notification and swearing in of Vice President Johnson as President, to plans for the disposition of the President's body. After Rowley's call reporting Kennedy 's death, I immediately telephoned Joe Fowler, who was acting Secretary of the Treasury in the absence of Secretary Dillon, who was en route to Japan with Secretary of State Dean Rusk, and told him It was very urgent that Rowley and I see him right away,

Upon learning of Kennedy's death, Fowler called the Air Force plane transporting Dillon and Rusk, recommending that they return to Washington. He also called the Secretary of Defense, Robert McNamara, to inform him of Kennedy's death. Rumors quickly circulated that the Soviet Union was behind the assassination. These rumors led McNamara to put the U.S. armed forces on a high alert. While we were with Fowler, I advised him that we should begin right away to assemble all the facts known to the Secret Service relating to the assassination in preparation for a government investigation that was certain to follow. Whereupon he telephoned Gaspard d'Andelot Belin, the Treasury's General Counsel, to come up to take charge of this task.

Returning to my own office, I telephoned Louise to decide what we should do about our celebratory, dinner-dance planned for that night. The news of Kennedy's death had spread throughout Washington like a black cloud, creating a sense of disbelief and shock, along with an almost paralyzing pall. As most of our friends who would be coming to our anniversary party that night were working in Kennedy's administration, I thought neither Louise and I, or any of the guests would be in a mood to be partying, and we both agreed we needed to cancel our party. But to our joint surprise, when we called everyone invited, many said they wanted to come and be with friends with whom they could share and discuss their sense of deep, devastating loss, sorrow and despair.

So our anniversary party that November 22nd evening turned into a wake for Kennedy. We sat up talking late into the night, drawing comfort from one another as we shared our mutual grief. And we speculated about his assassination, whether the Russians, with whom we had been engaged in a "Cold War" for two decades, were responsible, and the terrifying possibility of nuclear, "hot" war consequences for us, our country, and the world. While the early evidence for Kennedy's death focused on Lee Harvey Oswald and the findings of the official Warren Commission later led to the same conclusion, numerous conspiracy theories about others who might be responsible flourished and many intelligent and respected people here and abroad remained convinced that Oswald had not been acting alone.

I discovered that some of these skeptics included highly reputable, foreign law enforcement officials. Soon afterward I traveled on a business trip to Thailand and Turkey and, en route, lunched with my counterpart Interpol representatives in Tokyo and Hong Kong. In each instance, toward the end of our meal, each senior, high ranking police official laid down his utensils, leaned forward across the table looking directly into my eyes and asked in a quiet, confidential tone, "Now, tell me in confidence, who really was responsible for this terrible assassination—was it Johnson, the Vice President?"

And each time, after I had shaken my head to say, "No," and added that all our evidence had shown that Oswald had been acting alone. My luncheon companion sat back with a disappointed look to say in a cool, huffy voice, "Well, I'm sorry you can't trust me." This was understandable, for as professional, sophisticated police officers, both had naturally focused their trained suspicions on who would gain most from, President Kennedy's death. The logical person was his political successor, the Vice President.

This trip was also illuminating as an example how different branches of the U.S. Government can have totally different, conflicting national security objectives and priorities, sometimes resulting in one part of the executive arm of the Federal Government deliberately undermining and successfully sabotaging the foreign policy objectives and initiatives of another arm of the U.S. Government. In Bangkok I was attending meetings with Thai national police officials on the progress of our program providing them needed weapons and communications equipment to improve their capabilities for blocking the vehicles transporting opium from the Northern Shan states into Thailand, ending up as heroin smuggled into the U.S. In the course of our meetings, I learned that the opium convoys were now being escorted by military trucks driven by Thai military personnel equipped with heavier, 50 caliber machine guns that greatly outclassed the 30 caliber rifles and handguns we had been furnishing the Thai police. I was even more shocked to discover that these better armed opium smuggling transports and their military escorts had been financed by our own CIA !

Shortly after this discovery, when I was invited to an American Embassy party and introduced to the head of the CIA in Bangkok, it might be understandable that my sense of outrage led me to lose my cool. Pulling the startled CIA representative aside, I angrily, and naively, demanded to know how his agency could be undermining Treasury's efforts to interdict the narcotic drugs destined for the U.S. by helping these drug-trafficking enemies of America, the Shan opium smugglers. While noticeably taken aback by my hostile confrontation, the CIA's "station chief" tried to calm me down as he explained the facts of life in America's Southeast Asia world in the 1960s. He pointed out that we were in the middle of the Cold War where President Johnson, following Presidents Eisenhower and Kennedy, had been sending military advisors and assistance to oppose the Communist-led North Vietnamese regime that had defeated the French colonial forces in 1954. They were now seen to pose a serious domino-type escalation threat to America's and Western Europe's security interests in the region.

Accordingly, the CIA, in its efforts to prevent Communist forces from gaining power among the Burmese to Thailand's north, had been building allies among the native tribes in the Shan states. For centuries these tribes had grown and relied on opium as their only marketable export crop to sustain them. "We need the critical intelligence and the other assistance we are receiving from these tribes, and the only way we can get it is by providing them with trucks and weapons essential to marketing their opium crops." Having their help and support in blocking the Communists from gaining power was more important to America's foreign policy than helping the Thai police block their opium shipments, he told me. I could only shake my head in disbelief with a sad resignation.

The next day, I flew to Ankara, Turkey to meet with Turkey's Minister of Agriculture to get his help in suppressing the serious diversion of Turkey's opium crops by many Turkish farmers. These farmers, instead of selling the opium to the Turkish government as required after the United Nations had authorized Turkey to grow opium for legal medical use to sell only to licensed pharmaceutical companies, had been selling significant amounts to illegal drug traffickers at far higher profits. As a result, this legally grown opium was now ending up as heroin that was being smuggled into the U.S. and sold on our streets. In my meeting with the Agriculture minister, I emphasized how important it was to the U.S. to shut off the illicit flow of this Turkish opium which was converted into heroin for sale in U.S. cities. The minister told me he understood my concern, that he was very upset to learn of this illicit diversion by a few unscrupulous Turkish farmers. But, he assured me, he would take immediate action to correct this situation by cracking down on the farmers concerned.

Mission accomplished, I flew back to Washington with a positive report on the Turkish opium diversion. However, not long afterward I learned meeting efforts had been torpedoed by a ranking staffer in our American Embassy. He had his own, different agenda and had met with the Turkish minister after I left to inform him that the American Embassy sympathized with the difficult problem the Turkish government had in trying to control these farmers. The Treasury, he told him, only represented one small part of the American government, and he assured the Minister if he did nothing at all about this issue, the American Embassy and American government would understand.

When I had joined the Treasury Department in 1961, the Bureau of Narcotics was reporting less than 60,000 known narcotics addicts in the U.S. Essentially those using heroin were largely poor, urban, black and Hispanic, with more than 50% of them living in New York. And the number of persons using cocaine and marihuana was so small that they were not considered a problem.

This situation would change drastically, after Kennedy's assassination when President Johnson in 1965 dramatically altered the previous U.S. policy of limited military assistance to the anti-Communist South Vietnamese government. He dispatched tens of thousands of American combat troops to fight in North Vietnam and ordered the drafting of young men. These unpopular actions precipitated a protest march by an activist group of University of California students on their local draft board in Berkeley, followed by the burning of a number of student draft cards. These antiwar protests in turn triggered copycat burnings of draft cards and demonstrations, sometimes violent, among college students, academics and young professionals, throughout California that soon spread relentlessly East across the entire U.S.

As the numbers of American troops, casualties, and young men drafted escalated, a major symbol of those protesting against the government's actions was their blatant, defiant acquisition and use of outlawed drugs, such as marijuana and cocaine. Almost overnight, marijuana, cocaine, and the entire array of narcotics, stimulants, hallucinogens, and other dangerous drugs were being used by an enormous segment of American youth. These drugs became a protest symbol of opposition to the Vietnam War. In retrospect some 40 years later, I am appalled and deeply saddened to see how terribly misguided and tragic our governmental and publicly supported punitive attitudes were in the 60's and 70's toward the early rebellious use of narcotic and dangerous drugs.

Frightened and persuaded that all of these drugs were the work of the devil and endangered the general public, Congress enacted extreme punitive laws, including mandatory 20-40-year prison terms, for anyone caught buying, selling, or manufacturing them, and most states followed with their own tough laws. One cruel and unintended consequence of these excessive prison sentences was to overload our Federal and state prisons with thousands of young men and women many of whose primary motivation had been political opposition to the Vietnam war.

As a result, our country has created a monstrous, counter-productive and ultimately unsuccessful law enforcement approach to controlling narcotic and other dangerous drugs. The results have not been very different from legislating the prohibition of alcoholic beverages in

1920. In many respects, criminalizing the consumption and sale of alcohol and now drugs has created far worse consequences in human suffering, the corruption of police and other public officials and the growth and entrenchment of violent, armed criminal gangs that endangered the pubic safety of America's large cities. And we have to add the high cost and harm suffered by Mexico and our other Central and South America neighbors.

I was personally made aware of the detrimental impact of the overwhelming flood of new youthful prisoners on our Federal prison system when I was angrily accosted at a Washington social gathering by the Director of the U.S. Bureau of Prisons, James Bennett. A strong-willed and outspoken prison reformer, he could barely restrain his anger as he snapped at me accusingly: "Your Bureau of Narcotics is filling up my prisons to capacity with young drug violators. Most are just dumb college kids who are not dangerous or violent. But they're being sentenced for outrageously long terms, taking up short, critical space we need for the really more serious, dangerous and violent criminals."

At this time, the U.S. massive law enforcement emphasis on narcotic and dangerous drugs was not shared outside the United States. When I started attending Interpol General Assembly meetings in 1961, the chairmen of several European delegations, including the British, German and Belgian delegations, individually took me aside to complain about U.S. insistence on having a permanent Committee on Narcotic Drugs. Each one told me this committee was unnecessary and a waste of their time, as narcotic drugs were not a problem in their countries or Europe, only in the United States. My reply to each was the same: these were important crimes in my country, facilitated by criminals who were aiding and abetting them in other countries, and we believed it was an important enough crime to warrant having a special Interpol committee on this.

Several years later, however, the British delegation's chairman sought me out to speak to me privately. He surprised me by saying the British police wanted to work more closely with us to suppress trafficking in narcotic drugs. I told him I was pleased to hear that, but I was curious as to why they had changed their position. "The prime minister's grandson has become an addict," he explained. The same transformation was occurring throughout the other European countries, as the protests against the Vietnam War crossed the Atlantic to spread among European youth.

Meanwhile, back in Washington, the Kennedy assassination was having major repercussions within the Treasury and Joe Fowler, who now was the Secretary , believed it was essential to have a complete review of the Secret Service and its presidential protection responsibilities. To do this, he established a new position of Special Assistant to the Secretary (for Enforcement). In a press release on September 16, 1965 he announced the appointment of David Acheson, the U.S. Attorney for the District of Columbia, to this position with direct authority over both the Secret Service and my office. The effect was to reduce significantly my previous scope and independence.

However, in a follow-up Treasury press release the next day, Fowler announced my full-time assignment to serve as Treasury's liaison with President Johnson's newly created Commission on Law Enforcement and the Administration of Justice, stating: "This assignment will be Mr. Sagalyn's primary responsibility, in keeping with the high priority attached to the work of the Commission, which has been charged by the President with studying crime in the United States and recommending ways to reduce and prevent it. Mr. Sagalyn will continue as Director of the Office of Law Enforcement Coordination, which is now in the office of the Special Assistant (for Enforcement)."

I had already discussed working with the Crime Commission with Nick Katzenbach , the Attorney General and Chairman of the Commission as I was immensely interested in its mission. Therefore, I found my new primary responsibility more than agreeable and mutually satisfactory solution my changed situation. I continued to be Director of the Office of Law Enforcement Coordination, and remained in my office at Treasury, although spending most of my time working with the President's Commission located in the nearby Executive Offices of the President. This new, felicitous arrangement enabled me to develop a cordial relationship with Acheson and warm personal friendships with his two very bright and competent principal assistants, Bob Jordan and Tony Lapham, whom he had brought with him from the U.S. Attorney's office.

PRESIDENTIAL COMMISSION ON CRIME: 1965-1966

President Johnson's action on July 23, 1965, appointing a national commission to study America's crime problems, was in response to an alarming growth of crimes and violence in our cities and political pressures on the Federal government to "do something" to help. My law enforcement responsibilities and activities had required me to work closely with local police departments, making me familiar with their everyday crime problems and weaknesses. My additional experience working directly with the Cleveland Police and with Eliot Ness had also enabled me to evaluate the performance and needs of a large police department.

After four years in Treasury, the initial stimulation had faded and I found myself looking forward eagerly to exploring the primary factors responsible for the current ineffectiveness of the counter-crime strategies and tactics of most police departments. I hoped to help find innovative ways of improving police operations and bringing down those high crime levels. But I quickly discovered that my preventive "radical" approach and recommendations for various major crime problems were finding little favor with the Commission's executive director, James Vorenberg, a brilliant, Harvard Law School professor (later Dean) who had been brought to Washington by Attorney General Robert Kennedy to be Director of the Office of Justice. He was now serving President Johnson's new Attorney General and the commission's chairman, Nicholas de B. Katzenbach.

Since I was working at the Commission as the Treasury Department's liaison, I was a kind of free agent and felt that I was in an independent position and could express my own views and ideas. I believed my previous experiences, starting in Cleveland and more recently during my Treasury, Justice, and Interpol years, qualified me to do that. My first confrontation with Vorenberg occurred at one of the early meetings following the Commission's approval of a number of items on Vorenberg's agenda. I spoke up to protest and challenge the automatic passage and lack of any discussion of some of the matters. Pointing out that more than 75% of the Commission's membership were lawyers and judges, I explained that I thought their legal training tended to make them assume that they had all the essential facts and that it was not necessary to question the validity of various matters with which they were dealing.

"I believe some of your assumptions may not be entirely true, but nobody here is questioning any of them." Whereupon a very annoyed, but unfazed Vorenberg sought to educate me that lawyers were trained to analyze very complex subjects and to come up with rational findings and explanations, and that's what was being done. But I persisted there was always the danger that their basic assumptions may be wrong and it was important to have someone who was trained to ask questions, and if an assumption was in doubt, ask for proof. To shut me up, Vorenberg told me, All right, then you find these people."

Recalling the famed "Whiz Kids," the young group of systems analysts that Defense Secretary McNamara had recruited and brought to work at the Defense Department, I called my friend, Adam Yarmolinsky, who was a special assistant to McNamara, and asked if he could arrange for a contingent of their systems analysts to be assigned on loan to the Crime Commission. Adam came through. To his credit, Vorenberg put them to work, assigning them to a newly created science and technology task force, studying and analyzing the operations of the U.S. police, courts and corrections system as well as the criminal justice system. Alfred Blumstein, one of McNamara's most talented systems analysts led the group. Their invaluable findings and recommendations had a far-reaching impact through the application of new science and technology to those crime related agencies and to the administration of justice.

I devoted most of my time to my own agenda, focusing on selected crime areas and problems where I believed important contributions could be made by applying an innovative crime prevention approach, which I thought merited far greater attention and promised rewarding results. Taking advantage of my independent status, I set up meetings with representatives from various key businesses to obtain the basic information needed, along with their critical response to my ideas. Vorenberg's reaction to my freewheeling activities was to assign a trusted assistant director, Bruce Terris, to attend all my meetings to keep tabs on my maverick actions. For example, as auto theft was a major national crime problem and as 45 % of the hundreds of thousands of cars stolen every year were stolen by juveniles because it was so easy—e.g., the car's driver had left the key in the lock—I thought it would be productive to meet with representatives from General Motors to discuss what they could do to make it difficult to leave a key in the lock and to build other antitheft features into their cars. When I met with representatives of the U.S.'s largest car manufacturer, I told them the tendency of drivers to leave a car unlocked, with the car keys in the ignition, was creating an inviting, irresistible opportunity for an immature teenager to impulsively climb into the car and take off on a "joy ride," only to abandon the car later. Apart from the importance of preventing these tens of thousands of unplanned auto thefts, there were the personal losses to the car owners and the costs related to involvement of police personnel and to the public's safety.

In addition, I pointed out, they, as well as the American public, should be concerned that a large number of these juvenile offenders were getting arrested and ending up with criminal records that would brand them for life, in many cases pushing them into a life of crime. The result would seriously jeopardize their futures and opportunities to live normal lives as respected citizens, who would get jobs that would enable them to buy General Motors cars. I also argued that none of these costly auto thefts and consequences would have occurred had the car manufacturers made lock systems that made it very difficult to leave the key in the ignition lock when the car was parked. Another desirable change would be to reform GM's highly theft-vulnerable practice of equipping various car models, with common lock systems and keys that would fit all cars of the same model. My presentation met with a cool, noncommittal response and I was taken aback when one the GM representatives strongly defended this glaring security vulnerability, saying that the common key custom had been carried out at the request of law enforcement organizations who said they wanted easy access into cars in their line of duty.

Although I was disappointed by General Motors disinterest in my auto theft prevention proposals, I turned my attention to a different area and a problem that would meet with more success: creating a national emergency telephone number for summoning police or other assistance in emergency situations. After a series of meetings and telephone calls with representatives of the Bell Telephone Companies (AT&T), Federal Communications Commission (FCC) and the Associated Public Safety Communications Officers (APSCO), I wrote a memo October 21, 1965, describing the findings of this research on a national emergency phone number. To my great surprise AT&T said that a national emergency number already existed in every city—the single digit "0", labeled Operator, found on all phones. Anyone needing the police or other emergency assistance, they said, could quickly obtain it by dialing the "Operator," a person trained to immediately pass on this call to the police, fire or ambulance response service. (At that time, AT&T's Bell telephone companies, for all practical purposes, constituted a national telephone monopoly.)

Stating that the value of any national emergency telephone number "depends on the speed and proficiency with which such calls are passed on to the police or other emergency agency," my memo reported that "the AT&T representatives were asked to furnish the Crime Commission staff with answers to a number of critical questions, including: Do the AT&T companies now have or will they have enough operators to assure the expeditious handling of an anticipated larger volume of emergency calls; will all AT&T operators be properly trained in emergency procedures to ensure all emergency calls are transmitted promptly to the proper agency; assuming a heavy increasing volume of emergency calls over the coming years, will Bell want to transfer responsibility for handling such calls to the communities; if so, at what stage will they wish to relinquish responsibility and what cost will be involved to channel all emergency calls directly to a community emergency board.

I never heard AT&T's answers, as I was reassigned to attend the National War College for a year, but I renewed my active interest in establishing a national emergency telephone number two years later when I was serving as the Associate Director for Public Safety on President Johnson's newly appointed Commission on Civil Disorders (aka the Kerner Commission). The commission was to find out why the violent racial riots that broke out in Detroit and Newark in the summer of 1967 was followed by mass violence and destruction in numerous other cities, and what should be done to prevent them from recurring. Here, again, the urgent need for a national emergency telephone number that would enable the public to call the police in an emergency and receive a quick response was back on my agenda.

Although the AT&T representatives I had talked to at the Crime Commission had assured me that all such calls to "O" would be answered by an operator within 10 rings at the most, I had been told that a number of persons who had called the operator seeking emergency police assistance had very poor, frustrating experiences, waiting excessively long periods of time before an operator answered their call. Accordingly, I decided to check up personally on how well AT&T operators were handling an emergency call by dialing one myself. After making several different calls to "O," and waiting up to 75 rings without an operator responding, I gave up.

Distressed by these results, I called Lee Loevinger, the member of the Federal Communications Commission who dealt with public safety communications issues, and told him of my previous talks with AT&T and my own disappointing findings about their national emergency service. He asked me to write him a letter outlining the Civil Disorders Commission's interest in a national emergency number, and to enclose a copy of my October 21, 1965 memo on this subject when I was with the Crime Commission. Two weeks later, in a letter dated November 6, 1967, FCC Commissioner Loevinger gave me an encouraging progress report: He had spoken with H.I. Romnes, Board Chairman of AT&T as well as to the President of AT&T, Ben Gilmer. Gilmer had advised him that AT&T was conducting field tests of "techniques for making the telephone a more effective means of summoning aid in an emergency." He added that Gilmer regarded the delays that I and others had experienced in getting an operator were "inexplicable and inexcusable" and he would report back to Loevinger on the results of the field tests and his own investigation. Loevinger concluded, " I am confident that the officials of the company are concerned with this matter and will continue to pursue it," and that he would keep me advised.

True to his word, Loevinger wrote me on December 11, 1967, about the very long conference he had with AT&T's chairman, president, vice president and a few other AT&T officials regarding "making the telephone a more effective means of summoning aid in emergency situations." During the meeting "the officials of AT&T did concede that your original complaint was warranted and that the zero dialing for "Operator" as a means of securing help in emergencies is not, by itself, adequate." After discussing a number of possibilities, it was agreed that something should be done in the relatively near future.

I did not hear from FCC Commissioner again until March 7, 1968, when I received a brief letter, enclosing an 11-page memo Loevinger had written, signed as Defense Commissioner, FCC Commission, February 2, 1968, and entitled "THE UNIVERSAL EMERGENCY SERVICE NUMBER— The Problems and Some Answers." In it he described the long history of previous discussions and failed attempts to overcome the many complex, technical problems involved in establishing a universal telephone number to summon aid that was not only compatible with the boundaries of telephone exchanges, but also the political boundaries of the emergency agencies with their numerous overlapping jurisdictions. His memo recounted the Bell telephone companies' unsuccessful experiments in training their operators and advertising their "O" number as a national emergency aid service, only to discover that it was inherently limited and inadequate.

Although demands for establishing a universal emergency telephone number had been coming from members of Congress, and from the President's Commission on Law Enforcement, Loevinger's memo and covering letter to me revealed that it was my October 30, 1967, letter, with its citations demonstrating the inadequacy of Bell Telephone System's emergency call "O" number, that had finally "stimulated" FCC's Defense Commissioner Lee Loevinger and he had taken the initiative in spurring the chairman, president and vice presidents of AT&T, to become actively involved in solving this problem without further delay.

The resulting top priority efforts during the next two months by AT&T executives, with the active participation of Loevinger, produced an AT&T report to the FCC on January 11, 1968, on success in developing a universal emergency calling system, using the number 911. While it would take several years to change all of its switching stations, Bell System operating companies were ready to begin working with emergency agencies and municipalities throughout the U.S. to establish the 911 system and would give priority to large metropolitan areas. Most important, the more than $50 million estimated cost would be absorbed by the AT&T Bell Telephone companies.

I found it ironic that one of the few objections to establishment of the new 911 emergency call system came from the International Association of Chiefs of Police, the principal representative of U.S. police executives. They opposed it "because the multiple police forces and conflicting jurisdictions in many communities" would present "a spectacular problem" which was a "hat full of snakes." As the great majority of emergency calls (an estimated 80%) were seeking police assistance, it was logical for police departments to be the primary recipient of all 911 calls.

An unfortunate consequences of the initial, strong opposition of many police departments was their failure to educate the general public by issuing and publicizing guidelines which provided a clear definition of what kinds of "emergency" situations warranted calling the 911 number. As a result, many routine, everyday non-emergency calls were made by people who regarded their individual crises—such as the theft of a coat from an unlocked car or a cat marooned in a tree—as legitimate 911 calls for police assistance. So the emergency 911 lines of many police switchboards were clogged with trivial calls, thus overwhelming the capability of large municipal police departments to staff. The consequence in many large cities has frequently led to the delay of the quick, police response so important in true emergency situations. In addition, the sheer volume of non-urgent 911 calls often significantly reduces the number of police officers available for deployment to high-crime spots and neighborhoods that need more police protection.

THE NATIONAL WAR COLLEGE

A surprise telephone call on a clear, sunny Monday morning in early May 1966 was from A.E. Weatherbee, Treasury's Assistant Secretary for Administration. He was calling to ask if I would be willing to attend the National War College (NWC) for a year in nearby Fort McNair, starting in August. The person who had been scheduled to represent the Treasury Department in the War College class of 1966-1967 class had unexpectedly withdrawn and Treasury did not want to lose its one slot for representation that year. While completely unexpected, the opportunity to spend a year at the prestigious National War College studying national security policy and strategy with a highly select mixture of predominantly military and a smaller number of civilian government classmates, was both daunting and exciting. The distinguished service records of my classmates had led to their being chosen for special training as future leaders of the Armed Forces, State Department and other national-security-related civilian agencies. The challenge and opportunity inherent in this very different, highly intriguing kind of experience, was irresistible. "If I can be helpful to Treasury by attending the National War College," I told Weatherbee, "I'll be glad to go."

Early morning August sun was already heating up Ft. McNair when I arrived at the National War College's stately, pillared Theodore Roosevelt Hall to enroll as one of 140 members of the Class of 1967. There were only 30 civilian representatives of various Federal, national-security-related agencies, most of whom were from the State Department, while the balance ranged from the U.S. Information Agency, the Agency for International Development and the Commerce Department, to the Defense Intelligence Agency, National Security Agency and the CIA. The great majority, 110, were senior Colonels and Lt. Colonels from the Army, Air Force and Marines and Navy Captains, nearly all of whom had just returned from active duty in Vietnam. Their vivid war experiences and angry tirades that the Vietnam War was a political, not a military, mission that threatened to destroy America's Armed Forces, would later resonate in our after-class "bull sessions."

While my early military service as a "buck" private, and later as
a commissioned officer, had made me well acquainted with the
military services' traditional, treasured, and strictly-adhered-to
code, RHIP ("Rank Has It's Privileges"), I was agreeably surprised
to discover that, as the ranking civilian member of the class, I was
entitled to have one of the few and highly prized reserved parking
spaces at the War College. My Treasury Civil Service G-17 rating
was equivalent in military rank to a Major General's. This seniority
would later dictate that I would be selected to serve as "POTUS"
(President of the United States) in the NWC's annual, still experimental, politico-military "War Game." This was a highly rated
training exercise conducted at the end of the course and designed
to test the different players' national-security, analytical, strategic
and judgment capabilities. This would turn out to be one of my
most challenging, revealing, and traumatic experiences at the
War College.

The quality and intellectual stimulation of my instructors and classmates were unlike any other educational institution or student body
I had known. Our instructors included cabinet and top ranking military officials, while our visiting speakers included former President
and WWII European commanding general Dwight Eisenhower, former Secretary of State Dean Acheson, and the current top-ranking
military, foreign affairs and national security officials. They, together
with the knowledgeable, insightful, and spirited classroom discussions of my uniformed and civilian classmates, made my year at the
War College a truly wonderful educational experience.

That experience was especially enlivened by the freewheeling, can-
did, often emotionally charged small group "bull sessions" on the
Vietnam War. The career military participants had all been on active
duty there and, without exception, were deeply embittered about
this war, which they characterized as a disastrous decision. They
believed their civilian superiors had sent them on an inappropriate,
"political" mission, namely to win the hearts and minds of the civil-

ian Vietnamese population. They were fearful that the consequences would be the destruction of the warrior spirit, the vital kill-and-destroy capability of our armed forces.[21]

One of my most memorable and reassuring experiences was a discussion that followed the talk of the State Department's Assistant Secretary for Latin America who, in the course of his lecture, stated that while many of the rulers of Latin American countries were military commanders who had seized power by force, he praised them for bringing the stability to the region that U.S. policy sought. When he had finished his talk, he waited expectantly and confidently for questions. He was clearly expecting that this War College audience—composed largely of career, senior military officers—would support and react favorably to his pro-military comments. He was quite taken aback when an Army colonel rose to express his deep concern that the U.S. State Department did not oppose but actually appeared to approve when, in the name of stability, a nation's military leaders deposed their elected civilian president and took control of the government. "As career military officers," the Colonel said, "we were taught, and I fully support, the fundamental, democratic government concept that a country's armed forces stays out of politics and does not seize power by force if it disagrees with the policies of the elected leader. If I find I strongly disagree with a mission or order from my civilian commanders, I have two choices: I either say yes sir and carry it out to the best of my ability, or I can resign. But I never believe I have the right to lead or join a military coup."

The stunned State Department Assistant Secretary's discomfort increased even more when an Air Force colonel, followed by a Navy Captain also stood up to express similar strong disapproval of such military coups and their devotion to our American democratic gov-

---

21. *I was poignantly reminded of these bull sessions when the U.S. troops President Bush ordered to invade Iraq quickly found themselves in the middle of a disastrous civil war with a nonmilitary, occupation mission, to win the hearts and minds of the civilian population. I had fully expected our tragic Vietnam experience to evoke very strong protests and opposition from our senior career, uniformed officers, as well as angry protests and a political storm from the civilian population when the Iraq adventure turned into a deadly urban, civil war with many casualties. But that did not happen.*

ernment system of civilian control. I sat there elated, and proud of my military classmates, and the training and inbred beliefs of the career military establishment. I was simultaneously seething with disbelief at the discovery that order and stability trumped a basic, vital constitutional principle in our current U.S. foreign policy.

Arnold aboard a U.S Aircraft Carrier during a joint naval-military exercise.

One of my most colorful classmates, who became a good friend, was John M. "Mike" Dunn, an Army Lt. Colonel who had already distinguished himself in combat in WWII and Korea with a Silver Star, a Bronze Star, and a Purple Heart, then earned a BA at Harvard and a Masters and Ph.D. at Princeton. He had been serving with distinction in Vietnam as an assistant to U.S. Ambassador Henry Cabot Lodge, who was intricately involved in the South Vietnam government. Mike was a very bright, articulate, breezily irreverent individualist who was seen as a "maverick" in the traditional, tightly disciplined military bureaucracy. His strong, unequivocal (bordering on brash) opinions on all important issues were an inherent part of a personality that made him stand out and command the respect, if not the approval, of his fellow classmates. But Mike was also markedly different from everyone else in the class in the independence of his views and actions, which showed little respect for traditional military and government dogma, customs or rules. I was to discover how much his rare, independent qualities, along with his brilliant record of leadership, were prized by the highest commanders of the U.S. Armed Services in one of my courses where our speakers were the chiefs of staff of the Army, Navy, Marines and Air Force. We asked each one in turn this same question: What do you believe would be the most important achievement you could make as Chief of Staff? And to my astonishment, each one gave the identical reply, "Protect the maverick." Yet, ironically and unfortunately, reality proved that the dedication of our military services to the importance of unwavering allegiance to discipline and automatic response to chain-of-command decisions makes them incapable of tolerating mavericks, as Mike Dunn's experience would illustrate. Despite his future meteoric rise from Lt. Colonel to Major General, and attaché to two Vice Presidents, his continual frustration in battling the Army's obstacles to making innovative, needed changes, led him to retire to civilian life and an executive position in private industry.

Our acquaintance began early in the college year when I found myself the butt of his critical scorn and biting wit. We were both participating in a seminar on national security policy, where I had just finished listing the various economic, political, and other important options we needed to consider prior to ordering a military response. A very impatient, exasperated Dunn stood up and, pointing his finger at me, snapped "You're so well-rounded, Sagalyn, I don't know how you can stand up!" During the following months I got to know him better in our classes, and socially, after Louise and Mike's wife, Fran, discovered they shared many mutual interests, including being the mother of twins (Fran's being boys). We grew close as Louise and I became increasingly appreciative and admiring of Mike's penetrating, sharp humor and his entertaining observations and outlook on life.

As members of the National War College class of '67, my classmates and I were being prepared for "the exercise of joint and combined high-level policy, command, and staff functions and for the planning of national strategy." NWC's core program focused on the domestic and international contexts in which national security is developed and the formulation and implementation of national security policy. Our studies included an invaluable grounding in military strategy and operations, including field trips to military bases and an aircraft carrier, where we observed joint military exercises. For me, the major highlight of these field trips was a totally absorbing three-week overseas trip in April 1967. Our travels extended from the East to the West coasts of Africa, during which we visited eight countries that had been colonies of France, Great Britain, Belgium, Italy, and Portugal. We flew on our own Air Force passenger jet, accompanied by our own physician and a faculty and support staff of seven, one of whose jobs was to carry the gifts we were to present to the heads of state with whom we met.

It began with our landing in Rabat, the capital of Morocco, a kingdom which had retained strong French ties, where the King honored us with a spectacular cavalry drill demonstration of beautiful Arabian horses, followed by a mock battle. Following this, we met with Morocco's key foreign affairs officials and senior military commanders to learn of their security concerns, military capabilities, and perceptions of U.S. policy. We also met with the U.S. ambassador and CIA station chief to hear their views. Four days later we were in Abidjan, Ivory Coast, a former French colony, where we again met with its principal foreign affairs and military officials during our two-day stay. After that we flew on to visit the foreign policy and military leaders in Lagos, Nigeria, a former British possession that was currently in the middle of an extremely vicious civil war with its oil-producing Biafra region. I still have vivid memories of our brief, two-day visit there because of the extraordinary dinner two of my classmates and I had with the drunken, vociferous, bloodthirsty chief commanders of Nigeria's army, air force and navy.

My expectation of just a relatively short, friendly, collegial dinner turned into a rabid, nightmarish event in which our Nigerian military companions kept us up drinking until late at night, during which they described at length and in shocking, gruesome detail how they were planning to find and then torture their counterpart Biafran enemies. Each of them took enormous pleasure in telling us how slowly he would personally carve up his Biafran enemy's body into small pieces, and then eat each piece with great pleasure. For the next few days, I dined very lightly and principally on green salads.

Our next stop was Kinshasa, once known as Leopoldville, the capital of the former Belgian Congo. Originally claimed and run by King Leopold II of Belgium as his personal property, it was later ceded to and ruled as a colony by the Belgian Government for 85 years until 1960, when it declared its independence as the Republic of the Congo. But

Arnold questioning General Mobutu during a briefing.

its elected government soon broke down and internal strife between rival secessionist groups continued until November 25, 1965, when General Joseph Mobutu, the army commander, seized power. It was widely acknowledged that the coup had been engineered by the current CIA Station Chief there. We were to meet both the CIA representative and Mobutu. Kinshasa's main street was then very striking, with modern-looking buildings lining the paved thoroughfare, one of which was our hotel for which I was charged $5 a night and $2 for breakfast. I recall how disappointed I was when several of our group took a short cruise on the famed Congo River and, instead of the anticipated thick, overhanging foliage of an exotic African jungle, populated with monkeys and perhaps a local Tarzan, the Congo looked little different from many small New England rivers.

The most interesting and rewarding part of our Congo visit was the time we spent with General Mobutu, an arresting, flamboyant, and charismatic personality. It was fascinating to listen to him describe the extraordinary problems he was experiencing in trying to change the traditional behavior, customs and minds of an ancient tribal system. The tribesmen had no understanding of the concept, much less the meaning, of any individual loyalty or responsibility beyond that to one's family and finally the tribe. He told us the concept of an entity such as a country or state to which an individual, family or tribe owed any loyalty or collective responsibility was beyond his people's understanding and acceptance. He cited as a typical problem his difficulties in getting Congo tribesmen to stop killing foreign diplomats who have been assigned there.

The last part of our trip brought us to Kenya, where I witnessed the remaining strong, institutional and other evidence of deep British influence. I took advantage of the opportunity to join several of my classmates in a tour of the spectacular animal wildlife preserve in Nairobi, personally conducted by the park's chief ranger. Our next stop was the colorful capital city of Addis Ababa in historic Ethiopia. This city showed little influence from Italy's brief occupation and U.S. interest was now predominant. Our briefings here focused on the strategic importance of the moderating role of this ancient, absolute monarchy as the third largest, in population, of the African countries friendly to the U.S. The rest of our trip exposed us to the African east coast and the clear impact of Portugal on Mozambique, one of the few foreign colonies remaining.

Three days later we were in Lisbon for a three-day stopover, where we reviewed the official U.S. national security interests in Africa: our military interests in maintaining access to bases and strategic resources in denying bases to hostile powers, and in providing security to our citizens and establishments abroad. We also reviewed our economic interests, promoting the growth of trading partners economically capable of absorbing our products. Politically, we were told, we have an interest in attaining maximum African support for our worldwide objectives, along with a humanitarian interest in the standard of living that prevails in African countries.

I returned to the U.S. on an enormous high that greatly exceeded the 35,000-foot altitude of our four-engine jet, tremendously exhilarated by the adventure we'd just been through. My mind was stretched by the fascinating discoveries made while traveling 21 days and 17,000 miles throughout the once mysterious land of "darkest Africa", talking with the top rulers and key foreign affairs, military and intelligence officials. It had been a once-in-a-lifetime experience, traveling in great comfort and style with highly interesting companions, with every living and traveling need expertly taken care of.

But another rewarding experience was still to come. I was notified that I had been picked from among my classmates to be a member of the small, select team which would engage in a special, still experimental "War Game", a highlight of the NWC year's program. Furthermore, I was not only to be part of this team, but also to head it as POTUS, President of he United States. The game would be refereed by star-ranked general officers located in a remote control room where they would monitor by video our team's discussions and responses.

When I arrived at our team's War Game room, I found that with the exception of a State Department colleague, the other members of our team were military officers representing each of the armed services. We were presented with a written scenario reporting that reliable intelligence had just been received. This information confirmed earlier warnings of threats and related suspicious activities that the "Enemy" had started to move heavily armed tank and infantry divisions, backed by ground and air-support units, directly toward an East European country, a U.S. ally we had pledged to defend if attacked. Since the "War Game" would begin with our team's first reaction to this threat to our ally, as POTUS I took charge by stating that our first responsibility, after reviewing the "Enemy's" capability for successfully invading and defeating our ally, was to determine what the "Enemy's" actual intentions were. Only after that was decided, should we discuss our appropriate response, especially any military action. What followed was one of the most unexpected, emotionally charged experiences of my life. Early on in the course of the periodic, increasingly serious, threatening reports on the "Enemy's" movements, one of the Air Force colonels sitting across from me had kept insisting it was very evident that our "Enemy's" intentions were clear: to invade our ally. Becoming increasingly angry and frustrated by my refusal to agree, he suddenly burst out in an infuriated, very loud shout, "Let's not wait for that to happen, damn it! Let's "nuke" them now, before it's too late!"

I strongly disagreed with his assessment and maintained that our intelligence reports to date had not made a convincing case about our "Enemy's" deadly intentions. I insisted that before we took that extraordinary, ultimate step, we first had to exhaust all of our non-military options, ranging from political and economic measures to enlisting the United Nations. Our team was split on the "Enemy's" goals and the ensuing debate aroused intense, conflicting views among us. In the close confines of our "War Room," all members of the team became caught up in the life-like situation, and our outspoken differences of opinion became heated, revealing surprisingly deep-seated, personal feelings among virtually all of the team's participants. Our individual reactions to the "Enemy" threat had taken on lives of their own. My persistent refusal to commit our nuclear forces finally caused the highly aggressive, " nuke them," Colonel to go almost berserk, as he turned to me, pounding on the conference table dividing us. Leaning across it, his eyes furious and his face deeply flushed, he screamed at me, "God damn you Sagalyn, it's people like you who are selling America down the river!" His venomous outburst and the intensity of his anger hit me like an unexpected punch in the gut, leaving me stunned, speechless and shaken by his implication that we were in a war and I was a traitor for not "nuking" the enemy.

I later learned from a friend, Len Duhl, who happened to be in the War Game control room at the time, that one of the generals serving as a referee commented favorably on the aggressive spirit of the Air Force Colonel, saying, "That colonel has the right aggressive spirit we like to see instilled in our officers." Len added that the general had then grudgingly conceded, "Of course, we do have to listen to our civilian superiors." It was almost an anti-climax when my analysis and questioning of the "Enemy's" intentions proved accurate--the threatened attack was a bluff by the "Enemy" who hoped to achieve most of his objectives without any significant military cost. If the objective of the War Game was to test the aggressiveness of our future military leaders, as seemed apparent, I found it pretty scary and the emotional stress and reactions of the "nuke them" colonel very unpleasant and unnerving. But I was also reassured and happy that our military leaders are constitutionally subject to civilian oversight and orders.

In light of this and my occasional other differences with the military approach to national security threats, I was pleasantly surprised when the National War College's Deputy Commandant for Foreign Affairs, A. Allan Lightner, Jr., an Ambassador and senior State Department official who oversaw the civilian government members attending the War College, sent Treasury Secretary Joe Fowler a copy of their report rating my performance and contributions. They were much higher than I would have expected. After citing my active participation in the College program, Ambassador Lightner wrote that I had exercised forceful leadership" as commander of the U.S. team in the politico-military war game. He went on to say:

"Mr. Sagalyn made significant and thought-provoking contributions to the discussions in both the larger class assemblies and small discussion groups. He showed a marked sensitivity to the political aspects of national security problems and considerable independence of thinking, and he was forthright in presenting his views, even on highly controversial issues.

"From time to time he brought out viewpoints at variance with most of the other, predominantly military, members of the class, which added substance and spice to the discussions. Mr. Sagalyn thus helped stimulate harder thinking among the adherents of prevailing views on national security problems. . . He handled himself throughout with composure, presenting his views with conviction, basing them on reasoned arguments, and expressing himself with assurance and facility...."

HUD CRIME PREVENTION: 1967

My work on the President's Commission on Law Enforcement & Administration of Justice (Crime Commission) had me deeply involved in America's rapidly growing crime problem and had stimulated my interest in finding new and better ways to protect citizens and improve the capabilities of police departments, particularly in urban areas where most serious crimes were occurring. One major objective had been to tap the enlarging capabilities of science and technology to help enforcement agencies prevent or significantly reduce the increasing number of serious crimes that were daily plaguing American families. It was this growing crime problem that had led me to persuade, the Executive Director of the Crime Commission to bring in analytical scientists to demonstrate how these resources could be used to help solve the problems of crime and improve our country's law enforcement and criminal justice agencies. Prior to this, the Crime Commission reported, there had been virtually no contact in the U.S.

between criminal justice and science and technology and the Justice Department was "the only Cabinet department with no share of the roughly $15 billion Federal research and development budget."

I also had an active role in the National Symposium on Crime and Criminal Justice, the first national meeting of its kind to "help bring the tools of science to bear against crime," which had been co-sponsored by U.S. Attorney General and Chairman of the President's Crime Commission, Nicholas Katzenbach, and the Special Assistant to the President for Science and Technology, Dr. Donald Hornig. Five hundred experts from industry, higher education, and criminal justice were invited to participate in this historic, seminal event, held in the auditorium of the U.S. State Department on June 22-23, 1966. My featured talk on crime prevention at this national symposium had received a great deal of national publicity and focused on how many of our major crimes— ranging from home burglaries and car thefts to street robberies—could be prevented if we removed the opportunity for criminals to commit them. The Associated Press story was very succinct and somewhat deprecating in its characterization of my ideas as "gadgetry," stating, "The government's expert on modern anti-crime gadgetry called today for a massive scientific effort to 'take the opportunity out of crime.' Arnold Sagalyn... suggested an array of space-age devices to 'prevent many crimes by either removing the opportunity or making the crime so difficult and the risk so great that the would-be criminal is discouraged and deterred."[22]

My preventive approach to crime stirred up a lot of interest and provoked serious discussion within the law enforcement community. My responsibility for the training of Treasury's 4,000 criminal investigators included their proficiency in firearms. This sparked my deep concern about the limitations and high risks involved in police use of their principal weapon, the handgun, in protecting themselves against dangerous threats. The Federal criminal investigator as well as the local police officer's gun is unreliable in immobilizing a threatening person who is also armed with a gun due to the variation in the factors involved, ranging from the distance, visibility and movement of the target to the size, impact and destination of the bullet. A standard .38 caliber bullet that

---

22. *My talk was published in the principal U.S. police publication, The Police Chief.*

hits the body of a 160-lb. man may incapacitate him, but that same bullet may not stop a 250-lb. threat or someone under the influence of alcohol or strong drugs.

Moreover, the handgun is a poor, inappropriate weapon when trying to make an arrest if the Federal agent or a police detective is physically attacked close in with a knife, broken bottle, or other hand-held weapon. A police officer that uses his handgun to protect himself against someone threatening him with a knife or dangerous club runs the risk of facing police disciplinary action or prosecution for using unjustified excessive force.

I believed this vital need for a law enforcement officer to be able to protect himself against dangerous threats and the inadequacy and unreliability of his current handgun was critically important for the officer as well as for the community that depends on him for protection. I decided I should take on the task myself and try to find a better solution and replacement for the antiquated handgun. To create greater public and professional law enforcement awareness of the need to develop more effective, less-than-lethal police weapons, I started to make speeches[23] on this subject at various public and professional meetings around the U.S., including national symposiums on law enforcement science and technology.

Determined to do something that would provide our thousands of Treasury criminal investigators with an effective weapon to protect themselves against personal physical assaults or persons armed with knives or club-like weapons, I turned again for help to Adam Yarmolinsky, my friend in the office of the Secretary of Defense. Adam put me in touch with research people with whom I helped design a prospective solution. It was a 7-inch long, 3/4-inch round mini "police stick" made of solid steel with an attached strap enabling the police officer to hold it securely in his or her hand. Carried in a leather sheath attached to an agent's belt under his suit coat, when pulled out

---

23. *I also wrote an article, "Wanted: Police Weapons That Do Not Kill" for the September 17, 1967, New York Times Magazine, in collaboration with Joseph Coates, a futurist in science and technology. This article was reprinted and published in the February 1968, mass circulation Readers Digest.*

and snapped hard, the solid steel tube would extend to a 12-inch protective club capable of disarming by striking and effectively neutralizing the use of the hand and arm holding a knife, broken bottle, or other dangerous hand-held weapon.

Following my graduation from the National War College, Art Weatherbee, Treasury's Assistant Secretary for Administration, asked to see me. He had been a member of the Treasury Law Enforcement Board I had chaired and had been very supportive of my activities, including my efforts to develop more effective defensive weapons for Treasury agents. He also had been kept informed of my work on the Crime Commission and knew of my broader interest in preventing and reducing crime in U.S. cities. So I was not surprised that he raised the subject of my being loaned to another, recently created, Federal agency, the Department of Housing and Urban Development (HUD), to serve as Public Safety Advisor. My job there would be to help HUD improve the effectiveness of its crime prevention programs for public housing, develop innovative approaches to the prevention of crime and raise the level of public safety in urban areas. If I agreed to this new assignment, I would be detailed to HUD for a period not to exceed six months effective June 19, 1967, on a reimbursable basis. I was immediately intrigued by the opportunity to work at the top level in a new Federal department that was directly concerned with the increasing threat and level of serious crimes in urban areas and that welcomed "innovative approaches to the prevention of crime."

While I told Weatherbee I was very interested, I said I would first like to discuss and clarify my role and responsibilities there with Robert Wood, the Undersecretary of HUD, with whom I would be working closely. Following a satisfactory meeting and discussion in which I was asked to serve beyond the termination of my Treasury detail and transfer to HUD, I wrote a letter to Treasury Secretary Henry "Joe" Fowler to advise him of my imminent loan assignment. As my transfer to HUD would necessitate my resignation from Treasury, I wanted to thank him for all of the many kindnesses and support that had made these past six years so memorable. After writing a letter of resignation effective no later than December 16, 1967, and taking a week's vacation to spend with Louise and the children, I reported for work at HUD on June 19th.

In the intense, long hours that followed that summer, I became fully absorbed in HUD's many crime and public safety issues, starting with a trip to St. Louis to recommend what could be done to make safe HUD's crime- and vandalism-plagued public housing project, Pruitt-Igoe, sited on 57 acres in St. Louis' lower north side. Pruitt-Igoe was a massive high rise with 33 11-story buildings completed in 1958 and containing 2,870 dwelling units. It had reportedly been envisioned by the city's government and business leaders as a dazzling, look-alike high-rise Manhattan on the Mississippi. But a large construction cost overrun had forced its builders to drastically reduce the size of the apartments' rooms, the public space and other amenities, with the result that the anticipated middle-class white residents did not move in. The black residents, who did move in, quickly expressed their dislike of the drab, unattractive, institutional accommodations by vandalizing them and allowing them to become havens for drug dealers and criminal activities. Harvard urban historian Alexander von Hoffman would later describe Pruitt-Igoe as the "most infamous public housing project ever built" in the U.S.

My first impression visiting this public housing project was one of appalled disbelief, accompanied by revulsion at the universally vandalized state of buildings and hallways—widespread graffiti, broken light fixtures and a general sense of property disrepair and human despair. I discussed with the housing project management the various measures that could be taken to protect the light fixtures from future damage, discourage vandalism and make the grim corridors less hostile and more attractive. I quickly realized how useless it was to try to improve or rehabilitate such a monstrosity, and when I returned to Washington to report my findings, my recommendations were brief and clear: tear it all down. It could not be salvaged. Pruitt-Igoe was a crime against its inhabitants.

My first bit of business after my report was to call on the head of HUD's Public Housing Office to ask why they couldn't build attractive low-rise apartment buildings with balconies and other amenities, such as were common in many residential communities and whose residents took pride and care in looking after their apartments and the public spaces? The Public Housing Administrator looked at me as if I was crazy, before replying flatly and devastatingly, "Those kinds of apartments are too good for those people." (While my advice appeared to be ignored, I read news accounts with dramatic photos of the St. Louis Housing Authority blowing up three of the 11-story buildings five years later and the destruction of the remaining high-rise units the following year.)

My work brought me into close contact with two of Weaver's aides, Leonard Duhl and Charles Haar, who were unusually bright and who would become very good friends. Duhl was an innovative Public Health psychiatrist and an HUD senior consultant, who as a participant at the June 1966, National Symposium on Science and Technology, had spoken brilliantly on "minimizing crime-inducing factors by the design and construction of city areas." Haar, who had been on the Harvard Law School faculty and was an authority on real property development, was an Assistant Secretary and actively involved with HUD's Model Cities program, among others.

In a memo to Under Secretary Wood describing my views on crime and public safety as they related to HUD's mission to increase home ownership and support the economic development of urban communities, I told him that HUD needed to develop policies and programs that would create a safe, secure environment for those living and working in urban communities. This required planning and constructing special features, such as good lighting, locks, and other controls for all housing and commercial buildings. Lighting and entrance controls should also be part of plans for public spaces, such as parks, squares, and public transportation facilities. Design and construction features, which help insure that residences and commercial buildings are structurally safe and fire resistant, should also be required. And practical features that would meet the functional needs of the occupants and users should be incorporated, including safeguards against common criminal threats. These seem like obvious recommendations today, but the were novel ideas to the Public Housing Administration in 1967.

But my new job and my ideas for innovative approaches to preventing and reducing everyday urban crimes were fated to come to an abrupt halt in September, 1967, following a series of violent riots, primarily in black neighborhoods, where there was widespread looting and destruction of property in more than 150 cities. The most destructive of these large-scale riots, in which many buildings were burned, occurred during a two-week period in July in Detroit, where 43 persons were killed, 33 of whom were black (most shot by police officers) and Newark, N.J., where 23 were killed, 21 of them black. At the core of all of these riots were the many years of pent up tensions in black communities, arising out of years of frustration and anger against racial segregation and discrimination in jobs, housing and public services, including the frequent harassing and arrests of black youths by police. These riots were usually triggered when the local police were seen to have unjustly shot a black youth, or used excessive force in making an arrest.

President Lyndon Johnson was greatly alarmed by these race riots, which threatened to spread to numerous other cities where similar grievances and tensions were prevalent. Deeply suspicious and concerned that the Soviet Union might be fomenting these nation-wide racial disorders that threatened the maintenance of law and order and our national security, Johnson issued an executive order on July 29, 1967, establishing an 11-member Presidential National Advisory Commission on Civil Disorders (to be known as the Kerner Commission, after its chairman, Otto Kerner, Governor of Illinois). The Commission was directed by the President to get to the root of these disorders by answering three questions: "What happened? Why did it happen? What can be done to prevent it from happening again?" An interim report on the findings was to be sent to the President by March 1,1968, and the final report and recommendations no later than a year from the July 29, 1967 order.

To find the answers, the President appointed David Ginsburg, a close advisor and highly respected Washington attorney, as Executive Director of the Commission's staff. It was not long afterwards that I received a telephone call from David, saying I had been recommended by a mutual friend, Abram Chayes, a Harvard law professor and a very close personal friend, for one of the key positions on the Civil Disorders Commission staff, Associate Director for Public Safety. I would be responsible for the Commission's report on the role of the police, the National Guard and the Army in responding to and controlling civil disorders. Could we meet and talk about this?

In anticipation of my raising the problem of my current responsibilities and commitments to HUD, David said he had already discussed with Robert Wood, HUD's Under Secretary, his urgent need for me at the Commission and was confident arrangements could be worked out for HUD to loan me to the Commission, if I was interested. I replied that I believed his Commission's mission and task were extremely important and I would be very pleased to discuss the matter with him.

As I had earlier participated in a panel discussion at the Notre Dame Law School on the problems and role of law enforcement officials in the earlier Los Angeles Watts riots, I had given some thought to the prevention and control of such civil disorders, including ways to provide police departments and National Guard forces with less-than-lethal weapons and training them to respond with minimal use of force. As part of this, I had been warning in talks and articles against the inappropriate use of guns by the police, citing the demonstrated, counter-productive consequence of the use of the police gun. Such use had been seen as excessive, unjustified deadly force in many local communities, and had been primarily responsible for triggering the riots that had followed.

While I had been greatly attracted to taking on the many crime prevention opportunities offered by HUD's mission for developing and promoting safe urban environments, I found far more critical, the public safety crisis confronting the U.S. and its cities. I saw my new position on the Kerner Commission as offering a chance to play a significant role in developing a realistic, effective Nonlethal police and military response for the control of racial civil disorders and violence. I also recognized the need to address and develop solutions to the explosive racial grievances and discrimination problems in America. Accordingly, after a successful meeting with Bob Wood, I called David Ginsburg to tell him I would accept his offer to be Associate Director for Public Safety of the President's Commission on Civil Disorders.

KERNER COMMISSION ON
CIVIL DISORDERS: 1967-1968

Courtesy of the Washingtoniana Division, DC Public Library.

I had first become sensitized to the potential dangers of racial civil disorders when riots exploded on a hot summer day in many urban Black communities. In Los Angeles in August 1965, the police arrest of a Black driver for speeding, had precipitated a protest demonstration that escalated into stoning passing cars, beating white motorists, overturning cars and setting them on fire. Following mediation efforts, there was a day of calm but when talks between police and Black residents broke down, the violence and destruction resumed on a burgeoning and bolder scale, two miles away in the Watts business district. It soon spread into other areas, involving hundreds of women and children in five nearby housing projects, with widespread looting, firebombing and the destruction of targeted white-owned or white-occupied properties. When the rioting was finally quelled with the help of the National Guard, some 4,000 persons had been arrested, 34 people killed and hundreds injured, sending shock waves throughout the country, especially to those Americans who believed race relations had been improving.

Bill Parker, the L.A. Police Chief, had been a colleague when we both were in the Public Safety division of the U.S. Military Government in Berlin and later when I was at the Treasury Department, I had worked with him on a variety of criminal intelligence and other projects of mutual interest. Brought to L.A. as a reform chief, Parker earned a national reputation as an outstanding, highly professional police leader. However, when I read the news accounts of the Watts rioting, I was appalled by the L.A. police's heavy use of deadly firearms. His suppressive actions became clearer when I talked to him later and learned that he and his police force had not been adequately trained and prepared for handling such a large, and ultimately violent civil disorder. For Parker, controlling this civil disorder was an essentially unknown kind of law enforcement and order maintenance experience that had taken Los Angeles by surprise and at a terrible cost, and many other U.S. cities would soon find themselves to be in the same vulnerable position.

A year later, in the Spring of 1966 when I was still at Treasury, I had occasion to present my own views on the right and wrong ways of controlling a serious urban disorder when I was invited by the Dean of the Notre Dame Law School, Joseph O'Meara, to be part of a panel discussion on riots. Dean O'Meara expressed the view that the police and National Guard at Watts had "a moral as well as a legal obligation to use effective measures to protect the community," even if this meant shooting looters or curfew violators. I took a contrary position, saying that the police use of lethal weapons, such as handguns, to suppress a riot was not in the best interests of the public in situations where the lives of innocent bystanders is seriously endangered. This was especially inadvisable, I said, if, as experience has shown, the deaths of such innocent persons is likely to aggravate the community and escalate the violence and destruction.

I felt strongly that the Detroit and Newark riots, and the increasing number of civil disorders breaking out throughout the country, had dramatically demonstrated how seriously unprepared our local and state officials and law enforcement agencies were to understand, much less respond wisely, to these threatening emergencies. I welcomed the new Presidential Commission as the best opportunity and mechanism for finding a solution to this national emergency. I now hoped I could play a valuable part in helping to educate and sensitize police departments and National Guard forces to the dangerous consequences inherent in the use of deadly force in these civil disorders. At the same time, I believed, it was essential to provide them with the training and equipment that would enable them to help prevent or minimize violence, restoring peace by minimum, Nonlethal means.

I told David Ginsburg, therefore, that I believed it was important for me to attend the forthcoming annual meeting in Kansas City of the International Association of Chiefs of Police (IACP), of which I was a member. All of the chiefs and other top police officials of the cities and states would be there discussing and analyzing the Detroit and Newark riots, and it would be a unique opportunity to hear and discuss their views—not only about the cause of the riots, and the police response, but also the current vulnerability and preparedness of America's police officers nationally.

As I had expected, the racial riots and how to control them were the main topics of discussion at the convention, and it was clear that no city's police force was trained or equipped to deal with a major civil disorder. Moreover, every large-city police chief reported the existence of strong racial grievances and tensions in his community that could erupt into a violent riot any day.

What disturbed me the most, however, was my visit to the large display of police equipment and weaponry on view for sale to the nation's police departments. This year, however, the vendors were not featuring and recommending their usual police patrol cars, police sticks, 38 caliber handguns, etc. Instead, the dominating, eye-grabbing exhibits that stunned and chilled me were the rows of intimidating and frightening military-type vehicles and weapons. These ranged from deadly automatic assault rifles to armored personnel carriers, equipped with highly destructive heavy machine guns-- and even to army tanks! Equally, if not more terrifyingly, their sales representatives were telling the fascinated police chiefs that these deadly military weapons would give them the only sure, effective way to control and end a violent civil disorder successfully, and with low police casualties. Our local civilian police forces—inexperienced and unprepared to deal with this new civil violence—were being told, in effect, that they must be prepared and equipped to go to war.

I gathered a representative assortment of the colorful wall posters and large brochures advertising these armored military vehicles and deadly weapons and brought them back to Washington. When I went to my first meeting with the Commission, I taped the posters and brochures prominently on the walls of the conference room. When I started to address the commissioners and the principal staff members present, I could see from their startled, rapt faces that the grim images of the military tanks and machine guns had captured their full attention. Pointing to the menacing exhibits, I told them that these weapons of war were being displayed for sale at the recent convention of the country's top police officials and were being touted as the only effective way to control serious riots. I reported that every large-city police chief I had spoken to had acknowledged the highly volatile racial tensions in his city and that all of them had expressed great concern and a feeling of helplessness in their inability to suppress a serious racial disorder if it were to break out.

"Virtually none of our police departments are trained or equipped to control a serious riot," I told the assembled commissioners. And then I added my chilling warning, "If our police chiefs are persuaded that these military weapons and tanks are the answer to suppressing a violent, racial disorder, I believe their use would lead to a far more serious and dangerous threat: a racial civil war." I could almost feel their shocked reaction. I went on to explain that, unlike the standard police handgun, which usually fired only one bullet at a time, and normally only at an individual threatening the officer or another person, the military weapons were essentially automatic weapons of mass destruction, spraying out hundreds of lethal bullets a minute in a wide pattern. Such military weaponry would indiscriminately kill or seriously injure not only those nearby, but often at some distance from the shooting. Moreover, as large numbers of sympathetic bystanders, including women and children, tend to be attracted to the early, nonviolent stages of virtually every civil disorder, they too would be in the line of fire and, if shot by the police, their injury or death would almost certainly inflame the intensity and duration of the disorder. This harm to innocent bystanders would outrage not only Black, but White communities across the country, which young, angry, activists and provocateurs would undoubtedly exploit, with devastating national-security consequences.

I warned the startled commissioners that, in light of the existing grievances and tensions in Black communities in virtually every large city, and universal charges of discriminatory, harsh treatment by the police, that the police use of these highly destructive military weapons could very well lead to a bitterly divided country and a brutal racial civil war. The members of the Commission were stirring uneasily; visibly disturbed at the bombshell I had just dropped in their laps at the very start of their presidential assignment. "What can we do? What do you suggest," one of the Commissioners asked? I had thought hard and worried about this nightmarish problem ever since I left the police convention, and I now told the assembled commissioners that it was absolutely essential for them to arrange immediately a series of educational meetings with the police chiefs and their top officials of all cities with large Black communities. These meetings would stress the fundamentals of how to, and how not to, respond to and control racial civil disorders. And, because a civil disorder is a political as well as a police problem, the mayors and city managers of the cities must also participate in these meetings and discussions. The instructional seminars would explain the potentially disastrous consequences of using military tanks and automatic weapons, as well as the demonstrated ineffectiveness and counter-productivity of the police officers' handguns. They would emphasize instead the superior advantages of using Nonlethal chemical agents, CS and CN,[24] as the most effective and humane means of achieving the neutralization of a mob with a minimum of personal injury. I also believed these meetings could provide the police chiefs and their mayors with the basic essentials and guidelines for properly planning for, and hopefully preventing and controlling, civil disorders.

---

24. *These tear gases, named CS (chlorobenzalmalononitrile) and CN (chloro-acetophenone), are now commonly used by police and military forces called to control, without resorting to deadly force, disorderly and violent crowds that fail to disperse peacefully. Both CN and CS are irritants—they irritate mucous membranes in the eyes, nose, mouth and lungs, and cause tearing, sneezing, coughing, etc. CS is stronger than CN and more effective, although it wears off more quickly.*

In response to the questions that were troubling many of the commissioners, I told them that I had been assured we could contract with the experienced, professional Research & Training Division of the International Association of Chiefs of Police (IACP) to help organize these instructional meetings as well as provide the instructors and written materials. The Justice Department and its Law Enforcement Assistance section could handle the funding and invitations to the mayors and city managers. After a lively discussion, the commissioners unanimously approved initiating this orientation and training project. The Commission Chairman, Governor Otto Kerner of Illinois, and the Vice Chairman and Mayor of New York, John Lindsay, wrote a joint letter to President Johnson, recommending that he direct the Justice Department "to conduct a series of intensive training conferences this winter for governmental and police officials. This series would focus on effective measures for the maintenance of law and order and on programs to improve police-community relations."

Within a very short time, this crash project was underway, educating and sensitizing the nation's police chiefs and mayors to the inflammatory background of the current disorders, and the horrendous consequences of arming themselves with military weaponry. They were also advised that if it became clear that their limited police resources would be incapable of stopping the violence, to call their governors to send in the National Guard. The Guard has the disciplined manpower and resources required for clearing the streets and enforcing the curfew essential for restoring law and order.

These educational meetings proved to be invaluable in discouraging U.S. cities from buying tanks, machine guns, and other destructive and counterproductive military weapons, at the same time providing the cities' chief executives and police chiefs with a basic understanding of the underlying causes of the racial disorders and alternative enforcement methods. I believed then, and I still do today, that those intensive training seminars for the cities' mayors, city managers, and top police officials, together with the follow-up training sessions and instructional materials on controlling civil disorders with minimum, Nonlethal force, prevented widespread deaths in many American cities and the possibility of a devastating racial civil war in America.

While this interim commission recommendation and action took care of the immediate emergency of keeping the cities' police chiefs from stocking up on military weaponry, my principal problems lay ahead. For unlike the President's Crime Commission, which had 18 months to complete its report, the urgency to respond with effective, remedial recommendations to prevent or control the violent city riots had led President Johnson to direct the Kerner Commission to deliver its report and recommendations in only seven months, by March 1, 1968. And his Executive Order called for the Commission to produce a report addressing such issues as "the origins of the major civil disorders in our cities, including the basic causes and factors leading to such disorders," but also "the development of methods and techniques for averting or controlling such disorders," and "the training of state and local law enforcement and National Guard personnel in dealing with potential or actual riot situations, and the coordination of efforts of the various law enforcement and governmental units which may become involved in such situations." The Executive Order also specified that our report outline "the appropriate role of the local, state and Federal authorities in dealing with civil disorders."

Responding to these latter demands would largely be my responsibility and I quickly discovered that the task of ferreting out much of this required information would prove to be an extremely difficult task. For virtually no U.S. law-enforcement or military agency in recent years had been called on to deal effectively and humanely with the serious violence and sensitivity of the racial disorders that were now occurring. After exhausting all known, likely law-enforcement sources in the U.S. and overseas, however, I got lucky again. A good friend, Byron Engle who directed the U.S. Agency for International Development's foreign police assistance program and on whose advisory board I had served while I was at Treasury, showed up with the sought-after riot control response information. It was the planning, training and operational manual, (in English) of the British-controlled Hong Kong Police. Hong Kong was the only known city that was still experiencing—and successfully defusing and controlling peacefully, without deadly force—large-scale demonstrations by potentially violent and destructive mobs. After centuries of colonial experience, the British overseers had trained the Hong Kong police in how to organize, train, equip themselves and respond to possibly violent crowds who were protesting local grievances. The Brits had developed effective Nonlethal tactics and measures to vent pent-up anger and tensions, including the use of humor, music, and other diversionary devices. This Hong Kong police manual now provided us the basic principles and detailed guidelines we needed. Drawing on this invaluable crowd- and riot-control resource, and in cooperation with the IACP and Department of Justice, we were able to follow up our initial, crash series of seminars with other training seminars and informational materials.

At the same time, along with other related Commission sections and staffers, we conducted numerous meetings and interviews with major law enforcement and National Guard officials, and commissioned studies from knowledgeable academic and other expert consultants. I was especially fortunate to get as my Assistant Director for Public Safety an indefatigable and priceless deputy, Paul G. Bower, a young lawyer from a distinguished Los Angeles law firm, who took over and produced a major part of the important and sensitive chapter of the report on police conduct and community relations, "The Police and the Community."

This freed me to concentrate on writing the chapter on the "Control of Disorder", which provided desperately needed information for U.S. police departments on how to respond to and control riots with the use of minimum force. I also prepared a special supplement and appendix, "Supplement on Control of Disorder." Written primarily for the chief of police and his principal aides, it focused on "controlling disorders that have escalated beyond immediate police capabilities, and require a total community response," backed up by state police, National Guard and Federal military forces if necessary. It described the critical police planning, training, organization and equipment necessary to deal effectively with civil disorders, together with the Commission's recommendations for improvements in their traditional operations and practices. While stressing that preserving civil peace is the first responsibility of government and its police, who must take all reasonable and just means to insure law and order and protect the public safety, my report also emphasized the urgent need to improve police-minority community relationships. It described the complaints of abusive, improper police conduct against Black and other minority groups that had been a major source of grievance, tension and ultimately disorder. And it noted that Black communities usually received inadequate police protection and recommended that their calls for help be treated with "the same urgency and importance as those from White neighborhoods."

As the inadequate representation of Blacks in police departments had been found to be a major factor in the poor communications and hostility between the police and Black communities, we also urged the departments to intensify their efforts to recruit Black policemen. The police officer has a great deal of discretion in his contacts with citizens, and the poor judgment and improper use of that discretion by some policemen had contributed greatly to the volatile tensions and grievances responsible for many community disorders. Our report called for police departments to minimize friction with the community by issuing policy guidelines which covered many of the sensitive police-citizen contacts, such as a policeman ordering a street gathering to disperse or move on; the handling of minor disputes; the decisions to arrest which do not involve victims, like loitering and vagrancy; and instead to consider alternatives, e.g. a summons or the use of investigative techniques, such as stop-and-frisk. Our recommendations for police guidelines addressed safeguarding the constitutional right of free speech for persons engaged in lawful demonstrations and police protection of lawful demonstrations. They also spoke on my special interest, "the circumstances under which various forms of physical force--including lethal force--can and should be applied." All of these guidelines involved common, long-standing police practices in American cities that had been seen as discriminatory harassment, and were a source of resentment and friction between the police and Black and other minority groups.[25]

While the quality and contributions of the 11 individual members of the President's Commission on Civil Disorders varied greatly, (I found the statements of New York City Mayor John Lindsay and Senator Fred Harris of Oklahoma especially memorable and significant),

---

25. *The work on the control of disorders benefited greatly from the assistance of Daryl Gates, Deputy Chief of the LA Police Department. Lent to the Commission on my request, he had been the tactical commander during the devastating Watts race riots in August 1965.*

virtually every member of the Commission's highly competent and effective staff would merit an A plus, starting with David Ginsburg, the executive director. Several of the most outstanding Commission staff members I met would become and still remain good friends, including David Ginsburg; Steve Kurzman, deputy director for operations; and Mike Miskovsky, director of investigation. (His job was to prove or disprove President Johnson's deep concern that the Soviet Union was responsible for instigating many of the riots. He found they were not.) I also, came to know as an admirable friend, John Koskinen, Victor Palmieri's special assistant, with whom I later worked as the security consultant for the company he was then running, the Palmieri Company.

Working for the Commission turned out to be especially enjoyable because Victor Palmieri, the Commission's resourceful deputy executive director, had hired Louise to be in charge of the large number of important research papers commissioned from academia and other outside experts, including our talented, longtime friend, Abram Chayes, making the Commission feel like a family enterprise. More important, I saw continuing evidence that the Commission's combined efforts contributed significantly to our country's welfare.

WASHINGTON'S RIOT: 1968

When I returned to HUD to resume my work following the publication of the Commission's report to President Johnson in March 1968, I reviewed my original mission at HUD that was helping to make urban communities and their environment safer places to live and work. However, the grievances and tensions in African-American communities that had exploded into the riots, made me reconsider and my focus shifted to concentrating on persuading law enforcement to use of Nonlethal methods of controlling disturbances.

Now, less than a month after I had resumed working at HUD, I became the front-seat observer of a violent riot right here in Washington, the nation's capital, following the tragic and calamitous April 4 assassination of Rev. Martin Luther King, Jr., the charismatic Black civil rights leader. The first broadcast reports of this event, just after 7

Looted Store. Star Collection, DC Public Library; © Washington Post.

p.m., shocked all Americans in Washington and throughout the country, galvanizing large angry crowds of Black residents in more than 100 cities to pour into the streets demonstrating their outrage. Perhaps the most devastating and long lasting of these nationwide demonstrations took place right here in Washington, D.C. The turmoil and destruction started in the crowded, largely African-American, volatile intersection at 14th and U Streets, N.W., just 10 blocks from the White House. The first demonstrators included opportunistic youths and Black activists, some of who broke loose from the crowd and started to smash windows and steal jewelry, watches and TV sets from stores displaying them. Before long the looting had become widespread as more nearby residents arrived and joined in. It was midnight before enough police officers could be mobilized to disperse the rioters, which they finally did with the aid of tear gas. And it was dawn the next day before the police had the situation under control, with the strong, tearing odor of smoke and gas still in the air.

I had been following the progress of the rioting and looting on television throughout the night and it was clear that the situation was still very explosive and dangerous, given the multitude of angry, vengeful Black youths, activists, and sympathizers, and the city's essentially small, limited police force and riot-control capabilities. The police and city officials were reported to be apprehensive about the tension and widespread outrage in the African-American community and the calls for revenge for King's death that had been heard during the night's rioting.

The next morning I went to the emergency control center in City Hall, where I found Patrick Murphy, the city's Director of Public Safety. (This was a new position Mayor Walter Washington, the city's first Black mayor, had established to supervise and circumvent a deficient but hard-to-fire police chief.) Pat was an innovative and progressive-minded New York City policeman who had risen through the ranks to be Deputy Chief.[26] I had drawn on Pat's valuable New York City police experience while I was working at the Riot Commission and he was in full accord with my views against a police officer's use of guns or other deadly force, except in those rare situations where his or another person's life is in peril.[27] I had established that restriction as an official policy for all of the Treasury Department's 4,000 criminal investigators and had recommended a similar policy for all police officers trying to control civil disorders including civil disturbances such as large-scale riots.

When I told him I wanted to monitor what was happening on the streets and the police response, he led me to a nearby vacant office, which turned out to be adjacent to that of Cyrus Vance, Secretary of the Army, whom President Johnson had sent to the city's control center as his personal representative. Vance had been in charge of the Army troops that were dispatched to Newark and Detroit after the riots there the previous summer and he had a direct telephone connection to the White House and the President.

The city was relatively quiet all morning, and while the police had no reports of new fires or looting, nearly everyone in the emergency control center was on edge and the tension was almost visible. The police

---

26. *I had been instrumental in bringing him to Washington in 1965, when I recommended him to Jim Vorenberg to head the police section of the Justice Department's newly created Office of Law Enforcement Assistance (OLEA).*

27. *Pat would later return to NYC as Mayor John Lindsay's Police Commissioner to clean up police corruption scandal disclosed by the Knapp Commission.*

were worried about anything provocative that Black power advocate
Stokely Carmichael could say that might stir up trouble and rekindle
the rioting. Carmichael had scheduled a press conference later that
morning at an outdoor campus rally organized by student activists at
largely Black Howard University. Although Carmichael's news conference and his speech on the university's campus ended peacefully, there
was a warning of dangerous trouble ahead when police observers
alerted their headquarters to the suspicious actions of several large
groups of high-school students who had been standing on the fringes
of the rally. Numbering in the hundreds, these massed youths were
seen following one another sequentially down Georgia Avenue, N.W.,
toward 7th Street. The emergency control center's worst fears materialized when these teenagers were joined by large numbers of Black
sympathizers along the way to the heavily commercial 7th Street,
N.W., area.

The resulting crowd overwhelmed the capability of the city's much
smaller assembled police force who tried to block their passage, and
the crowd spread out to the H Street, N.E., corridor. The local television stations were soon showing youngsters breaking store windows,
followed by looting. Before long, TV viewers could see the dark,
smoke rising from buildings that had been set on fire. The responding
firemen were pelted with rocks, bottles and other missiles.

Secretary Vance was now getting calls from the White House, and
I could overhear his calm, reassuring responses to a very upset and
querulous President who was being plagued by angry telephone calls
from worried members of Congress, as they witnessed the looting and
burning, while sympathetic violent mobs were calling for vengeance
for Martin Luther King's assassination. The President was getting calls
from senior legislators who could not understand why the police were
standing by and permitting this. Typical of these calls was that of the
Georgia Senator Richard Russell, the powerful chairman of the Armed
Services Committee.

"Why aren't they shooting these looters and arsonists?" the outraged
senator complained to the President. I could hear Vance trying to
soothe and explain to the frustrated President why the efforts of the
city's vastly outnumbered police force to control, much less arrest, the

estimated 20,000 rampaging, rebellious rioters, were futile. Shooting them would only inflame the crowds and result in an even greater number of deaths and more widespread destruction, Vance explained. The police had to wait for the arrival of thousands of nearby Federal troops, who were now in the process of being called up, to provide the necessary numbers of trained, equipped, and disciplined forces essential to cordon off and subdue these thousands of District rioters.

Police clearing the streets. Star Collection, DC Public Library; © Washington Post

But by the time some 13,000 Federal troops had been mobilized and equipped and arrived in Washington, supplemented by 1,750 Federalized D.C. National Guardsmen, and had dispersed the thousands of rampaging rioters, cleared the streets, and helped the police restore law and order, more than 1,000 buildings, including many stores, had been burned in Washington's predominantly Black neighborhood. Twelve people had died, mostly in the fires, while more than 1,000 people were injured, and some 6,000 people were arrested. However, not a single person was shot by a police officer or soldier, which was a great tribute to the discipline and wise policy of both the city's police and Federal military officials. Damage to the city's African-American community and economy would prove devastating and long lasting, and nearly 40 years later, in 2007, numerous blocks remained in rubble. Many businesses never re-opened and thousands of jobs were lost. In addition, the increase in insurance rates and crime led many

African-American middle class residents, as well as those of other minorities, to move to suburban communities, depriving the city and its large African-American community of much needed professional services, as well as political and civic leaders.

The many cities which suddenly found themselves under assault from the their angry Black communities was a wake-up call not only for them, but for every other American city with sizable African-American communities. Their political, business, civic, and religious community leaders could no longer ignore the pent-up, smoldering grievances of their Black citizens. The shocking reality of these widespread riots had suddenly made all U.S. cities aware of and deeply concerned about their need to understand and respond appropriately and effectively to this crisis, and to prevent future civil disorders of this magnitude.

As a result, I now found myself devoting a lot of my time responding to requests to speak at law enforcement and criminal justice conferences and to write articles on our findings and recommendations for preventing and controlling riots. These talks and articles were reaching police and law enforcement officials in publications such as *The Police Chief*, the monthly publication of the organization representing the country's police chiefs and senior officers, *The Journal of Criminal Law and Police Science*, and *Law Enforcement Science and Technology*. They were also widely covered by the Associated Press and other wire services and appeared in newspapers across the country, ranging from The *New York Times* and *Philadelphia Inquirer* to the *Chicago Tribune* and the *Portland Oregonian*. In all of these speeches and articles, I emphasized the importance of curtailing abusive and harassing police practices, and the need to restrict the use of police hand- guns to those situations where the life of the officer, or another person, was in imminent danger.

But not all of my comments and recommendations were well received by local officials, as I was to discover when I visited Chicago shortly after that city, like Washington, had experienced violent demonstrations and rioting following Martin Luther King's assassination in April 1968. I was in Chicago to speak to 800 law-enforcement officials and scientists attending a National Symposium on Law Enforcement, Science and Technology, and, in response to a reporter's question about the city's recent riot, I praised the commander of the Illinois National Guard for not using deadly firearms to quell the riot. But Chicago's Mayor Daley was furious when he learned that I had praised the Guard's restraint. He told reporters that the next time there was a riot and looting in Chicago he would "order the Chicago police to shoot to kill" arsonists and maim looters, adding that no "out-of-town expert" like me would tell him how to deal with such lawless rioters.

The next day's Chicago Tribune, which had asked for my response to Mayor Daley's angry "shoot-to-kill' edict, quoted my reply: "Those who talk seriously of being tougher and urging freer use of firearms by police and guardsmen are ignoring the disastrous realities of such a course." The Tribune reported my pointing out that there are more guns in the hands of private citizens than there are in the hands of all policemen, guardsmen and Federal troops combined and, I warned, "This fantastic private arsenal of weapons and other means of destruction in the hands of private citizens, Black as well as White, constitutes a potential for national calamity." The Tribune went on say, "Sagalyn said most police and military commanders used good judgment in keeping tight control over the use of firearms by their forces. The lives saved by this policy were not just those of the rioters—the lives of many policemen and soldiers were at stake. It seems clearly wise public policy not to deprive a person of his life, particularly without even a trial, for a crime that may involve property worth only a few dollars."

Fortunately, Mayor Daley's 'shoot-to-kill' views were not widely shared by the press, as demonstrated in the *Washington Post* report by Joseph Kraft, respected, nationally syndicated columnist. In an April 9th column headed Disorders Here Taught Control Without Bloodshed, Kraft commended Washington's response to the riot that followed Martin Luther King's death: "For Washington controlled with a minimum of bloodshed what could been a mass slaughter. This city was able to do that mainly because it had been following some of the recommendations of the President's Commission on Civil Disorders. It had moved toward the right conditions for meeting the critical black and blue problem--the problem of how the police deal with the Negro community during a period of extreme racial tension."

CONSULTING YEARS
1968-1990

Chapter 12

*The true secret of giving advice is, after you have honestly
given it, to be perfectly indifferent whether it is taken or not and
never persist in trying to set people right.*
  Hannah Witall Smith

ARTHUR D. LITTLE

My job at Treasury was as perfect a job as there is in government. I
loved what I was doing and the people I worked with, and for the
most part I was my own boss, with no one looking over my shoulder or questioning my decisions. What little oversight and bureaucracy there was had been very supportive. However, even though I
had been allowed a great deal of independence, I found working at
HUD much less rewarding. As a new Federal department with new
missions and new managing players, but with entrenched midlevel
officials from old-line agencies who were very resistant to change, it
had been a frustrating process getting important decisions processed
and implemented. So I was once again predisposed for a change when
I received a call in June 1968 from Michael Michaelis, whom I met
when he was on the staff of President John Kennedy's White House
Science Advisor. Michael was now head of the Washington office of
Arthur D. Little, Inc. (ADL) that was based in Cambridge, Mass.
He was telephoning to ask if I would be interested in joining ADL's
professional staff in Washington.

I learned that ADL, founded in 1886, was the world's first and oldest research management company and had a distinguished record
of pioneering achievements combining innovation, technology and
strategy to solve complex business problems for many of the Fortune
500 companies. Employing more than 1,000 professionals with skills
ranging from science, technology, management and finance to opera-

tions research, it had more than 30 offices in the U.S. and abroad. Michaelis felt that the growing highly publicized crime, public safety, and security problems in all nations demonstrated an opportunity to provide ADL's consulting capabilities to governmental agencies and private corporations confronted with criminal and security threats. He had been following my career and thought I was qualified to start and lead ADL's entry into this new consulting field.

Since I felt that my effectiveness in developing programs for crime prevention programs at HUD was greatly impeded by the department's restrictive legislative authority, I was intrigued by the opportunities offered by ADL. I agreed to meet with Michael to discuss working with him in Washington. After an initial, exploratory meeting with him and satisfactory follow-up discussions with the principal ADL officials in Cambridge, I informed HUD Undersecretary Bob Woods that I was leaving and submitted my resignation. July and August was spent with Louise and our girls at our house on Martha's Vineyard, and the day after Labor Day I started my new job with Arthur D. Little.

As the sole senior staff associate working in the area of crime prevention and public safety, I was expected to develop contracts for our services. I soon had my first contract: to update and improve the U.S. Army's guidelines for handling civil disorders and violent riots. As this was a very familiar subject and all the essential information was still fresh in my mind or at hand, I was able to produce a report and recommendations without any outside assistance. But when I started to explore larger and more complex potential consulting projects with other governmental agencies and large private corporations, projects that would require the assistance of additional ADL associates and skills, I ran into a surprising but critical problem. ADL operated on a system in which most professional associates were responsible for developing their own projects, or else would work on a regular basis as a member of the team of a fellow associate. But every professional associate was free to accept or decline a request to work on any project, and no one could be required to work on another associate's case.

After I had completed my report for the Army and had started to recruit a team to work with me on a very promising large contract on public safety, I discovered that none of the ADL associates I had approached would be available. Mystified, I telephoned one of the bright, younger ADL colleagues in Cambridge—they all seemed like very young kids to me—whom I had met, liked, and thought would be able to assist me. "Why don't you want to work on this case?" I asked. His answer was blunt and completely unexpected: "I don't like 'cops' and I don't want anything to do with them. They are all pigs!" he said.

This intense animosity against police and law enforcement organizations turned out to be virtually universal among the youthful ADL associates whom I would have to draw on in future crime- and security-related projects. Only now, in recalling that conversation, do I remember how strong, angry, and prevalent opposition to the Vietnam War and the draft had been among college and post-college young men. And their use of illegal drugs as a symbol of their war protest brought them into devastating conflict with the punitive laws passed against anyone caught buying or selling illegal drugs. The resultant bitter anti-law-enforcement antipathy now appeared to be reflected in the attitudes of many of the recent college graduates working at Arthur D. Little.

Apart from this disinclination of the Cambridge ADL associates to work on any projects relating to crime and law enforcement, the Washington office was a very pleasant place to work. I found Michaelis and the other people there were unusually interesting and very supportive, and a number of them became part of our growing circle of friends, particularly Peter Labovitz and his wife, Sharon. Peter had been one of the key ADL associates who had interviewed me on my initial visit to ADL's headquarters in Cambridge, and had now moved to work in the Washington office, bringing his wife and their two young daughters, Erin and Tara. Peter was young, bright and impressive, a recent graduate of Harvard who had been teaching a graduate course on urban planning at Harvard. Louise and I found Peter and Sharon especially compatible company, and we soon formed a friendship with them that would grow and expand into our partnership with Peter and Peter's brother John; and then Louise and Sharon's partnership in a country store in Washington, Virginia. Unlike his ADL associates in Cambridge, Peter's interest in urban problems and his recognition of the importance of achieving safe living conditions in U.S. cities, resulted in his taking a supportive interest in my crime prevention and other public-safety ideas and consulting projects. So it seemed natural to discuss with him my frustration in getting other ADL associates to work with me and the limitations that existed at ADL in taking advantage of the increasing needs and opportunities I saw in my field.

An unexpected opportunity came one day in a telephone call I received from a Washington acquaintance, Frank Loy, senior vice president for international affairs of Pan American Airlines, the dominant U.S. international airline carrier at that time. Would I be interested in conducting a security investigation of Pan Am's international airlines facilities and operations? In light of my experience at ADL, I had been thinking for some time about organizing my own management research and consulting company specializing in crime prevention, security and risk management, and this seemed the break I had been waiting for. Within a relatively short time I contacted a number of highly qualified people with whom I had worked who expressed their availability to work on this and similar future projects.[28] For a large-scale sensitive project like Pan American's worldwide operations and facilities, I believed we now had a very impressive, unusually well qualified team. Since Peter indicated that he would be interested in joining us, as did Louise, I resigned from Arthur D. Little and with Louise's help, found a suite of offices at 1225 19th Street.

---

28. *They included Courtney Evans, a former Assistant Director of the FBI with 25 years of service in Federal criminal investigations and security; Lester Johnson, the former U.S. Commissioner of Customs and for many years prior to that the deputy Commissioner in charge of criminal investigations and enforcement; Howard Anderson, Director of Personnel and Training of the U.S. Secret Service and an Assistant Chief of the White House protective detail; Wesley Pomeroy, former Special Assistant for Law Enforcement to the U.S. Attorney General and Associate Administrator of the Law Enforcement Assistance Administration, Department of Justice (and, prior to his Federal service, the Under-Sheriff of San Mateo County, Cal.); and Lt.Col. (Ret.) Leroy Weygand, former Chief of the Physical Security and Industrial Defense Branch of the U.S. Army.*

SECURITY PLANNING CORPORATION

However, while we were still in the middle of moving into our new
quarters and organizing the new consulting firm, Security Planning
Corporation, I received a devastating telephone call from Pan American's senior vice president for operations for whom I would be
working. He had just been informed that Pan Am had experienced
some large, unexpected losses that would require him to lay off
hundreds of their employees, as well as to postpone our consulting
project indefinitely.

Security Planning Corporation , President.

Our fledgling consulting enterprise had just been grounded and we
would have to postpone our big plans and hiring the large staff we
had lined up to handle the challenging Pan American project. Though
disappointed, I was still confident that there was a need and market
for a consulting company offering specialized capabilities and services
in crime prevention and security and I decided, with Louise, that we
would still go ahead, but on a smaller scale. We put the start-up of
Corporate Security Planning in temporary deep freeze and, instead,

we would start by taking on smaller projects that Louise and I could handle alone or with the help of only one or two others on a contract-by-contract basis.

Our first consulting, and unsolicited, client was the Hechinger Company, a pioneer in do-it-yourself home hardware, lumber and garden chain stores, whose CEO, John Hechinger, had just learned of my new consulting service through a mutual friend. His company was experiencing continuing losses from shoplifting and internal thefts in its Washington area stores and he called to ask if I could conduct an investigation and report my findings and recommendations to him personally. Enlisting the assistance of Lt.Col. Weygand, with his many years of experience in protecting U.S. Army property, I spent the next few months visiting every section and inspecting every phase of the Hechinger stores' operations. When I presented John with my detailed report of where, how and why these costly losses were occurring, I was uncertain and a little uneasy about what his reaction would be to my conclusion that laxness and failure on the part of his key managers was largely responsible. Handing him my report, I told him bluntly, "You have to tell your managers that they are responsible for your losses because they are not following company policies and enforcing company regulations." To my great surprise, he expressed his satisfaction with my findings, but then handed the report back to me, telling me he wanted me to come to a meeting with all his top managers, so that I could tell them the results of our investigation. When I replied that I thought he was the proper person to tell them this, he persisted, and I did end up giving the managers my conclusions.

My widely publicized articles and speeches advocating the greater use of technological preventive measures to reduce crime had attracted the interest and friendship of New York Congressman James Scheuer, a 13-term representative and a wealthy real estate owner. Upon hearing of my new consulting company he telephoned to request my assistance in improving the safety and security of several large apartment buildings and their tenants in Washington and Puerto Rico.

By the time I had completed this and similar small projects, Peter Labovitz had also left Arthur D. Little and was ready to join Louise and me, as was his brother, John, a talented lawyer and writer.[29] The time now seemed propitious for organizing and implementing the larger, more resourceful consulting organization we had previously discussed—a corporation that could qualify for large government and private industry contracts. The result was our activation of Security Planning Corporation (SPC). The goal was to meet the increasing needs of business, government and other organizations to develop comprehensive security systems providing effective prevention and control measures and take into account the full range of environmental, human and physical factors that influence security. SPC's prospectus stated it would provide cities, states, and Federal agencies with "expert consulting advice in evaluating existing crime prevention and law enforcement programs and in developing more effective approaches." Its services would range from studies of law enforcement and criminal justice agencies and assistance on internal theft, fraud, prevention of shoplifting and vandalism to guidance for architects and developers in the planning and design of buildings.

Over the next several years Security Planning undertook a wide range of interesting and challenging crime and security related projects. One of the first was a pioneering study for the National Science Foundation (NSF), "Nonlethal Weapons for Law Enforcement: Research Needs and Priorities."

During the previous several years, I had been giving speeches and writing articles advocating the development of more humane and effective weapons to replace the policeman's obsolescent 19th century handgun. I had pointed out that the police gun was too inflexible and delivered excessive force for dealing with most police situations. It was not only killing minor law violators and innocent bystanders, but it's use was becoming counterproductive, triggering riots that have resulted in many wanton deaths and destruction of property. We now needed to turn to science and technology to provide an alternative that was both Nonlethal and highly effective in suppressing dangerous threats to the police officer and the community.

---

29. *We called John "the fastest pen in Washington" because of his skill and speed delivering written material.*

I had written an article on this subject, in collaboration with Joseph Coates, a Futurist, that was published in the *New York Times Magazine* and the *Readers Digest*. The attention they attracted and Coates's employment by the National Science Foundation (NSF)were influential in Security Planning being selected by NSF to undertake a pioneering research study on Nonlethal Weapons for law enforcement. (Pick up with Our investigation was)

These alternatives have ranged from chemical, electrical, and acoustical devices to rubber bullets and liquids that create slippery or sticky surfaces. But virtually all of them have limitations with respect to their immediate effectiveness in neutralizing a threat and the potential risks of serious injuries. All of these approaches are dependent on the accuracy, kinetic force and vulnerable location of the "weapon's" impact (such as eye, neck, heart) and the size/weight and health of the individual involved. Thus a rubber bullet that hits someone's eye, the potentially fatal shock of a Tazer on a person with a weak heart, or the harmful effect of some chemical such as Mace on an asthmatic, all have the potential for severe injury. The electric-shocking Tazer weapon, for example, has resulted in a number of deaths, leading many police chiefs to ban or severely restrict its use.[30]

Nonetheless, a number of the new developments now offer very valuable alternatives and the adoption by most large police departments of policies restricting officers' use of guns, along with strict accountability requirements if a gun is fired, has dramatically reduced the often counterproductive use of handguns. At the same time, government-funded efforts are continuing to develop better, practical, effective, less-than-lethal means of immobilizing a dangerous physical threat to a police officer or citizen. However, until a substitute for the police handgun is found that is as light, portable and demonstrably reliable and effective in neutralizing a deadly threat, police and other law enforcement officers will continue to carry and utilize their traditional 19th Century handgun.

---

30. *Ironically, the ACLU objected to most Nonlethal weapons arguing that they are more likely to be abused by police officers.*

Another major government contract was the first comprehensive research and analysis study on residential security, a joint 21-month research project of the Department of Justice–Department of Housing and Urban Development. Over the following months (nearly two years) SPC evaluated existing measures, products, and approaches for providing security to residents of single and multifamily dwellings, with a wide range of detailed recommendations for making homes safer. These included having local law enforcement agencies initiate residential security inspection programs and insuring that security considerations be included in site planning and subdivision regulations. A *Washington Post* story on SPC's findings reported, "the federal government's most important role for helping homeowners and apartment renters to make their homes more secure against burglars is to provide 'accurate and useful information' about security measures."[31]

In the years that followed, we were asked to investigate and provide assistance on current as well as potential crime and security problems of numerous major corporations and governmental agencies throughout the U.S., ranging from IBM and the World Bank to the Department of Justice and Seven Flags entertainment parks. The scope of our consulting expertise included evaluating the impact of high intensity street-lighting of the District of Columbia and developing for their Highway Department a specialized computer program to measure the effectiveness of such lighting in reducing specific types of night crime in D.C.

For the Special Action for Drug Abuse Prevention in the Executive Office of the President, SPC interviewed state, county, and local officials and prepared a report summarizing their objectives for drug abuse control as well as an analysis of the variation in priorities, roles, and constraints in urban and rural areas. And on behalf of the Federal Bureau of Narcotics and Dangerous Drugs, we undertook a study designed to strengthen the international controls available to them

---

31. *I found it fascinating in rereading our standard government contract at the time to discover the relatively low rates of compensation in the 1970's. Peter's and my top pay rate, as Senior Principals, was only $18.75 an hour, or $150 a day, while the top pay for a skilled secretary was $4.25 an hour or $34 a day.*

to prevent the illicit importation of dangerous drugs into the U.S. As part of a study for the National Aeronautical and Space Agency (NASA), SPC identified major law enforcement problems to which NASA space technology might be applied.

Peter's background in urban planning and mine in crime prevention and security won us a contract to develop a security plan which included integrating crime prevention and security measures in the site plan for a planned community—Ft. Lincoln, a new community development to be built in Washington, D.C.'s Northeast area. The success of this planned community is reflected in a recent 2007 advertisement by a major D.C. real estate broker announcing the 2009 construction of a 40-acre Fort Lincoln retail project stating, "Fort Lincoln New Town was the brainchild of President Johnson, who wanted to create a 'new town in town.' He envisioned a model, planned community that would reflect the ideals and diversity of his 'Great Society.' The result was a combination of more than 1,300 condos and apartments built around a cultural center, elementary school, recreation area, and park."

THE BURLINGTON NORTHERN RAILROAD

One of our most interesting and adventurous undertakings was our consulting project in 1978 on the Burlington Northern Railroad's security problems. These included cargo and property theft, vandalism and trespassing, internal pilferage, wastefulness and fraud, freight damage claims, derailment and train/cargo protection. Originally named the Northern Pacific Railway and chartered in 1864 by President Abraham Lincoln, it was the first northern transcontinental railroad in the U.S. It was envisioned by its founders as a follow-up to Lewis and Clarke's exploration of America's northwest by opening up commerce and settlement to the thousands of miles of unsettled territory stretching from Lake Superior, across North Dakota and Montana, to Washington State and Puget Sound. During much of the late 19th century and early 20th Century, most of this Western frontier lacked any organized law enforcement and, except for the few widely scattered U.S. Marshals, the railroad police were the only

available law-enforcement organization in the "wild West" territories
through which the railroads operated. Later, when these territories became states, they all empowered the railroad police with the authority
and duty to preserve the peace and make arrests. The primary mission
of the early railroad police forces was to protect the railroad's trains and
passengers against the notorious outlaws who terrorized the Western territories. In those lawless days, the principal qualifications for a
railroad police agent were said to be his toughness and courage and his
skills shooting a gun and following the trail of a railroad bandit's horse.

At the time of our study, the railroad had become the Burlington
Northern (BN), a railroad empire covering 33,000 route miles in 28
states and two Canadian provinces and including the Chicago, Burlington and Quincy RR, the Great Northern, and the Spokane, Portland
and Seattle Railroads and their subsidiaries. With the establishment of
public police and sheriff forces in the newly created Western states and
cities, train robbers were no longer a serious problem. The primary mission of BN's police force had devolved to the protection of its passengers, cargo, and facilities from theft and vandalism. Our assignment was
to assess the operations and effectiveness of BN's 293-member Security
Department that was responsible for protecting the railroad's widespread facilities, its property, personnel and cargo. BN's Security force
was divided between the (1) patrolmen stationed to guard the various
protective and inspection functions at the railroad's numerous yards,
shops and other facilities and (2) special agents, who handled protective and investigative problems, responded to emergency problems, and
often had supervisory responsibility over the regular employees.

A long reigning, highly respected but autocratic director, who had
grown up with the proud traditions of the earlier railroad police,
directed BN's Security Department. Although he had instituted
organizational and operational reforms to address the railroad's new
priorities, he had ignored the need for security personnel to be skilled
in risk analysis. They needed to follow the paper trails of thieves and
embezzlers instead of the horse trails of train robbers. But the tradition
of strong, tough and domineering leadership still prevailed, and was
reflected in the autocratic, centralized management style of BN's long-
reigning Security chief.

We learned that the Security Director's failure to delegate authority over past years was now a serious concern. The Director was planning to retire the following year, leaving no qualified successor with the executive management skills and experience to replace him. This concern was a major factor in our being hired to help solve the CEO's problem of finding a successor to take over the Department.

Peter and I recognized that obtaining the cooperation of the retiring Security Director was essential. As that gentleman was very proud, opinionated, and accustomed to being treated with great deference, we needed to approach him carefully. Fortunately, my own national and international law-enforcement background was beneficial in gaining his respect and cooperation, and we also succeeded in helping him recognize his own stake in preserving his good reputation and record of achievement. This included leaving an efficient, productive, and praiseworthy Security Department as his legacy. As a result, we succeeded in getting him to agree to focus the year prior to his retirement on BN's priority to decentralize the Security Department's management system and to identify and train his best-qualified security personnel to assume leadership roles. This involved developing an executive management training program for those Security personnel he identified as meriting promotion to major command posts, including his successor as chief of security.

For me, the most memorable and certainly the most interesting part of this project was the many days and nights Peter and I rode on Burlington freight trains, from Chicago and St. Paul, Minn., to Seattle, Washington, and Vancouver, BC, traveling thousands of miles during bitter cold winter months, and sleeping fitfully in the no-frills, often chilly, caboose cars attached to the rear of the trains in which the off-duty train crews rested. These trips involved hiking through a multitude of BN facilities, talking to hundreds of employees and their supervisors as we inspected indoor and out-of-doors frigid freight yards, warehouses, freight trailer parks, and loading and unloading operations. Fortunately, in anticipation of working in frigid, rugged outdoor conditions, I purchased from an Eddie Bauer catalog an extremely warm, windproof parka in a bright red color that would make me highly visible to any approaching train engineer.

NEW ORLEANS SUPERDOME

Peter and Sharon Labovitz.

An equally challenging, but with physically warmer working conditions, was an earlier consulting assignment in late January, 1976,
that entailed traveling to New Orleans to evaluate the operations and
management of the city's new sports stadium and convention center,
the Superdome. Established by the state legislature in 1956 and less
than six months old, the government was besieged by complaints
from outraged customers. The ensuing unfavorable publicity about its
poorly managed operations and services had led the Governor to appoint a Superdome Management Advisory Committee to investigate
and recommend corrective measures. At the core of this problem
was the divided responsibility and political nature of the Superdome's
managing board, a 17-member troika commission representing the
State, the city of New Orleans and the two parishes (counties) concerned. Their inevitable patronage practices had resulted in many key
jobs and important functions being filled by unqualified, incompetent
personnel whom individual board members felt obligated to protect.

The Advisory Committee quickly concluded that the best and quick-
est way to meet the Governor's request was to assign this task to a
professional, research management consulting company. My involvement was precipitated by a telephone call I received from one of my
former ADL colleagues in Cambridge, who was heading an ADL team

competing with several other major firms for this Superdome contract. Would my firm be available to handle the Superdome's severely criticized, critical security problems for ADL? And, if so, as ADL was scheduled to meet with the Governor's Advisory Committee in New Orleans later that week, it was crucial I attend to make the important security presentation.

I arrived in New Orleans a day early and conducted a thorough inspection of the Superdome, identifying a wide variety of current and potential security risks, ranging from patrons' vulnerability to physical assault and entrapment in exiting in emergency situations all the way to serious fire hazards and other threats to life and property. Consequently, my presentation to the Governor's Advisory Committee the next day not only addressed the known criminal offenses and related security problems that had been an important factor in the Committee's appointment, but also exposed many other, far more serious, fire and other physical threats to the Superdome and its patrons. This report left the committee visibly alarmed and shaken.

The next day, after a jubilant ADL team leader informed me that my dramatic security revelations had been a decisive factor in the Advisory Committee's decision to award ADL the Superdome project, I returned to Washington and called to tell Peter Labovitz that I needed him on this job. As a week in New Orleans in January sounded appealing to Louise and Sharon, they decided to accompany us on what turned out to be an enchanting and memorable working vacation. Although Peter and I had serious work on the Superdome's security report during the day, we found time to party with our wives in the evening.

Our only disagreement with the other ADL team members arose after we had left New Orleans to write our respective reports and met to review and finalize our investigation's recommendations. Peter and I thought we had general agreement on rooting out the source of Superdome's notoriously inept management and operations: fire the political 17-member Superdome Commission and change it to a five-member board of private citizens with management experience, then appoint a director to manage the Superdome who was experienced in operating a major sports/entertainment facility.

However, the majority of our ADL colleagues now argued that it was unrealistic to think that the Governor and local political leaders would like or approve of such a recommendation. We had to modify our tough surgical recommendations and our criticism of their role, they said. I was surprised and angered by their position, saying we had a professional and moral responsibility to tell them what we really believed.

After a long and heated discussion, the others finally agreed with our position. But as we were preparing to fly back to New Orleans to deliver our report and recommendations, a jolting telephone call from a reporter I had met there tipped us off to an unpleasant surprise awaiting us at the airport—a subpoena for all of the copies of our final report. The reporter told me that rumors that our report was recommending the removal of the political representatives from the Superdome Board had created an angry backlash, and the District Attorney had been motivated to intervene and to suppress the release of our report.

Thus forewarned, we took an earlier flight, evaded the subpoena, and arranged for a quick, well-attended press conference, at which we read a summary of our report and recommendations before the assembled TV cameras, radio microphones, and print media. Copies of the full report were concurrently delivered to the waiting Superdome Advisory Committee. The deed was done and there was nothing anyone could now do to suppress our report. To my complete amazement, when the news media immediately followed up asking the mayor, the presidents of the two parishes, and the Lt. Governor for the their responses to our bombshell recommendations, their comments were very mild and dismissive as only the opinion of "some outside experts."

As I learned later, all of the members of the Board felt a tremendous sense of relief, because they had become increasingly frustrated and unhappy with their inability to rectify the Superdome's continuous problems and the political dilemma they had faced in their helplessness to appease the unending complaints of their political constituents about the Superdome. Now, ADL's report had taken them off the hook. The news media praised the report's recommendations.

the Board members could now blame the "outside experts" when all those incompetent Superdome employees they had hired started to receive the inevitable discharge slips and came to the Mayor, Parish Presidents and the Lt. Governor expecting them to fix everything. They could simply tell the discharged workers that they were very, very sorry—but there just wasn't anything they could possibly do about it. Peter and I took pride and satisfaction in our job well done.

It is often remarked that all good things come to an end, and so it did for our SPC partnership when Peter walked into my office to announce he and his brother John were both leaving to start new careers. The lure of battling crime and raising the level of security for others had finally diminished. John had decided it was time for him to begin practicing law and he would be joining Steptoe & Johnson, one of Washington's major law firms. That I could understand, but when Peter told me he was going into real estate development and now planned to build houses, I was startled. "What do you know about building houses," I asked? Looking slightly surprised at my questioning his qualifications, he replied matter-of-factly, "I'm going to read a book." Actually, Peter joined forces with a very experienced builder, and ended up as a successful real estate developer.

IMPEACHING NIXON: 1974

President Richard Nixon.

President Nixon's impeachment and consequent resignation in 1974 was an historic event. My personal high point was my participation as a member of the Congressional Impeachment Inquiry, established by the House Judiciary Committee to investigate the evidence for impeaching President Richard Nixon for "high crimes and misdemeanors" arising out of his involvement in the infamous Watergate break-in. The work of the Impeachment Inquiry Staff resulted in three Articles of Impeachment. The next step was a vote by the full House of Representatives, to be followed by a trial in the Senate. However, his complete lack of support quickly led to Nixon's resignation, which took place before the Senate trial.

My initial interest in Nixon dated back to his vicious 1950 Senate campaign in California against liberal Democratic Congresswoman, Helen Gahagan Douglas. He won the election by charging her with being pro-Communist. In those ugly, paranoid "Cold War" years, when the American public was terrified by the threat of nuclear attacks by Communist Russia, calling someone pro-Communist was akin to calling him or her un-American and a traitor. Nixon attracted national attention with his success demonizing his political opponent by tagging her pro-Communist. His unscrupulous political tactic intimidated his would-be critics, just as it did that same year for Joe

McCarthy, the demagogic, newly elected U.S. Senator from Wisconsin. Nixon's dirty tactics won him the nickname "Tricky Dick" and he exploited this type of aggressive campaigning to win the GOP's nomination as Eisenhower's vice-president in 1952 and later the presidency in 1968.

Long before Watergate, Louise and I heard scary stories about Nixon's strongly expressed views against Jews and other racial minorities, as well as his near schizophrenic behavior believing that as President he was above the law. He instituted an "enemies list" and sought measures, including IRS audits, against those he felt opposed him. This combination of hatred of the Jews and his strong belief that he had arbitrary power and immunity from any law raised chilling memories of recent German history and fears that it could also happen here. I remember discussing these concerns about Nixon one evening with some close friends who were also aware of these reports and shared our concerns that this was becoming a very dangerous country to live in. But if things became too dangerous for us, as Jews, where could we go? After a long discussion we all came to the sad realization that there really was no other place we wanted to go where we could be certain that it couldn't happen there, too. We finally decided all we could do was stick it out and try to do whatever we could to prevent this threat, including electing a new president.

Louise clearly recalls my comments to her after reading the *Washington Post*'s front page account on June 17, 1972, of the Watergate break-in. I told her, "This burglary story is crazy. It doesn't make any sense. Why would anyone break into the Democratic National Committee's office? All they had to do was ask for the information and it would be given to them freely." And I had concluded, it looked to me "like the kind of thing the CIA would do." My guess was confirmed by a later Post article reporting that one of the principal burglars had been identified as a former CIA agent, and that the Watergate burglary was part of a large-scale "dirty tricks" and sabotage project carried out by Nixon's 1972 re-election campaign committee (CREEP—Committee to Reelect the President), funded with money controlled by Nixon's Attorney General, John Mitchell.

The continuing *Washington Post* articles by its investigative reporters, Bob Woodward and Carl Bernstein on the illegal activities of
Nixon's reelection committee and attempts to cover up the Watergate burglary, led Senator Sam Ervin (D-N.C.), chairman of the
Senate Select Committee, to open nationally televised Watergate
hearings in May 1973 to investigate these allegations. The parade
of witnesses called produced damaging evidence against Nixon,
especially the bombshell testimony of Nixon's White House counsel
John Dean, when he revealed that President Nixon was personally
involved in paying hush money to the Watergate break-in burglars.
Dean's startling evidence resulted in the resignation of Nixon'
four top aides, Chief of Staff Bob Haldeman, Domestic Affairs Assistant John Ehrlichman, Attorney General Richard Kleindienst and
Dean himself.

My concerns about Nixon's paranoid, lawless behavior and the imminent threat to our constitutional rights were expressed in a *Washington Post* article on January 8, 1973, following the revelation by
a White House aide, Tom Huston, that he had authored a "clearly
illegal intelligence plan" approved by Nixon in 1970. This included
provisions for opening sealed letters and burglarizing a large number
of "security targets," as well as recommending the surveillance of
college campuses and of students traveling or living abroad. The
Post interview reported, "Arnold Sagalyn, who headed the Treasury's law enforcement agencies from 1961 to 1967, said he was
'horrified' by the 1970 memos because they reflect such a 'cavalier
attitude about ignoring the law.' . . .The Huston plan, he added,
'set up an agency that is, in effect, lawless--not accountable to anyone. It was no different from setting up a Gestapo. It was a highly
dangerous situation.' "

Perhaps the most damaging testimony in the Senate hearings came
from an Air Force colonel assigned to the White House staff, Alexander Butterfield who, in response to a routine question, unexpectedly and to everyone's great astonishment, stated that he had
installed in Nixon's Oval Office hidden microphones to record
all conversations. And then he added the critical "smoking gun"
information, that most of Nixon's conversations had been recorded
on audiotapes! The immediate consequences of Col. Butterfield's

revelation was the extraordinary legal battle that came to be known as the "Saturday Night Massacre." This event was triggered when Archibald Cox, who had been appointed Watergate Special Counsel by Attorney General Elliot Richardson, subpoenaed the Nixon tapes. Nixon refused to surrender them and ordered Richardson to fire Cox. But when Richardson refused and resigned as Attorney General, and his deputy, William Ruckelshaus, also refused, Nixon turned over Cox's firing to the willing Solicitor General, Robert Bork. When a Federal District court ruled Bork's action invalid, Nixon finally agreed to the appointment of Leon Jaworski, a prominent Texas lawyer, as Special Prosecutor. On July 23 the Supreme Court unanimously ordered Nixon to surrender the tapes, which might furnish proof of Nixon's role in obstructing the Watergate investigation. However, when Jaworski sought to subpoena 64 of the tapes, Nixon refused to surrender them, claiming "executive privilege," whereupon Jaworski took the case back to the Supreme Court. On July 23 the Justices unanimously ordered Nixon to surrender the tapes, which provided proof of Nixon's role in obstructing the Watergate investigation.

Three days later the Judiciary Committee approved the first Article of Impeachment on "Obstruction of Justice," followed shortly by a second charge, "Abuse of Power," and a third Article on "Contempt of Congress." The disclosure of these shocking and possibly censurable acts by Nixon on national TV before Senator Ervin's investigating committee, together with the intensive coverage by all the print, radio, and TV media, had led to widespread Congressional and other calls for impeachment. A few months later, on February 6, 1974, the House of Representatives, responsible for the initiation of any impeachment, passed Resolution 803, authoring its Judiciary Committee to investigate whether "sufficient grounds exist" to impeach the President.[32]

Rep. Peter Rodino, the Committee's chairman, had appointed John Doar to be Special Counsel to the Judiciary Committee and director of the Impeachment Inquiry staff. I had known him when he was the very competent deputy to Burke Marshall, the Assistant Attorney

---

32. *This would be the second impeachment in U.S. history since that of President Johnson in 1868, although Johnson was later acquitted by the Senate.*

General for Civil Rights. He won wide respect then and later for his ability and integrity. On April 26, I signed a contract with the Judiciary Committee's Chairman to be John's Security Consultant.

Doar told me his Impeachment Inquiry mission required a large number of highly classified and sensitive documents from the White House, Justice Department, and other Federal agencies, including the FBI and CIA. In many cases these documents were going to be given reluctantly and only after being subpoenaed. His great concern was that any document leak or loss would result not only in serious accusations of violating classified security laws, but also in the immediate refusal to turn over any future documents vital to the Inquiry staff's work. Doar said he was looking to

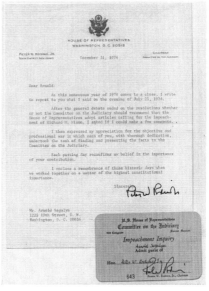

Appreciation letter from Chairman Rodino of the House Judiciary Committee.

me to establish a totally secure document control and accountability system for the Impeachment Inquiry staff that would insure that (1) no unauthorized person had access to any of these files or documents, and (2) no Inquiry staff file or document would ever be lost or leaked to anyone outside the authorized staff.

The offices of the Impeachment staff were in the former Congressional Hotel, just a block south of the House office building. During the next few weeks I designed a comprehensive physical security plan covering not only the Impeachment staff offices but also the perimeter of the offices and building. These included the roof, rear grounds, parking areas and their lighting as well as the building's windows, stairways, freight and passenger elevators, entry to telephone panel room, corridors and basement, and power, heat, and other utility areas. Additional security would be provided by the special Capitol police force as needed. Twenty-four hour access controls, including guards, were provided to ensure round-the-clock security of the staff offices. All the classified and highly sensitive documents would be in separate files and locked in the Federal government's top security, fire resistant steel cabinets located in a specially partitioned, secured section of the file room. Access to these files was severely restricted and limited to those members of Doar's staff with a "need to know." The files were maintained by a full-time document control officer stationed in the file room, who was responsible for ensuring that every time an authorized staff member needed a file, he/she was required to sign a document control register listing the document file ID, his/her name, and the date and time the document was removed. The same document control procedure and information had to be followed when the file was returned. Moreover, as no document could be copied or removed from the file room, workspace would be provided for staff members within the restricted, secure file center.

To ensure the effectiveness of this document control system, I recruited the full-time assignment of a thoroughly screened retired Army colonel. His job was to oversee and enforce the file center's security and accountability regulations. No classified or sensitive document stored in this file center was ever reported leaked or lost.

As noted above, the work of the Impeachment Inquiry staff led to the House Judiciary Committee's recommendation of three Articles of Impeachment which, with Nixon's forced release of other damaging evidence a few days later, made his conviction and removal by the Senate inevitable. Nixon's impeachment by the House of Representatives, as John Labovitz (one of John Doar's stars on the Impeachment Inquiry staff, and my former partner at Security Planning Corporation) wrote in his authoritative book, *Presidential Impeachment*,[33] published four years later, "a virtual certainty" had not "Nixon become the first president in our history to invoke another constitutional procedure—resignation from office." In a copy of his book inscribed to Louise and me, John wrote, "With fond regards and hope you will never need to refer to this book."

---

33. Labovitz, John R., *Presidential impeachment.*, New Haven: Yale University Press, 1978

It seems as if times and the corruption of power never change, for 43 years later we heard again angry outbursts from members of Congress and legal critics with calls for impeachment of yet another President who had been acting as if he were above the law and no longer subject to the U.S. Constitution. President George W. Bush's "dirty tricks" included deceiving the Congress and the nation that Iraq was allied with the 9/11 terrorist organization and was arming itself with nuclear and other deadly weapons of mass destruction which seriously threatened our national security. Then, claiming his authority as President and Commander-in-Chief, Bush proceeded to flout existing laws that protected the constitutional rights of American citizens. But unlike Nixon, his assumption of extra-legal powers as necessary to protect the country in a time of war, won enough support from members of his own party to insure that none of his lawless acts would be subject to Congressional censure.

MY ASSIGNMENT TO INVESTIGATE
THE F.B.I.

Three years after my work with the Nixon Impeachment staff, I was asked by the Chairman of the House Judiciary Committee to consult on a completely different subject, the FBI. This request was in response to a to a study by the government's General Accounting Office (GAO) that found serious deficiencies in the information the FBI was providing the Judiciary Committee, which it needed to evaluate the FBI's performance. The GAO's findings concluded the FBI reports on its accomplishments were "of limited value" and concluded that the FBI information on its accomplishments were "not a firm basis for measuring the effectiveness of past operations, determining where resources were used or planning future operations."[34]

My assignment was to provide the Committee with their own, independent capability for an annual assessment of the FBI's investigative activities and performance. A comprehensive, standardized

---

34. *For example, the FBI took credit for the multimillions of dollars worth of stolen cars, recovered every year by local and county police departments, on the justification it had conducted fingerprint checks for the various police departments*
.

questionnaire and reporting form was drafted which focused on those specific categories and types of information essential to a responsible and complete evaluation of the FBI's operations and allocations of its resources, essential to the Judiciary Committee's ability to carry out their oversight and legislative responsibilities. I reduced the number of questions and the amount of information requested, making the questionnaire short, not burdensome and reasonable demand on the FBI's manpower resources, which had been a principal concern. It was agreed that when major problems with the FBI were identified in the future, to the extent possible the GAO would be brought in to perform an audit that the Committee could follow up with hearings, if warranted.

FBI DIRECTOR J. EDGAR HOOVER OPENS A FILE ON ARNOLD SAGALYN

Looking back now, I find it ironic that the House Judiciary Committee asked me to help monitor and appraise the activities and performance of the FBI. For when I was a sophomore at Wesleyan, J. Edgar Hoover, the FBI's Director, had incredibly targeted me as a potential, dangerous foe and opened a FBI file on me that would grow to 108 pages of inaccurate, unsubstantiated, derogatory information that a later FBI Director and former Federal judge, would order expunged and destroyed.

J. Edgar Hoover

It all began when I needed a paper for my political science class and, intrigued by a news story on the success of the FBI in curbing bank robberies in the Midwest, I had written the FBI's office in Boston requesting information about the FBI. As I learned later, the agent in-charge (AIC) sent a memo directly to

Hoover informing him of my letter and asking if it was o.k. to send me the information. Hoover's return memo instructed him to check me out, whereupon the AIC sent an investigative agent to Wesleyan, verified I was an enrolled student there and also talked to my political science professor, who confirmed my term paper requirement and the appropriateness of the FBI's activities in bank robberies as my subject. My FBI records showed that after receiving this report, Hoover had not only informed Boston's AIC he was authorized to send me the FBI information, he also ordered a permanent file to be opened on me in Washington!

A few years afterwards, Director Hoover ordered another FBI investigation on me, this time I was a reporter on the Cleveland Press assigned to cover civilian defense after the Japanese attack on Pearl Harbor. I wrote an unsolicited article questioning the wisdom of the FBI in rotating its agents to a new post every two years. With the U.S. now at war with Germany and Japan and the FBI responsible for protecting us against espionage, I thought it did not make sense to shift FBI agents just as they were becoming knowledgeable about their area and were developing valuable intelligence contacts in their community. I discussed this frequent reassignment policy with a number of current and former FBI agents I knew, and all agreed with my conclusion.

Although the Press had not run my proposed article, Cleveland's FBI agent in charge had been quickly tipped off by one of the agents I interviewed, and he wired Hoover immediately. The next day an FBI Inspector from Washington, accompanied by Cleveland's AIC, called on my editor, Louis Seltzer, telling him that publishing my article would raise doubts about the efficacy of the FBI at a critical time in the war. They added that Director Hoover would like to invite Seltzer to be a speaker at the FBI Academy. Louis was a fervent patriot and quickly assured his visitors that the Press would never publish the critical article.

At the same time Hoover dispatched the FBI Inspector to Cleveland, he ordered a full-scale investigation of the audacious Arnold Sagalyn, this time to inquire about my character and loyalty to the United States. FBI agents visited Oberlin as well as Wesleyan and the FBI agent sent to Wesleyan included in his report a derogatory claim by "an anonymous informant" that I had read Communist literature when I was a student at Wesleyan.[35] As a result, when Clayton Fritchey asked me leave the *New York Times* to join him at the Pentagon, the Defense Department (DOD) investigators checking out my character and loyalty in the FBI files, found this informant's claim that I had been " a reader of Communist literature" at Wesleyan. This charge was also found by the Secret Service agents investigating my employment for the Treasury Department during their routine check of the FBI's files in Cleveland. In both cases, the FBI's informant's charge had the potential of killing or blocking my appointment indefinitely, pending hard proof of my loyalty to the USA.

I was saved from this potential fate because the FBI agent did not classify his informant as "reliable," and did not obtain a confirmation of the Communist literature charge from a second reliable source, as required by Federal investigators when evaluating a derogatory charge. As a result, both the DOD and Treasury investigators and security officers dismissed the FBI informant's claim as lacking any creditability. Moreover, every one of the multitude of other persons interviewed about me commented very favorably about my loyalty and character. The end result was I passed the DOD and Treasury loyalty and character tests with flying colors and was issued each Department's Top Secret security clearance.

Soon after I was sworn in at Treasury, and held my first meeting as Chairman of he Treasury Enforcement Board, I learned that some of the Treasury agencies had operational issues with the FBI. When it was suggested it would be helpful if I could arrange to meet with the FBI's Director, J. Edgar Hoover, to resolve these problems, I telephoned Hoover's office and arranged for an appointment for the following week.

---

35. *In the 1950s and 60s, the accusation of being a Communist, or even a Communist sympathizer, had serious consequences for a Federal government employee and most likely would have prevented the appointment of a job applicant, particularly anyone in a sensitive or important position. For the United States was then deep into the "Cold War" with the Communist Soviet Union (USSR), our former ally against Hitler's Germany. This atmosphere of fear had been politically exploited by Senator Joe McCarthy in his infamous televised Congressional hearings in 1953-54, in which he accused State Department and Hollywood personages with being pro-Communists and security threats. Thus, the FBI informant's charge that I read Communist literature would have been sufficient reason for Hoover to cite me as a security risk and ineligible for the sensitive or important position.*

Although I went to that meeting with a list of the subjects I was asked to take up with the Director, our discussion was an entirely one-way conversation. After greeting and telling me that the FBI had been receiving excellent cooperation from Treasury in recent years, he then proceeded to talk nonstop. I was unable to intervene with one word, much less address any of the matters we needed to discuss, until the end of our meeting time, when an aide knocked and entered the room to escort me out.

That was the first and last time we ever met. Thereafter, all future business I had with Hoover's office was handled by the FBI Liaison Section agent, who was assigned to visit me in my office periodically to exchange information and discuss matters of mutual interest or concern. These Liaison meetings were always very cordial and productive, as were my relationships with my Liaison and numerous other FBI officials with whom I worked over my years in government.

Although I had no specific evidence, there were a number of indications that the FBI's Director had a strong personal animus towards me that had adversely impacted on some of my activities while I was in the government, including a broached presidential appointment by an aide to President Johnson that never materialized. When I mentioned this one Fall day in 1977 to Mitchell Rogovin, my brilliant lawyer and a close friend, he suggested I might learn a great deal about this through the Federal Freedom of Information Act (FOIA), which empowers a person to obtain from government agencies all unclassified personal records. I thought this was worth trying, so he wrote a letter for me to the FBI's FOIA representative.

Several months later, after paying a fee of ten cents a page, I received a large envelope containing copies of 108 pages in my FBI files. Despite the many redactions, I was both greatly surprised and shocked to discover the scope and depth of Mr. Hoover's continuum of weird suspicions of my Treasury and Interpol activities and motives, bordering on paranoia. He not only interpreted some of my Interpol comments as attacks on the FBI, he also believed my motive for the various speeches I gave at law enforcement and criminal justice conferences, and the articles I wrote, was to supersede him as the senior representative of U.S. law enforcement.

Even more serious, Mr. Hoover believed I was trying to persuade foreign police agencies to communicate only through my National Central Bureau office and to stop communicating directly with the FBI and its Legal Attaches, stationed in U.S. embassies in many foreign countries, as they had previously been doing. This appalling misinterpretation had its origin in the 1962 Interpol General Assembly, when I had informed the delegates of my setting up a U.S. National Central Bureau, as required by Interpol, to serve as a U.S. clearinghouse for all foreign inquiries to the U.S. Then, at a later meeting of the Chiefs of the National Central Bureaus, in explaining that now that our NCB was operational, their inquiries to the U.S. could now be sent to my office at the Treasury Department. But I also stressed there was "no change in any of the established procedures between any foreign police agency and a U.S. government agency," For in addition to the FBI, the U.S. Secret Service, Narcotics and Customs Bureaus also had offices in a number of foreign cities, and would continue to deal directly with foreign country's law enforcement agencies.

Hoover's misunderstanding of what I had said at the meeting of the NCB's chiefs was all the more incredible as I had gone out of my way to improve the FBI's access to Interpol members and had facilitated their direct communications. As no FBI representative had been a member of the U.S. Delegation when I went to my first Interpol General Assembly, to rectify this omission, I took the initiative to personally invite thereafter the FBI representative in the country or region where Interpol was holding its annual meeting.

Fortunately, my FBI Liaison representative raised this issue at our next meeting, and my explanation and assurance there would be no change in the FBI's previous procedures with foreign police agencies satisfied him. Nevertheless, the FBI's record of Mr. Hoover 's response to his Liaison agent's report of our meeting was "The Director instructed 'Give Sagalyn a wide berth'."

James Rowley, the Chief of the Secret Service, encouraged Hoover in his mistaken beliefs about my ambitions. I learned this much later from a FBI Memorandum dated 2/19/63, reporting a Liaison Section discussion of my Interpol activities. "In October, 1962 Chief James E. Rowley of the Secret Service told Assistant Director Malone that he feels Sagalyn is trying to set himself up as the representative of all American law enforcement in the eyes of foreign nations. The Director noted His 'growing pains' should be carefully watched."

My FBI files made it clear Hoover wanted no record of his having any direct relations, much less recognition, of my official existence. Adherence to this policy, however, created a dilemma for him and his staff when, on March 20, 1963, Louise and I were at a Washington reception and stopped to chat with Cartha "Deke" DeLoach, one of the FBI's most senior officials. As Vassar College alumnae were about to begin their annual sale of donated books, and Louise's assignment was to obtain autographed books by well-known authors who reside in Washington, Louise took advantage of this opportunity to mention the Vassar sale and that its proceeds helped provide scholarships for students from the Washington area. "It would be wonderful if Director Hoover would autograph his recent book, which I would provide him. The Attorney General, Robert Kennedy, is contributing an autographed copy of his recent book, Just Friends and Brave Enemies", Louise said.

DeLoach was very cordial and suggested writing him a note explaining the request, together with a copy of the Director's book for his signature, which was done. What happened afterwards as recorded in fourteen pages of my FBI files can only be viewed as an unbelievable series of comically frenetic efforts to deal with this Vassar book aka hot potato problem. After Mr. Hoover read the letter, his first response was "Check out Vassar." Informed that one of the Assistant Directors had very good relations with Vassar and could vouch for the college, the Director's next instruction was to check out Louise Sagalyn. A Memorandum reported criminal and national security files showed no records on Louise. With those two concerns out of he way, and as the Attorney General was autographing a book, Hoover's staff recommended it would also be appropriate for the Director to autograph his own book for the sale.

Then a series of memos between the Director and his principal staffers pondered how to deal with the problem of getting the signed book from the Director to Louise Sagalyn without any record of my being involved. Finally, following several more exchanges of memos, an agreed solution was found. The autographed book was sent to Liaison Section and the agent who liaised with me personally delivered at his next meeting.

At the same time he encouraged a close watch and reports on my activities. The file showed this resulted in a steady stream of FBI memorandums from various FBI personnel and informants, passing on calumnious, untrue gossip and derogatory charges about me. After discussing with Mitch my desire to challenge the defamatory damaging nature and scope of the allegations in my FBI files, he wrote a Privacy Correction Request to the chief of the FBI's Records Management Division, petitioning the Federal Bureau of Investigation "to expunge completely all records" pertaining to me.[36]

On April 11, 1978, William H. Webster, Director of the Federal Bureau of Investigation, wrote Rogovin that my files would be destroyed, declaring;

> *It is our view that the information pertaining to Mr. Sagalyn in our records is not relevant and necessary for current purposes of this Bureau. Subject to approval by the National Archives and Records Service, we will arrange to expunge these file materials from the FBI central records system. In addition we will notify any agencies to which this information previously was disseminated of our expungement action.*
>
>
>
> *I hope the above will be of assistance*
> *Sincerely yours,*
>
> *William H. Webster*
> *Director*
>
>

---

36. *After citing the FBI's violations of the Federal law governing the FBI's maintenance of its records, and the grounds for the deletion of their files on me, the petition stated:*

> *If there were even the slightest doubt that any of this material bore any pertinent or relevant relationship to legitimate agency purposes, it is put to rest by the Bureau's own records. In a December 21, 1961 letter from J. Edgar Hoover to A. Russell Ash concerning Mr. Sagalyn's appointment to the Interdepartmental Committee on Internal Security, Mr. Hoover wrote "our files contain no pertinent information which can be identified with him." Thus, in the Bureau's own view, there is no possible reason for retaining the information complained of.*

On September 13, 1978 , a letter from the FBI advised that the National Archives and Record Service had authorized the destruction of my FBI records.

CARTER YEARS

Gratified by the work of the Impeachment Staff helping to terminate, as many of us saw it, Nixon's "Reign of Evil," and infuriated by his successor, Gerald Ford's immediate pardon, I looked forward to the coming 1976 Presidential election as an opportunity to help the Democratic Presidential nominee unseat Ford and restore a Democratic presidency. So when I was asked to direct the campaign's Crime and Criminal Justice Committee of the Democratic aspirant, Georgia Governor Jimmy Carter, I accepted without any hesitation and went to work enthusiastically.

Carter was relatively unknown and seen as a long shot, so I had some initial difficulty recruiting a high quality, experienced team. But calling on old friendships and with a lot of persistence, I succeeded in assembling a talented, first-rate campaign committee that included Patricia Wald, a Hollin Hills alumna and brilliant lawyer who was largely focused on injustices and helping needy causes; Henry Ruth, who as Jim Vorenberg's deputy, kept the Crime Commission running smoothly and Patrick Murphy, an old friend and innovative, visionary police leader who had come up through the ranks of the NYPD and later served as its police commissioner as well as police CEO in Detroit and Washington, D.C. Although I managed to get the requisite position papers produced and sent to Stu Eisenstat, the domestic advisor at the Carter campaign headquarters in Plains, Georgia, the only trip planned for me to meet and brief Carter was cancelled at the last minute because their latest polls showed that crime was no longer a big issue in the campaign.

Apart from my great delight in Carter's election, I couldn't deny some disappointment in not receiving any attractive offers for my efforts as often occurs when one plays a role on the winning side. But I did enjoy a very brief 24 hours as a celebrity with a paragraph in a

President Jimmy Carter.

national news magazine to show my grandchildren. As Andy Warhol once noted, everyone in the world can attract enough attention to become a celebrity and experience 15 minutes of fame.

My 15 minutes occurred shortly after the announcement of Carter's victory when I just reached my office and was starting to read the rash of post-election stories in the morning Post and Times. Ever since the confirmation of Carter's narrow victory, the news columns and the TV political Gurus had been busily engaged in the aftermath analyses of the election results, and competing in their speculative prognostications as to whom the new President-elect would appoint to his cabinet and other important, top political posts. I was startled when the phone rang because I didn't think many people would be at work this early and surprised when I heard the astounded, virtually speechless voice of a law professor at George Washington University who had been a colleague on my Criminal Justice campaign committee. "Have you seen the new Newsweek story about your being considered for attorney general?" he asked, his voice shaking with shock and disbelief, "Don't they know you're not a lawyer?"

Having difficulty understanding the reality of what he was saying, I muttered something unintelligible, put down the phone and rushed out to a nearby shop that carried the news magazines. Spotting the Newsweek's "Election Special" with Carter's picture on the cover, and the caption, "The New Look," I grabbed a handful of copies and rushed back to my office. There it was, on the bottom of page 34, in an article speculating on who among Carter's file of "10,000 resumes on computer tapes" would be selected to be Cabinet Secretaries and the other "top 200 appointees," a paragraph with the bold-faced heading, Attorney General, that read, "Among the possibilities, insiders say, is former U.S. Fifth Circuit Judge Griffin Bell, 58, who left the bench this year... There is also talk about Harvard Law Prof. James Vorenberg, 48, Burke Marshall, 54, who headed the civil-rights division at Justice under Robert Kennedy, and Arnold Sagalyn. 58, a Johnson Administration veteran who directed Carter's task force on Criminal Justice."

A flood of congratulatory telephone calls poured in all day, some that were from acquaintances who were lawyers and dumfounded, and some sounding upset that the new President would even think it was o.k. to contemplate appointing a non-lawyer to be the Attorney General. My conclusion after the initial shock had faded, was that those "insiders" who were responsible for my name being put in play had just assumed I was a certified lawyer because of all the criminal justice related positions I had held. In the meantime Louise and I had a good laugh about it and I enjoyed tweaking some of those who indicated it was akin to lèse majesté to entrust a non-lawyer to the government's top legal post, by pointing out there was no law requiring the attorney general to be a lawyer. But President Carter ended the speculation by soon announcing he was appointing his fellow Georgian, Griffin Bell, to be the country's top legal officer.

I was absolutely delighted when Carter appointed Pat Wald to be an Assistant Attorney General for Legislative Affairs and that in turn would later lead to her appointment to the U.S. Circuit Court of Appeals District of Columbia Circuit, the most important Federal court next to the Supreme Court, where she served with distinction for 20 years, including five as Chief Judge. She later was appointed to the International Criminal Court at The Hague.[37]

FEMA

My involvement with the Carter Administration was indirect. In 1979 when John Macy, who had just been appointed by Carter to be the first Director of the Federal Emergency Management Agency (FEMA), called to ask if I would help him organize it.[38] Established to serve as a national contact and Federal response center for major emergencies, such as hurricanes, floods and other disasters that exceed the capabilities of local and state governments, FEMA started by absorbing the remnants of the Defense Department's former Civil Defense division. This agency had earned some notoriety during the Cold War for its advocacy of American families building underground shelters in case of a Soviet nuclear attack. In the absence of any overt Russian attacks and the essentially ignored public response to this and other civil defense measures, the Civil Defense mission and staff had largely atrophied and most of the remaining personnel were unwanted cast-offs of other Defense agencies who were prevented from firing them because of their Civil Service protection. Now there was an urgent need to create an effective, national communications capability to meet FEMA's emergency operations needs. As I acquired a great deal of knowledge in this area as a result of my work on the President's Commission on Civil Disorders, as well as work on the 911 national emergency system, I took on this assignment. As assistant to Macy, I learned that FEMA's emergency responsibilities included acts of terrorism and I added that task to my consulting mission. One of

---

37. *Her husband Robert was also an old, good friend. Louise and I visited with them in Holland where Pat gave us a fascinating personal guided tour of the International Court.*

38. *Macy had been a year ahead of me at Wesleyan and had been the chairman of the U.S. Civil Service Commission under both Presidents Kennedy and Johnson, and I previously worked with him as a consultant to explore the various options for financing the new private, non-profit national public television network, when Johnson asked Macy to be president of the new Corporation for Public Broadcasting.*

my chief contributions in this area was to commission a classified study to identify the most serious vulnerabilities to America's major vital service systems, such as energy, communications, transportation, banking, etc., and whose destructive impact would be regional and even national, extending far beyond an individual city.

Not surprisingly, the resulting report showed that virtually all of these critical, potential targets were only designed to be protected against regular, known hazards, such as fire, lightning, accidents, and extraordinary weather conditions, such as hurricanes, tornados and earthquakes. It was discovered that virtually none were safeguarded against any deliberate effort to seriously damage a vital service facility. The reality was that our open society had created a wide-open industrially developed nation, whose infrastructure and key service components—including its air, water and surrounding environment—were extremely vulnerable to successful sabotage and far-reaching devastation by anyone with the knowledge, resources and the will to carry it out.

Not many efforts were made to alter these critical facilities, undoubtedly due to the lack of any serious attack against them. This changed after the 9/11 attacks and these dangerous vulnerabilities have been materially reduced.

ADVENTURES IN BUSINESS
Chapter 13

It is better to be born lucky than rich.
  Old Spanish Proverb

While I was the beneficiary of good luck finding meaningful work throughout my life, the same good fortune was never in evidence when it came to my occasional excursions into business and investments. I always found this ironic, because my father was a highly successful and visionary businessman, and at his death on June 2, 1949, the Springfield Daily News ran this banner headline on top of page one: "Raphael Sagalyn, Local Industrial Leader, Dies". However, I never inherited any of my father's business aptitude.

Reviewing the personally rewarding types of work and the careers that attracted me, I realize that, with the exception of journalism and politics/government, none of the traditional professions and business endeavors ever interested me. I grew up leading a very comfortable life for which my father provided everything I needed or wanted. But after I left home to go to college, I knew that I did not want to return to Springfield to work and live in a house nearby that my father had bought or helped buy. That was not for me. Though I deeply loved my father, mother and all my brothers and sisters and wanted to keep in close communication, I was determined not to return to Springfield after I graduated and to be completely independent thereafter.

So, when I was finishing college, I thought about what kind of job I could find that I would not only find interesting and enjoyable, but one which would also pay enough to support me without any assistance from my generous father. As high school and college had made it clear, I had no aptitude in the sciences. In college I found myself attracted to political science, my major. I also discovered, when I was offered the opportunity to write a regular column for the Oberlin College student paper, journalism seemed very appealing with its opportunities for obtaining and publishing information that was in the public's interest. And the sense of independence it afforded was additionally attractive. These two areas drew me into my lifelong involvement in government and journalism-related jobs and enterprises.

While I thought it was desirable to have enough money to be able to live comfortably and provide children with a good education, I never thought money itself was very important. Nor had I any particular interest in the sort of job where one could make a lot of money. Happily, I was always lucky in everything in life that's really important and matters most—in my love of Louise and our family, and in our many wonderful friends. Unfortunately, I found the developmental stages of new business ventures exciting and challenging, but my sense of accomplishment tended to dissipate, when the challenges were succeeded by the routine managerial chores that required sitting at a desk and on the phone, or in meetings for long periods of time.

Nonetheless, when I look back and reflect on my various business experiences, I find that I actually had an extraordinary knack for envisioning a number of outstanding business and financial opportunities.

PHOENIX AIRPORT

My first investment opportunity with the potential to make a lot of money was a joint real estate venture in Phoenix, Arizona in the 1950s with Jacobo Eisenberg, a prosperous businessman in Venezuela and Georgette Klinger's husband.[39] Foreseeing the city's rapid growth and expansion, and following its decision to build a new, larger airport farther away, Jacobo had obtained an option to buy the large acreage of the old, close-in airport and asked me to be his

---

39. Like a growing multitude of other aging residents of cold-winter states, my mother, in the early 50's, had been attracted by Arizona's warm dry climate, and had started spending her winters in Phoenix, where I would regularly join her for several weeks. I had met Georgette (Klinger Eisenberg) the summer of 1954 when I was on an ocean liner to France, enroute to Lou and Polly Cowan's rented country house, where I had agreed to look after their young children while they were visiting friends. My meeting with Georgette had developed into a close friendship with her and Jacobo, and had been renewed when we discovered they, also, were wintering in Phoenix. I later would serve on the board of her chain of skin-care salons company, Georgette Klinger.

partner in acquiring and developing this prime desert area. Even an
idiot businessman could recognize the potential for future financial
rewards in this enterprise, but it would require me to move to and
live in Phoenix. While I found spending short periods of time there
in the winter with my mother and socializing with interesting people
like Georgette and Jacobo, the idea of spending most of the next few
years in this quiet dullsville community with its terribly hot, pre-air-
conditioning climate seemed too high a price to pay just to make a
lot of money. Regretfully, I told Jacobo I appreciated his partnership proposal, but didn't think I was the right person for this project
and that he should go ahead without me. However, Jacobo said he
was only interested in taking on this project if I joined him, and he
dropped his option.

MOUNTAIN FIR LUMBER & WESTERN FOREST PRODUCTS

My next business opportunities came after I had move to Oregon,
and on Dan Goldy's recommendation, I had financed the purchase
Dan and my partnership interest in Mt. Fir Lumber, a small, mod-
erately successful Oregon company with three operating mills. Dan
had been confident he could increase Mt. Fir's profits significantly by
persuading its CEO to stop buying its timber at Forest Service and
BLM sales, and instead purchase and own the timber it cut, thereby
entitling the company to the highly beneficial Federal depletion tax
deduction. But Dan was unable to persuade Joe Crahan, the CEO,
Mt Fir's profits and value remained the same, and I never received
any dividends or other financial benefits. (My Treasury position later
required me to sell my partnership interest.)

I was now living on the income from the sale of my interest in my father's estate plus other savings, and I had to look elsewhere for more
income. Before long I became involved in starting a new lumber venture in Montana, Western Forest Products, which, in addition to Dan,
included Jebbie Davidson, a former Assistant Secretary of Interior
and Dan's boss in Washington, and Jack Kaplan, the wealthy owner of
Welch's Grape Juice, and Jebbie's father-in-law. Jebbie had moved to

Portland and was focusing a lot of his new law practice on becoming an entrepreneur, and continuously looking for attractive capital investments in the Northwest and Alaska. The Montana project, however, had grown out of a new lumber-mill mechanism Dan had learned about that could produce high-value pine paneling out of lodgepole pine, a tall, thin, pine tree that had long been believed to be essentially worthless except for its primary use as low-value telephone poles. The key to this venture's success was to buy up—quickly and quietly—large, substantial amounts of the relatively limited, privately owned Lodgepole tracts in the region. Although the lodgepole pine project had great financial potential, it was ill-fated as a result of Dan sharing our plans with a former U.S. Forest Service employee he saw as a valuable ally. We were dismayed to learn he had secretly informed a large, rival, Oregon lumber group of our discovery and activities, with their promise that he would be rewarded far better then he could ever expect from us. The result of this unexpected, well-financed competition was to elevate the purchase price of the former, lowly regarded pine tree too high to justify our pursuing the venture. In addition to my investments in Mt. Fir Lumber and the Western Forest Products venture in Montana, financial success in Oregon would also elude me in all of my trusting, fairly substantial outlays in Jebbie Davidson's enticing oil and energy quests.

ELECTRONIC DATA SYSTEMS

A few years later, after I had returned to Washington, D.C. to start the *Northern Virginia Sun*, I went into another business venture with Dan, who had also moved back to work at the Commerce Department following Kennedy's election, and was living only a few blocks away. We decided to set up a joint stock market investment fund, Danalyn, with a respected broker and friend, Harry Kahn. This fund had the objective of acquiring equity in high-tech, startup companies with high potential for financial success. Soon after that, Harry called to recommend our buying stock in a new company called Electronic Data Systems (EDS) that was being started by a former salesman at IBM, Ross Perot, to provide data processing services for large organizations. Harry believed this company had great promise for the new

world of computers and was therefore an excellent investment opportunity. After conferring with Dan, I called Harry back and told him
to buy for Danalyn $25,000 worth of equity in EDS. Harry reported
that since we would be buying "letter stock" (which meant it had
not yet been registered with the Securities and Exchange Commission), we would have to hold it as a long-term investment, because it
couldn't be sold to the public legally.

Soon after, Dan heard a discouraging report about our recent EDS
investment and pressed the panic button. Perot had tried to sell his
data processing idea to IBM, who had rejected it as impracticable
and without merit. Now we became concerned we were stuck with
our money in what appeared to be another high-tech loser and we
couldn't sell it and cut our losses. I agreed to call Harry Kahn and see
what might be done to salvage our $25,000.

Not surprisingly, Harry was quite huffy that we were questioning
his professional judgment in recommending EDS and asking him to
get our money back after he had fully informed us when we bought
it that its letter-stock status prevented its public sale. But Harry was
an old friend of Louise's, as well as her broker, and he reluctantly
agreed to see what he could do, although he was not hopeful. A few
days later he called to say that he had, with a great deal of difficulty,
finally managed to cancel the sale of our letter stock. My record of
bad business judgment was to remain unblemished. A few years later
when EDS went public, the value of a share of the stock listed at $16,
in a short time shot up to $160, thereby making our initial $25,000
investment worth $250,000.

And soon the company's success in selling its data processing service
to large corporations and winning a contract to computerize Medi-
care's records made a joke of the wisdom we had shown jettison-
ing our investment in EDS. Whatever business judgment ego I may
have had left completely vanished in 1984 when General Motors
purchased EDS for $2.4 billion. In those days a million dollars was
a lot of money, and a BILLION dollars was a lot of money to divide
among those original shareholders who had not lost their confidence
in EDS's future. In retrospect, while my business judgment was zilch
when it involved my having faith and sticking with an investment, I

like to console myself that I might have inherited a small particle of my father's gene when I initially envisioned EDS's future success.

THE PROJECT THAT SPAWNED AOL

The same ability to spot a promising new business venture was reinforced not long after, in 1981, when I was mesmerized by the future potential of new technology and became a starting investor in a company that was eventually to morph into an even more financially successful business venture than Ross Perot's EDS. It all started when I had lunch with a friend, Marguerite Owen, the managing partner of the law firm, Nussbaum & Owen, and she mentioned that she had just sublet almost all of the unused office space to a visionary entrepreneur, William F.von Meister. The law firm would be serving as general counsel. Only a few years earlier Bill founded the Source, the first popular online service for the sale of airline reservations directly to consumers, a system that later became CompuServe. But Von Meister had a falling out with his principal financial backer, and Michael Nussbaum, Marguerite's partner, had defended and admirably extricated von Meister in the messy, publicized lawsuit that followed.[40]

Now, Marguerite and her law partners were helping the flamboyant von Meister start up his latest, exciting high-tech enterprise, Digital Music Company, which von Meister was calling The Home Music Store. It would provide very high quality musical entertainment at a low price to subscribers served by cable television. As a nationally transmitted, commercial-free network, it would offer digital audio programming whose sound quality would substantially exceed the best FM reception currently available, achievable through the transmission of digital data and the use of a proprietary decoder.

I was captivated by the accounts of this and von Meister's previous innovative exploits and impulsively decided I wanted to meet him and learn more about this project. I walked Marguerite back to her office

40. *Michael was also a good friend of mine, as well as of Dan Goldy, whose house he had bought just a few doors away from us on Albermarle Street.*

after lunch and was introduced to Bill von Meister. My first impression of him was of a young, very large, blond and energetic fellow, who proved to live up to his reputation as an accomplished promoter and persuasive salesman. During the next 35-40 minutes, he explained the merits and exciting future of digital music and the Home Music Store. He described the concept and vision, together with the operations and promise of his new high-tech venture, including the radically new method of distributing recorded music at substantial savings in distribution costs. He told me he was currently negotiating with the major record companies to obtain the licensing for distribution of their recordings via the Home Music Store system. A contract had been signed with American Satellite Company granting Digital Musical Company a protected transponder capacity on one of its Westar satellites to transmit Home Music Store's music to a commercial-free network, providing a pay service to cable TV subscribers. Plans called for the "recording" channels to carry up to 1,600 album-length selections per month, with subscribers billed for each album recorded at a price 40-60% less than current retail prices. Initially there would be five stereo "listening" channels, two stereo "recording" channels and two monaural channels for news, previews, data and other undetermined services. The programming for the "listening" channels would range from a rock/"top 40," country and western, jazz and blues channel to contemporary pop/"easy listening" and a classical/opera channel. The superior quality of the music would be achieved through the transmission of digital data and the use of a proprietary decoder developed by the new company, Digital Music, Inc., which von Meister was sub-titling and marketing as the Home Music Store.

According to von Meister, the company's principal business would be to sell a service that provides superior high fidelity stereophonic musical programming distributed to cable TV subscribers as a pay or "premium" service. The company's programming would be digitally encoded in a studio facility in Los Angeles and transmitted by satellite to earth stations of CATV operators, whose subscribers would receive the signal over a cable TV channel. At this point, it would be converted by a decoder to an analog signal suitable for listening and recording on the subscriber's existing stereo equipment. The company's proprietary digital decoding, encoding, and transmission equipment, along with computerized control systems, guarded against unauthor-

ized reception and recording of The Home Music Store's programming. The system also provided a "feedback" mechanism
so that royalty payments due to the record companies could be
precisely calculated.

Despite the large gaps in my technological understanding, I recognized the technological advance von Meister was offering in trans-
mitting a superior quality of music by satellite directly into people's
homes, with the additional capability of enabling the recipient to
record the music at a significantly lower cost than buying it at a retail
record store. And when von Meister followed his briefing with a stunning audio demonstration that compared the appreciably higher quality of a digital recording of a Brahms concerto with that of a regular
record, I found myself agreeing to return soon to discuss not only
investing in Digital Music Company, but also joining von Meister to
help carry out his new venture.

Michael and Marguerite—in addition to serving as general counsel to
the new company—with a few of her partners, would also be investing
in the company in a limited partnership. I also talked at great length
with Louise about my attraction to the adventurous nature of the
new company and the challenge of working with its creative, colorful
CEO. A few weeks later, Louise and I had made a significant investment in the private, restricted letter stock of Digital Music.

I found von Meister impressive, fascinating and a continually interesting colleague and after a short time he asked me to be on DMC's
Board. Irwin Steinberg, a pioneer leader in the music industry and
most recently Chairman of Polygram Records was serving as Board
Chairman. But I was very concerned about the personal risks my family and I would face in such a new, financially insecure company, and
declined. Instead, I persuaded von Meister to appoint a very bright
and level-headed old United Press acquaintance, Bob Graff, who had
recently married a very wealthy widow and whom I had interested in
making a large investment in DMC.

For someone who liked a sense of adventure in his work, the weeks
that followed were never dull and often could best be described as a
virtual roller-coaster of daily surprises and challenges. Bill's energy

seemed inexhaustible. When he wasn't working, he was playing tennis on his own court, racing fast cars or chasing attractive women. And in the course of the many weeks of working closely with him, I quickly learned that while he was a bright and innovative pioneer with an outstanding record as a promoter and entrepreneur, he was too often seriously lacking when it came to making good business judgments and managing a business.

I was a first-hand witness to one of the early demonstrations of his critically bad business judgment. Von Meister had contracted with a securities firm, Kidder Peabody, to raise an initial $15 million through a private placement of two million shares of common stock of Digital Music Company to cover estimated cash requirements for the company's first year. But the stock sales had been slowed because of a storm of protests and adverse music industry publicity generated by retail music stores. They feared that marketing music as the Home Music Store would put them out of business. As a result, the record retailers threatened to stop selling the records of any company that licensed Home Music Store to distribute its recordings. At this low point in funding DMC's start-up, von Meister had a call from a top Sony executive in Japan expressing Sony's strong interest in the applications of digital transmission. He reported that Sony was deeply involved in developing digital and related equipment and had learned of von Meister's digital transmission project.

The Sony executive told von Meister he would like to meet with him in Washington to discuss Sony's investment in the Digital Music Company and to contract with DMC in turn to manufacture and provide the various components of DMC's digital transmission system. Sony's strong financial stature and technical manufacturing capabilities, looked to nearly everyone like the answer from heaven to our current funding problems. We were assured of Sony's seriousness by the fact that it was rare for top Sony officials in Japan to come to the U.S. to meet and negotiate an agreement, instead of using their U.S.-based representatives.

Our luncheon meeting was in the downstairs dining room of what is now the Vidalia Restaurant on M Street, just a block or so from DMC's office. There were five or six of us from DMC dining with the smaller Sony delegation, with most of the business discussion consisting of the Sony representatives questioning Von Meister about DMC's digital transmission technology, particularly its proprietary data processing. Von Meister answered lucidly and fully, to their clear satisfaction. As the Japanese visitors grew more relaxed and looked increasingly pleased at what they were hearing, my own excitement grew correspondingly. After weeks of depressing rejections of DMC's efforts to obtain the critical licensing agreements with the major record companies, I now saw a bright ray of hope for DMC's current financial problems by securing a deal with the interested Sony envoys.

Then von Meister asked his questions: When could Sony start manufacturing the essential components of DMC's digital transmission system? I suddenly felt my rising high spirits chill, as von Meister's face slowly reflected disappointment on hearing their timetable. "A year! We can't wait that long. We're moving too fast," he told the surprised Sony and astonished DMC attendees. He stood up, signaling that the discussion was over. I was appalled, as were the others in our group, von Meister was blowing our one chance of being rescued.

But von Meister was adamant and would not listen to any opposing opinions. His credentials as an inventor, entrepreneur and promoter did not extend to his business judgment. Our financial problems only increased as the threats of the retail record increased, effectively discouraging would-be investors. The death knell to The Home Music Store came when Warner Records—who had previously told von Meister they wanted to invest in Digital Music and signed a licensing agreement—now informed von Meister that the threats of the retail record stores forced them to renege on their agreement. Moreover, when the Board of Directors agreed on a plan to rescue DMC from looming bankruptcy by selling its valuable satellite asset and use this money finance a more profitable venture for DMC's innovative digital transmission technology, Von Meister disregarded the Board's decision. He was determined to prove his business acumen and continued on the obstinate course that ended in the loss of the satellite and a bankrupt Digital Music Company, aka The Home Music Store.

At the end of the tense meeting at which Warner Records informed von Meister their licensing agreement was cancelled, an official from

Warner Communications, the record company's parent, walked over to von Meister and brightened his day by offering him an alternative market for Digital Music's technology. It was the Atari Corporation's popular and profitable video games, owned by Warner Communications. Atari's innovative 2600 model, had been a sensational success when it was released during the 1980s and von Meister saw the home video game market as an attractive outlet and market for digital transmission and equipment capabilities. He quickly shifted gears and incorporated a new company, Control Video Corporation (CVC), to focus his efforts on invading and capturing a major, profitable position in the hot video game business. (The shares Louise and I held in Digital Music Company were converted into CVC stock, which now owned Digital Music's proprietary digital transmission system's equipment and related technology.) Von Meister moved CVC into new offices in nearby Vienna, Virginia, and in an incredibly short time, the brilliant, inventive von Meister had developed—and was introducing at the annual Consumer Electronic Show—CVC's s new on-line service, the GameLine Master Module, which would distribute video games over telephone lines to a special cartridge plugged into the Atari 2600 game system. Von Meister's entry into the video game business was an instant hit and CVC was swamped with orders for tens of thousands of its GameLine module.

Still the consummate entrepreneur and promoter, von Meister swung into action, mesmerizing and signing up major investors, including Citicorp Venture Capital, Hambrecht & Quist, Kleiner Perkins, Imagic, Hamco Capital, and Bell South. All of them were attracted by his vision for his new digital technology: the transmission of all kinds of information by telephone into people's homes, not only to play the enormously popular and profitable video games, but also to digitally transmit stock reports, sports news, banking transactions, and e-mail. One admiring victim of von Meister's fabled salesmanship was later quoted as noting that he could raise money from the dead. As for Bill's view of any personal fiduciary responsibility, Mike quoted him as saying that contracts were only needed "to make the *other* party aware of his responsibilities".

But CVC's success and Bill von Meister's role as president and CEO were fated to be short-lived. The over-saturation of the video game market resulted in the Great Video Game Crash of 1983. And the end for von Meister came when CVC's vital flow of revenue dried up, along with the tolerance of CVC's Board and major investors. His extravagant spending habits and poor business management were no longer acceptable. The urgent need to find a capable replacement for Von Meister led to the appointment of Jim Kimsey, who had built up a group of successful restaurants and bars in the Washington area

 I remember those gloomy days after the collapse of CVC's video game market in 1983 and the dispirited CVC meetings I attended in the depressingly empty company offices following the laying off of all except a few employees. With no money to pay its numerous bills, CVC was receiving an increasing number of anxious calls from creditors. Everyone was now looking to Kimsey for his plans to revitalize the near bankrupt CVC and resolve this crisis. Kimsey moved quickly, switching its business of making video game modules to a new focus on marketing online communications, and by calling it Q-Link to stress its new online communications mission.

A few years earlier, Dan Case, whose venture capital company was a major investor in CVC, had introduced to Von Meister his younger brother, Steve, a quiet, unimpressive looking youth in his mid-20s, with a marketing background. Von Meister hired him as a marketing consultant at a reported $20 an hour. But Kimsey, hard pressed for funds, now made the young Steve Case director of marketing and dispatched him to Apple Computer's office in California to sell them CVC's Q-Links services. Case surprised everyone by signing up Apple. He followed this achievement by getting IBM and Tandy to modify their modems so that their PC users could communicate via telephone with Q-Link services. While Steve Case returned to Virginia with his new Q-links sales to a more cheerful and hopeful meeting with CVC's investors, Kimsey was still confronted and struggling with CVC's strangling debt problems. Also, most CVC's investors were expressing mixed feelings and a low level of confidence in the company's future viability, especially me. As Kimsey and Case continued to hold off the hordes of creditors and change CVC's course for a more financially successful future, I stopped going to their meetings.

It would be nearly 10 years later when I learned that a few months after my last meeting with CVC investors, Kimsey and Case had transferred CVC's digital transmission and related technology into a new corporate entity, Quantum Computer Services, and that a few years later Quantum would start calling itself America Online. I discovered their earlier connection to von Meister and CVC when I heard that Michael Nussbaum and Marguerite had both been beneficiaries of AOL's success. As Michael much later explained it to me, von Meister had called asking him to invest in a new company, Quantum Computer Services, that was replacing CVC. Von Meister was trying to impress Kimsey that he could still be of great value to them by demonstrating his talent for raising capital. He told Michael that if he could bring in two prominent Washington lawyers such as Michael and Marguerite, it could be very persuasive for the new Quantum. Michael had demurred saying he was a lawyer, not an investor. But when Von Meister pleaded with him to give him something, had agreed he would send him a check for $300 if Bill promised never to ask him to invest in one of his ventures again.

 Michael said he had forgotten about this until years later, when he needed to make out a new, up-to-date financial statement. When his secretary brought him his financial file, she also handed him a large box filled with correspondence and documents dating back a number of years, explaining that these all related to the $300 check he had sent to Bill von Meister. When he telephoned AOL to inquire about the status of his Quantum letter stock, he learned that his $300 investment was now worth more than $300,000.

When I heard this, I was curious and called AOL's corporate office to find out if there existed any value in my shares of Control Video Corporation, Quantum's and AOL's predecessor. I was informed it was only valuable to an unlikely corporate history buff interested in AOL's former corporate history. I resisted the impulse to go on E-Bay to find out.

TRUSTEESHIPS
Chapter 14

*Advice is like snow; the softer it falls, the longer
it dwells upon, and the deeper it sinks into, the mind.*
     Samuel Taylor Coleridge

Cornell Capa.   © *Photo by Karsh*

CORNELL CAPA AND THE ICP

Towering among my many good fortunes during my lifetime have
been the extraordinary friends with whom I've been blessed, and
outstanding among them has been the friendship of Cornell Capa. He
was an irresistible Hungarian charmer, whose spellbinding magnetism
and contagious good humor and wit always made it rewarding and
fun to be with him. A charismatic visionary and dedicated humanist
he used his remarkable, sensitive skills as a "concerned" photojournalist to reveal and improve the lives of the world's less fortunate.

After the death in1954 of his famed, war- photographer brother, Robert Capa, by a Vietnam War landmine. Cornell gave up his own distinguished career as a Life and Magnum photographer to pursue his remaining life's mission: to preserve and promote the memory and photographic images of his brother, and three close eminent friends, who also died on photographic assignments. Initially, he focused his efforts on projects within his financial means and personal capability, which included the publication of their photographic works, as well as arranging for their exhibition in the few museums who recognized photographs as a form of art worthy enough to be exhibited.

But Cornell envisioned a unique, grander and permanent memorial, endowed with the mission and capabilility of generating an appreciative national and even international audience: the International Center of Photography (ICP). He founded the world-famous museum, school and archive in 1974. And he asked me to help him, as one of its 23 founding trustees, to carry out what many experienced observers were predicting was "Mission Impossible

My friendship with Cornell was initiated on a bright sunny morning in 1952, when I was working on Adlai Stevenson's presidential campaign staff in Springfield, Illinois. Cornell, who had just arrived to cover Adlai for Life Magazine, dropped by my office to ask if he and Ray Scherer, an NBC news reporter, could borrow for a few hours my new Chevrolet convertible that was parked outside with the top fastened down. Although I had just met Cornell and Ray, I had said sure and handed him the keys to the car.

Just before noon, Cornell returned, looking crestfallen, and when he handed me back the car keys, he told me there had been a slight accident. He had been smoking a small cigar, and had tossed it out behind him when he had finished. But instead of landing on the road, the cigar had landed on the folded canvas and burned a hole in the top. Our friendship bloomed when I assured the upset Cornell not to worry, that it was only a small hole.

It was only a matter of time before Cornell's bonding contagious gift of friendship had spread throughout the Sagalyn family. Soon after that, Cornell met my younger brother, Bobby, when both were vacationing in the Virgin Islands and the encounter developed into a very warm friendship that resulted in Cornell volunteering to photograph Bob's wedding to Avital Schwartz. Bobby on his part helped Cornell by collaborating with him in 1968 and writing the text for *The Concerned Photographer*, which displayed the photographs of Werner Bischof, Robert Capa, Andre Kertesz, David Seymour, Dan Weiner and Leonard Freed. This friendship led to Bob's daughter, Michelle, a student at Bennington College, who worked for Cornell as her 1975 winter term project and lived with Cornell and his wife, Edie, sleeping on a mattress in the storage room of their third floor walk-up apartment at 275 Fifth Avenue.

It was only natural when our daughter, Laurie, became interested in photography that she, too, worked for Cornell (she later achieved acclaim as a fashion photographer for Women's Wear Daily and W magazine). She made it her personal agenda to persuade Cornell that fashion photos warranted being exhibited as well as those of "concerned photo journalists." And tours of service with Cornell by our daughter, Rita, and nephew, Rafe, would follow them.

Making Cornell's vision for the ICP a reality was an extraordinary, Herculean task, as I can attest. Start-up money was not only in very short supply, it was non-existent when several other trustees and I met in response to a call from Capa to approve the $500,000 purchase of the landmark Willard Straight mansion at 1130 Fifth Avenue, a prime museum location. Previously, it had been occupied by the Audubon Society. Its commodious, high-ceiling halls and rooms met ICPs needs for offices and exhibitions, as well as classrooms and labs for the new school. As we did not have the money to pay for it, we had to approve taking out a mortgage for the $500,000.

At this point, one of founding trustees, who had been very quiet, now looked deeply concerned at the sudden realization of the magnitude of the high risk each of us would be assuming for the $500,000 mortgage, spoke up. "We must be crazy! Where will we get the money to pay for this?" However, the other trustees and I were reassured her, saying, we have Cornell-- he is our big asset. And the one-half million-dollar mortgage was approved

That's the way the ICP started, with no money, a large mortgage on the Fifth Avenue townhouse and the faith of the original trustees to support Cornell. It was a remarkable tribute to his brilliant vision, leadership and his capability to inspire others.

When Cornell first began to plan seriously about establishing the ICP, he asked me to be one of the founding trustees and telephoned me periodically to discuss the funding and other concerns, using me as a sounding board. My earlier background when I worked as a reporter for Life and knew his brother Bob, and then as picture editor for the Sunday *New York Times*, had created a warm rapport between us, which was strengthened by our closer extended family ties.

Although Cornell relied heavily on his local associates and advisors, the fact that I was living in Washington and not involved or had a personal stake in Cornell's or the ICP's affairs, I was in a position to be more objective. This resulted in a special relationship and bond of trust that led Cornell to seek my counsel and advice when he was uneasy about a critical issue. For example, it was natural for him to draw on his friends and associate photographers for his Board, but few had the ability to fund raise. I explained to him that the Board was responsible for the financial well being of the Museum and he needed to recruit members who could commit to that responsibility.

The trustee's faith in Cornell's ability and magic was continually tested during ICP's early, formative years as the demand for more money to pay ICPs staff and all the other monthly bills outpaced the flow of income from fund-raising activities. I still have vivid memories of those soft-spoken, but disquieting telephone calls from Cornell, reporting, "Arny, we don't have enough money to pay the staff next week. What do we do?" And I would review with him possible options to tide us through that week's financial crisis, as well as what measures might be initiated to improve the long-term income status. No matter how gloomy the outlook, Cornell remained optimistic. I always reminded him that I was a short-term pessimist, but a long-term optimist and we ended our conversation on a cheery, upbeat note.

Cornell, with the help of his recruited, invigorated board of trustees committed to producing a significant amount of revenue annually, succeeded in building the ICP into a financially strong, world-class, photographic museum-school-archive that helped influence art critics and museums to finally recognize photographs as an art form that merited their display and permanent collection. Another Cornell Capa monument was his legacy as a selfless mentor to a generation of young aspiring photographers who were captivated by his passion and dedication to employ the camera to show the beauty and wonders of the human spirit, and to "contribute to the understanding or the well-being of humanity."

Young photographers came from all over the world to talk and learn from Cornell, who, with his childless wife, Edie, opened their door and hearts to them, nourishing their minds and stomachs and, if necessary a place to sleep. "Edie's army, as they were called, all became devoted members of the Capa family.

One of Cornell's most difficult and courageous tasks was to relinquish in 1994 the direction and management of the ICP, his creation and full-time life for 20 years to his handpicked, groomed successor, Willis Hartshorn. Although he lived another 7 years after Edie's, death in 2001, he lost his zest for life and his deteriorating health confined him to his apartment. But his faithful, devoted friends continued to visit him regularly. I would keep in touch by mail and telephone, and periodically travel to New York where I joined a small coterie whose core included Karl Katz, a founding trustee, and Phil Block, ICP's Director of Education, that regularly lunched with him on Saturdays. He died peacefully in his bed on May 23, 2008 at the age of 90.

In its obituary, the *New York Times* noted, "Capa had three important incarnations in the field of photography: successful photojournalist; champion of his older brother Robert Capa's legacy among the greatest war photographers; and founder and first director of the International Center for Photography, which since it was established in 1974, has become one of the most influential photographic institutions for exhibition, collection, and education in the world.

GEORGETTE KLINGER, INC.

Georgette Klinger.

One of my life's fascinating and rewarding discoveries has been to find how a casual meeting with someone far from home can lead to a surprise reunion thousands of miles away and then develops into a close, valued, lifetime friendship. That was true of my early relationships with Clayton Fritchey and Dan Goldy and later, even more unlikely, with Georgette Klinger, whom I met in July 1953 on an ocean liner.

I was traveling to France to house sit the Cowen children in their French country house, while Polly and Lou were visiting friends on the Riviera, and Georgette was en route to Switzerland with her young daughter, Kathy.

Her striking beauty and charm attracted me, and her elegant European style gave her a commanding presence whenever she entered a room. Her story of growing up in Czechoslovakia, her flight when the Nazis invaded and her successful enterprise in America intrigued me. Her business career was precipitated after winning a beauty contest that awarded her some cosmetics that irritated her skin. As a result, she made herself an expert on skin care, studying with European dermatologists and other skin care experts in Vienna, Zurich and Budapest in addition to Prague.

Georgette developed her own treatment products and techniques and in 1938 opened a salon. However, when Hitler invaded, she used her stunning, blonde Nordic appearance to pass through the border and smuggle her three brothers out of the country with her and fled to London. Two years later, in 1941, she opened her first Georgette Klinger Salon on Madison Avenue in New York. Eventually there would be nine salons, extending from coast to coast.

My friendship with Georgette really developed after we met again with her husband, Jacobo, in Arizona where we all were winter vacationing. Jacobo was a successful businessman in Venezuela, commuting to their New York home, and I became good friends with these two warm and attractive people. I visited them on my periodic trips to New York, and they both came to Washington to attend my swearing-in at the Treasury Department. When Lisbeth was born, we asked Georgette to be her godmother.

From time to time during trips to New York I would meet Georgette for lunch at her Madison Avenue office. She took pride in showing me her salon and talking about her plans not only for expanding Georgette Klinger salons throughout the country, but also to build her own laboratory and produce her own line of Georgette Klinger skin care preparations. All of these ventures were very successful, including a second salon in New York and ones in Washington and Chicago, thereby enabling Louise and all our daughters to become regular devoted Georgette Klinger patrons.

In the course of these lunches and conversations, I learned Georgette had lost confidence and trust in the recommendations of her able, but highly ambitious chief operating officer, Tony, whom she could not fire because he had a long-term employment contract. As Georgette kept her business affairs completely separate from Jacobo's, she now started to ask my opinions and counsel on how to deal with Tony and other troubling problems. After awhile, when she found my judgment helpful, she asked me to be on her small Board of Directors. Then, following Jacobo's death in 1976, I agreed to serve as guardian for her daughter, Kathy, whom she was grooming to be her successor at the Georgette Klinger Company.

During the years that followed, I read the continuous stream of praise of Georgette and her skin care philosophy, treatments and techniques from the country's leading beauty and fashion publications, always referring to Georgette as the "Dean of skin care".

Georgette always believed that her primary mission was helping people develop an attractive and healthy skin, and that was more important to her than making a lot of money. When the success and fame of the various Klinger lotions brought extremely lucrative offers from top department store chains to display and sell them, as they did for Revlon and other top brands, with the promise of enormous life-time profits, Georgette turned all of them down.

She explained to me that each person's skin condition is different and required a careful analysis by someone properly trained and fully knowledgeable about the customer's skin condition, before deciding on the appropriate and effective lotion. Until the department stores' sales personnel possessed this knowledge, she felt it would be morally wrong, and put making money more important than providing the customer with the best, effective treatment for her or his skin.

It was not surprising that Georgette would receive attractive offers to purchase her lucrative company, which she always declined. But one day, following a board meeting and her request I stay to discuss a matter, she told me she would like me to discreetly inquire how much she might expect to receive if she agreed to sell the company. She was thinking of the future and the fact that Kathy had told her that while she was comfortable managing the Beverly Hills and Dallas salons, she now had a family and life in Beverly Hills and she was not interested in moving back to New York to take over the direction of the entire company.

With Georgette's approval, I talked with the company's lawyer, a member of one of New York's most prestigious firms. We quietly obtained information about what a skincare company with revenue of $20 million might expect, who might be the most likely bidders and, most important, which of these would Georgette feel most comfortable about owning and operating her creation.

Shortly afterwards, I had to curtail my activities and board membership and only found out later that when Georgette informed her
daughter, Kathy had implored her not to pursue a sale, that she had
changed her mind about running the company. Consequently,
Georgette ended up turning over control of the Klinger Company
to her daughter.

Georgette and Arnold at Kathy's wedding.

Georgette had one firm rule for herself: she personally would not
provide skin care treatments outside of the salon. Although she had
constant appeals and enticements from top Hollywood, Broadway
and TV stars, as well as from some of America's most distinguished
citizens to come to their hotel or home, she adamantly and
politely refused.

She broke this rule, however, for Lisbeth's 16th birthday when she volunteered to be the centerpiece for her birthday party. I don't believe that Louise, Lisbeth, I or any of her invited friends will ever forget that memorable birthday when Georgette arrived at our Albemarle Street house, accompanied by one of her top cosmeticians from her Madison Avenue salon, carrying large suitcases packed with enough skin care treatment and make up kits for the individual facial and makeup treatments she and her assistant gave to Lisbeth and each of her invited friends. They received a lecture on how to care for their skin, followed by individual facial treatments and lessons in applying makeup. Georgette also presented each young girl with a special gift box of Georgette Klinger skin care and makeup products to take home. The amusing side factor was the very early arrival of the mothers to pick up their daughters in order to meet and greet Georgette. Eight years later, Georgette returned again for her goddaughter's prenuptial dinner and wedding to Matthew Stone.

The *New York Times* obituary following her death in 2004 at the age of 88 reported: "Miss Klinger, whose own complexion was a pampered milky white, began by treating the skin as a tender, living organ, not a surface in need of decoration, an approach that revolutionized cosmetic skin care. Her techniques for doing facials set the standard, as did her early use of herbal treatment, nutrition and exercise as part of skin care. Before Miss Klinger, beauty treatment involved getting one's hair or makeup done, her daughter said. The new techniques Miss Klinger brought from Europe and further developed herself to revitalize skin helped lay the foundation for today's multibillion-dollar spa industry, and she widened the universe of those who enjoyed facials, devising treatments for men and teenagers."

YOU CAN GO HOME AGAIN
Chapter 15

The early 90s found us returning to the Berkshires in the summer. The lure was familiarity, gorgeous scenery, family and old friends, as well as the Tanglewood music, Jacobs Pillow's dance concerts and few Washingtonians. And with our grandchildren growing up, Louise and I wanted a summer and year-round retreat where family members could gather and vacation free of their daily pressures and those of their children's school.

The Berkshire House.

For a few years we rented a summer house, but found it difficult to find one that met our needs. So when our friends Toni and Abe Chayes decided to buy a second home there, we started to look too. They ended up finding a farmhouse compound that suited their needs. Soon afterwards, we found and purchased a nearby contemporary Shaker farmhouse in Canaan, New York on the Richmond, Massachusetts border that was ideal for us. The house sat on a 6 1/2 acre lot on Shaker Ridge Drive, a new community developed on a former Shaker hill, that was only 12 minutes from Tanglewood, 15 minutes to most other Berkshire towns, and 5 minutes to the Chayes compound.

Both Louise and I had pretty much retired by this time and planned
to spend the entire summer away from Washington. We could return
during the Fall to watch the gorgeous colors of the New England
countryside, and again at Christmas with the snow. But most of all,
this was a wonderful place to catch up with our children and watch
our grandchildren grow up during the summers and occasional holi-
days. The accessibility of several nearby skiing resorts was an added
attraction during the winter months, and the proximity of the Shaker
Ridge house enabled our New York City daughters to use it in our
absence as a convenient weekend retreat. It was also available to our
Chicago daughter and her family when our grandsons were on
winter breaks.

And for Louise, and myself, the large gentle sloping green acreage
bordered by very tall thick pine trees provided quiet privacy. It also
enabled Louise to fulfill a lifelong craving for a summer garden. She
proceeded to create colorful, enchanting gardens both in the front
as well as back of the house, which she happily tended part of each
day; and to plant an attractive, landscaped entrance lined with sen-
tinel trees along the long driveway to the house. A wide permanent
walking path was mowed in the surrounding fields that led from the
green lawn to a circular gazebo that offered a tranquil, comfortable
shady place to read or to chat on a warm sunny day. The path then
circled parallel to the wire fence of our Massachusetts neighbor across
the rear of our property and followed a row of bordering pine trees
towards the front of our house.

Family and friends.

A large, wide wooden deck extended from the rear of the house with a set of wide circular steps descending to the garden and a large open lawn which served as a playing field for our grandchildren to fly kites, pitch horseshoes and other games. It also was the site of the junior Olympic games, which we organized with the Chayes for all our grandchildren.

Two years after we purchased the house, we were visited by a devastating tornado on a Fourth of July holiday weekend, when all the children were expected. There had been tornado advisories all day that kept us home, but when the radio reported an all clear, we decided to use our Tanglewood tickets for that evening's concert. Just a few minutes before the concert was due to begin, an usher came to our seats and called out our name and pointed our attention to our friends, Abe and Toni Chayes who were standing and waving at us from the other side of the music shed. We were both terrified that something dreadful must have happened to one of our children, and seeing the stricken look on our faces, Abe called out reassuringly, "Your children are all right--it's only your house!"[41]

The aftermath of the tornado.

---

41. *Chris Toupin, a close friend who lived directly below us on the main road, witnessed the tornado striking our house and lifting its roof off while she was enroute to her storm cellar. After the tornado died out, she ran up to our demolished house to see if anyone was inside who needed help. She then telephoned the Chayes, whom she knew would know where to find us to report the destruction of our house.*

The house was nearly completely destroyed and pieces of the roof that had been our garage were found 5 miles away at the Pittsfield airport. We were lucky to find a bed for everyone during the busiest weekend, and a rental house for the rest of the summer. As we absorbed the magnitude of what had happened, we had to decide what to do about our wonderful house of which we had grown so fond. After assurance by the regional director of the U.S. Weather Bureau of the low probability of another tornado hitting our house, and the agreement of our insurance company to pay the full replacement cost, we were very lucky that the original builder, Roger Mitchell, offered to come out of retirement to round up and supervise the very scarce skilled laborers to rebuild our house.. And we took this opportunity to adjust a few aspects of the house that Louise believed would make it utterly perfect.

We spent our time in the Berkshires in a very different relaxed way than our life in DC. There was so much cultural activity from which to choose. While Tanglewood was the centerpiece, we went often to Jacob's Pillow to see its world famous dance groups, to the Clark Museum in Williamstown and nearby MassMoCA, and visited and dined with my family and old Berkshire, New York and Boston area friends. Louise painted, joined the Board of the local Art School and tended her garden. And we always looked forward to family visits.

It was as close to perfect as a vacation place could be. But ultimately all things change, Ben, Mitchell and Emma were growing up and their summers shifted to camp and other adolescent activities. Soon family visits were difficult to schedule and became less frequent and increasingly shorter. Also, our own trips to our Shaker Ridge house in the Fall and winter months became less enjoyable as driving became difficult as darkness descended early in the afternoon and we confronted poor weather conditions. And the frequent snowstorms made it an onerous problem to keep clear our driveway to the house.

The net result was to hold a family council to discuss the future status of our house. Everyone spoke of his/her love and enjoyment of the Berkshire house and visits, but confirmed the changed conditions and interests of our daughters and grandchildren that negated our original motive and the getaway value of a Berkshire residence. We had previously incorporated the Shaker Ridge property into a Family Partnership, and its membership now agreed to a sale. We were fortunate to have made this decision before the housing climate changed and achieved highly successful financial results from the sale.

A race in the Jr. Olympics at Shaker Ridge Drive.

However, summering in the Berkshires was part of my heritage and fondest memories. From the time I was born, I had spent every summer at our family farm there. And even after I left home, I always returned to the Berkshires in the summer to visit my parents and siblings at our farm. The sale of our house in Canaan did not terminate my love and devotion to this special New England place. Happily, Louise shared my feelings about the Berkshire, and we have continued to return to spend part of every summer there, first in a B & B Inn and later rented a house to have room for any family member who wanted to visit us. As I had stopped driving, after my 90th birthday, we found a house in town, primarily in Lenox, where I could walk to get a *New York Times*, Berkshire Eagle, groceries or a restaurant.

EPILOGUE

July 2009

Let us be up and doing,
With a heart for any fate;
Still achieving, still pursuing,
Learn to labor and to wait.

     Henry Wadsworth Longfellow

This memoir fulfills my promise made many years ago to Laurie, Rita, Lisbeth, Benjamin, Mitchell and Emma to record the stories I used to tell them about my life growing up, and the various and often adventurous careers and enterprises that followed. They were my inspiration and my prod for this review of my life.

I was very fortunate to grow up in a large close-knit family with loving parents and supportive siblings. And when I researched my own family history and probed the files and memories of other family members and acquaintances, I rediscovered how fortunate I was to have such extraordinary caring father, mother, brothers and sisters.

Writing my memoir has given me many surprising insights about myself and those who greatly influenced and assisted me on the paths I took to my various destinations. They included the importance of my Wesleyan professor, who urged my transfer from Wesleyan to Oberlin, a rare move in those days, which brought me to Cleveland where it all began. And it was a revelation how just the chance choosing of a topic for a college course paper had such major consequences. It led to a stimulating, rewarding career in law enforcement, a remarkably strange and unlikely calling for someone with my family, social and economic background.

It was a field that offered opportunities to be of public service and to stimulate law enforcement thinking to prevent and reduce serious crime. I was enabled to champion the use of nonlethal weapons in situations where the firing of a policeman's handgun gun could result in a major riot with a great loss of life and commercial property; to provide police departments with the training to anticipate and prevent a major riot and, in the event of a serious civil disorder, the training and equipment that would enable them to control it with minimum loss of life and property.

I also had the opportunity to promote the need for law enforcement officials to focus more on the preventative aspects of major crimes by limiting the opportunity to commit a crime. I was also instrumental in getting the Federal Communications Commission and AT&T, then the U.S. telephone monopoly, to create 911, the national emergency telephone number.

I came to appreciate the importance in my professional life of Eliot Ness, Clayton Fritchey, Keith Wilson and Dan Goldy, all of whom I first met in Cleveland, and who became treasured friends. It led to a career in the Federal government, beginning with Eliot Ness's venture in Washington, then at the Defense Department, and my remarkable military assignment to the U.S. Military Government headquarters in Berlin, culminating in my appointment to the Treasury in the Kennedy-Johnson era and the rewarding time at the National War College and two Presidential Commissions. And all this happened because I transferred to Oberlin and wrote a paper about Eliot Ness.

My career in journalism also started in college where I wrote a weekly column for the college newspaper and discovered how much influence there is in the written word. The challenge in ferreting out and communicating valued information and the reporter's independence motivated me to pursue my career in journalism, where my coverage of many eminent people and historic events made for a great adventure.

I wanted to call this book "A Fortunate Life", but looking back, I realized that there was more to it than that. From the time I was only five or six, once I set my mind to achieve a goal or obtain something I believed was extremely important, I would keep after it with a relentless persistence until I was successful. Mrs. Sullivan, our housekeeper, referred to me as "the nudge".. But, I also, came to learn how irritating this trait could be, so early on I realized the absolute necessity to soften this approach.

In the final analysis, I realized that whatever I may have achieved in each of my careers had been dependent on my own efforts. While I clearly experienced a number of critical lucky breaks throughout my life, each time the reality was the same: I had to help make the break and be prepared with the requisite experience, skills and qualifications My mentors may have opened a door, but from there on I had to prove my capability to handle the job creditably..

Although I was blessed with many wonderful friends, this memoir essentially focused on my professional life, and thus I have not mentioned some of my warmest and most memorable personal friendships that helped make my life whole. I was lucky to meet several friends through work and they have been briefly mentioned. Undoubtedly it was those friendships that made my work more fulfilling. Others were neighbors, who remained important and valued even when we moved away. Another source were the parents of my children's friends, and as they grew older, some of my children's friends have become mine as well. And Louise brought some of our very closest friends with her to our marriage.

Our last move to an apartment at the Watergate has been more than satisfying. We were lucky to find a wonderful, convenient final home with a first class view of the Potomac River, the adjacent Rock Creek Park activities and lovely neighbors. While I have been busy writing this memoir, i continue to be involved in many things, though not nearly as extensively as in the past. Paramount and towering over all my many blessings has been my marriage of 52 years to Louise and the joy with which she has so completely enriched and fulfilled my life. My family, which in addition to Laurie, Rita and Lisbeth has expanded to include Matt and Eric and my beloved grandchildren, Benjamin, Mitchell and Emma, has given my life the purpose and meaning I long sought as a bachelor for 39 years. My final observation: my wonderful family personifies the super lucky man I am.

THE END

ACKNOWLEDGMENTS

When my accomplished and enterprising film maker nephew, Dan Sagalyn, persuaded me to let him interview and videotape my stories for more than 12 hours, it became evident that accessing this medium and the long viewing hours involved proved intimidating. I reluctantly recognized I would have to write down my memoir and make it available as a convenient book. And so I have Dan to thank for starting me on this journey to leave a recorded narrative of my life's wanderings.

But I never expected to need all the invaluable help I received. Beginning with my Springfield family who had carefully saved my youthful letters from college and through the war and later years, I have to thank my mother in particular for thinking those letters were worth saving.

I owe an enormous debt of gratitude for the magnificent assistance of Carla Sykes, a dear friend and talented editor. Her beneficent generosity and skillful, sensitive and thoughtful editing made this memoir a reality.

I am also deeply indebted to John Solorzano, my extraordinary computer guru, who transcribed the edited pages and continually came to my rescue with his resourceful computer skills whenever my rogue iMac stopped functioning. Without John, I would have had to take my old Remington typewriter out of storage and be countless months away from finishing this.

I also want to acknowledge the early and important assistance of Kenny Wapner in editing the first group of chapters, whose professional counseling helped me make my memoir a more interesting narrative of my life experience.

In addition, I want to express my deep appreciation to my nephew, Rafe Sagalyn, the consummate book agent, for his enormously helpful and timely critique. Thanks to Ellie Horowitz for her comments, and special thanks to Anita Jones for proof reading the final draft, and her extremely helpful advice. And my appreciation for the artful contributions of the book's gifted graphic designer, Yordan Silvera.

I could never have completed this memoir without the loving, constant encouragement and invaluable critiquing of my wife, Louise. She was always there when needed with her crucial support and wise counsel and made finishing this book a true partnership. Finally I am grateful to each of my children and grandchildren for their supportive understanding and comforting patience these past years as they waited for me to finish their promised memoir.

Portrait by Annette Polan